The House of Lords and Ideological Politics:

Lord Salisbury's Referendal Theory and the Conservative Party, 1846-1922

Corinne Comstock Weston
Professor of History,
Herbert H. Lehman College
The City University of New York

American Philosophical Society
Independence Square • Philadelphia

Memoirs
of the
American Philosophical Society
Held at Philadelphia
for Promoting Useful Knowledge
Volume 215

Library of Congress Cataloging in Publication Data
Weston, Corinne Comstock
The house of lords and ideological politics
includes index
ISBN 0-87169-215-5
1. Lord Salisbury 2. Parliamentary history–U.K.–19th C.–house of lords 3. Conservative ideology 4. Political Science

ISSN: 0065-9738 94-78524

To Kit and Gerald Comstock
and family

By the Same Author

Two monographs: *English Constitutional Theory and the House of Lords, 1556-1832* (1965) and with Janelle Greenberg, *Subjects and Sovereigns: The Grand Controversy over Legal Sovereignty in Stuart England* (1981). An American fellow of the Royal Historical Society, Corinne C. Weston is also author, with Robert L. Schuyler, of two Anvil Paperbacks: *British Constitutional History since 1832* (1957) and *Cardinal Documents in British History* (1961). She has also published numerous articles in scholarly journals. Three of them, reprinted in *Peers, Politics and Power: The House of Lords, 1603-1911* (1986), ed. Clyve Jones and David Lewis Jones, center on the house of lords in Victorian and Edwardian England. Another article, "The Royal Mediation of 1884" was at the center of a debate in the *English Historical Review* (January, 1991). Dr. Weston is also author of an essay entitled "Lord Selborne, Bonar Law and the 'Tory Revolt,' in *Lords of Parliament: Biographical Studies, 1714-1914*, ed. R.W. Davis (1995).

Contents

Preface vii

1. Introduction 1

2. The Emergent Theory, 1846-68 13

3. Salisbury and the Irish Church Bill 51

4. "Legislating by Picnic" 81

5. The Great Scenario 117

6. Selborne and the Imperial Factor 153

7. The Closing Door 189

Preface

Writing on the declining efficiency of parliament, young Mr. Gladstone in 1856 offered the bold prophecy that for the foreseeable future administrative rather than constitutional reform would be seen as the key to good government.[1] He could hardly have been more mistaken. In the wake of Lord Salisbury's stunning electoral victory in 1895, had he recalled his earlier prophecy, he must have been compelled to admit man's fallibility when it came to forecasting the future. Yet Gladstone's failed prophecy is understandable. After all, how could he have anticipated that Salisbury by the 1890s would be the beneficiary of a sea change in public perception of the house of lords, one that the Conservative leader had himself generated? For Salisbury's activity had given rise to a lively ideological debate that bore no relationship to good administration, centering in fact on the pattern of political power at Westminster. The skill with which Salisbury redirected public perception of the houses of parliament provides this study with one of its leading themes.

In the course of writing the study I have incurred numerous obligations. I am happy to acknowledge, first of all, my gratitude to Her Majesty the Queen for access to materials in the Royal Archives and also for permission to refer to and quote from letters of Sir Arthur Bigge (Lord Stamfordham), one of George V's two royal secretaries; and in this connection I wish also to thank D. M. Blake, European Manuscripts Curator, Oriental and India Office Collections of the British Library, who as holder of the Crown Copyrights gave permission for the use of these letters. I am likewise indebted in this matter to Oliver Everett, Royal Librarian at Windsor Castle, who assisted me in this and other ways.

My thanks are also extended to the following for their permission to quote from letters and other documents in which they hold the copyright or which they have in their possession. I am indebted in particular on this point to the marquis of Salisbury and the earl of Selborne, as readers of this study will quickly per-

---

1. Gladstone's essay was published in the *Quarterly Review*, 99 (June to Sept. 1856), 521–70.

ceive, and also to the duke of Northumberland though it has not been necessary to call upon him to the same degree. Let me express my appreciation as well to Ann Lambton, who was helpful with regard to the Robert Cecil papers, and to the late T. D. Wragg, formerly Keeper of the Devonshire Collection at Chatsworth and his successor, P. Day, for their kindness.

Among the institutions that were generous with their assistance were the British Library and its India Office Library and Records; the Bodleian Library, and the libraries of the Universities of Cambridge and Birmingham. Though it is possible to list only a few names in this connection, I wish to thank by name the following: Colin Harris of the Bodleian Library, which houses the Lady Clarendon "Diaries" and the voluminous Selborne papers; and J.F.A. Mason of Christ Church, Oxford, and Robin Harcourt Williams of Hatfield House, skilled librarians, who guided me through the Salisbury papers. I am grateful as well to Dr. B. S. Benedikz for assistance with the Joseph Chamberlain papers at the University of Birmingham and to Patricia Gill, County Archivist, West Sussex Record Office, which has the papers of the fifth duke of Richmond. Access to these papers and permission to publish from them for the purposes of this study are "by courtesy of the Trustees of the Goodwood Collections and with acknowledgements to the West Sussex Record Office and the County Archivist." Finally, it is a pleasure to express my obligations to Bridget Taylor, the Institute of Historical Research, University of London, who helped me in diverse ways, and also to Professors John Weiss of the City University of New York, and R. W. Davis, Washington University, St. Louis for their timely advice.

My gratitude is also due to the Syndics of the University Library, Cambridge, for granting access to the Crewe papers, which the University owns. I have incurred further obligations with regard to the papers of Andrew Bonar Law, Lord Willoughby de Broke, and John St. Loe Strachey, which are in the Record Office of the House of Lords. I wish to thank the Clerk of the Record Office for permission to make use of these papers and also the present Lord Willoughby de Broke and Charles Strachey.

It would be remiss of me not to express appreciation for

the opportunity to read and quote from two unpublished doctoral dissertations: David Robert Fisher, "The opposition to Sir Robert Peel in the Conservative party, 1841–1846" and Patricia Kelvin, "The development and Use of the concept of the electoral mandate in British politics, 1867 to 1911." Both were completed at the University of London, the first in 1970, the other in 1977. I have also profited from conversations with Dr. Kelvin; and although I have had no opportunity to discuss his dissertation with Dr. Fisher, I have used it extensively in my own work and am happy to express at this time my deep sense of obligation to him for his generosity in this regard.

Research for my study was supported (in part) by repeated grants from the Faculty Research Award Program of the City University of New York. Without its generous support, it would have been very difficult for me to make the trips to England that were required. I was also the recipient in 1986 of a "Travel to Collections Grant" from the National Endowment for the Humanities; but other attempts to secure financing from foundations were unsuccessful. I was of course seeking grants as a woman well before the development of the present social climate, and in the circumstances it was fortunate for me that there existed in the City University a Faculty Research Award Program.

I was also fortunate in having access to the skilled and gracious assistance of Deborah Trepp of The New York Public Library. On countless occasions her contribution to preparing my typescripts for publication has been indispensable. I wish also to acknowledge with thanks the willingness of Jeanne Hodgson of Herbert H. Lehman College, CUNY, to borrow through interlibrary loan countless books otherwise not readily available to me; and the care and facility manifested by Jacob Goldstein, who presides over the 57th Street Copy Center in Manhattan, in duplicating endless pages of typescript as the book took shape. In their individual ways, all of them were very helpful to me.

Finally, I wish to express my deep appreciation to my husband Arthur Weston, who has consistently supported and encouraged my scholarly interests. He has always understood their importance to me; and despite the daunting presence of countless boxes of papers in our home never lost his patience and good humor.

One

Introduction

The taproot of Conservative ideology in late Victorian England was the belief that the house of lords had a referendal function. It was based on the concept of direct democracy and supported by a referendal theory that enabled the lords to exercise freely an independent legislative veto in an age of mass politics. According to the theory, it was the lords' constitutional duty to refer measures to the electorate for its decision when in their judgment the commons lacked a mandate for the proposed legislation. Whatever the nature of the electoral verdict, the lords, it was said, would accept it; but in doing so they bowed not to the commons but to the electorate. Although the theory was usually invoked to block Liberal legislation, it ran a surprisingly prosperous course, despite its partisan cast, in the late nineteenth and early twentieth centuries.

The author and promoter of these political ideas was Robert Gascoyne-Cecil, third marquis of Salisbury (1830–1903), referred to in this study as Lord Salisbury. He was in electoral terms the most successful nineteenth-century Conservative leader, serving for fourteen years as prime minister and for twenty-one as party leader. Although he shared the party leadership with Sir Stafford Northcote from 1881 to 1885, Salisbury was the dominant figure. This tenure of power, coupled with a strong personality, a gift for trenchant public speaking, and high intelligence, creates the expectation that he left a strong imprint on his party; and this seems the more likely in light of Robert Blake's description of him as "the most formidable intellectual figure that the Conservative party has ever produced."[1]

Since writing in this vein, Blake has changed his mind.

1. *Disraeli* (London, 1966), 499. Hereafter no place of publication is given if it is London.

He now writes in the terms made familiar by Paul Smith, who finds that "though the Conservative party enjoyed what was in many ways its heyday under Salisbury's leadership, it is hard to say that his role was crucial to its success or that he gave it any distinctive...policy that can be accounted fundamental in its development."[2] Adding that Salisbury conspicuously lacked the "creative impulse," Smith states that there was "no element in the party's personality, no article of its creed or item of its policy, no turn of its thinking that can be said to have originated with him." In office, "he seemed to men like Lord Randolph Churchill to be unsympathetic to the cultivation of mass support made necessary by the extension of the franchise [in 1867]."[3] Peter Marsh, in his study of Salisbury's domestic statecraft, strikes the same note: the object of his endeavors "was stability, to be produced by well considered and firm resistance to radical change."[4] Donald Southgate agrees, writing that "It was too much to expect Salisbury to act in the spirit of democracy." And further, "he lived essentially from day to day. He imparted no impulse. He developed no doctrine–except one of caveats. He left no legacy, except his brilliant eccentric sons."[5]

Yet the nature of Salisbury's policy for the lords puts these judgments in doubt, suggesting in fact a political leader more on the order of that promised by Blake's initial description. Nor was the adoption of the referendal theory the impulse of the moment; rather it was part of a carefully thought-out strategic plan that had been prepared over a long period of time. That Salisbury took up the theory at all and gave it widespread popularity makes for hesitation in describing him as basically impervious to change. In this instance he seems to have welcomed it, embracing it almost recklessly at times. With high energy and maturing political skills, Salisbury undertook to cement a firm alliance between the authority of an aristocratic, hereditary house and the popular

---

2. *Lord Salisbury on politics: a selection from his articles in the Quarterly Review, 1860–1883* (Cambridge, 1972), 1. Blake's more recent statement is in the introduction to *Salisbury: the man and his policies,* ed. Lord Blake and Hugh Cecil (New York, 1987), 7–8.

3. Smith, *Lord Salisbury on politics,* 1, 105, 108.

4. Peter Marsh, *The discipline of popular government* (Hassocks, Sussex, 1978), 14.

5. *The Conservatives: a history from their origins to 1965,* ed. with an introduction and epilogue by Lord Butler (1977), 224.

will;[6] and the ingenuity and pertinacity with which he pursued his goal led to a distinctive Conservative ideology that shaped his party's policy in the decade before 1914. An examination of the history of the referendal theory reveals a political leader of uncommon tactical skill and political inventiveness. That this can be said of Salisbury is the more remarkable because some of his personal characteristics seem to militate against this assessment.

His decision to proceed in this way was at bottom due to his fear that parliamentary reform must make the house of commons increasingly stronger even as the house of lords grew feebler. Unless the process could be reversed, that house would become a cipher in the constitution just when the lords were needed to check a Liberal house of commons. What he feared was radical change, in particular the adoption of direct taxation, which he viewed as a manifestation of class warfare.[7] Salisbury, a man of great pride, also deeply resented membership in a house unable to withstand the pressures of a house of commons dominated by William Gladstone in alliance with Radicals such as John Bright and Joseph Chamberlain. To cap it all, he seems to have had a personal dislike and distrust of Gladstone.[8]

Very probably the emphasis on the importance of public opinion so evident in the referendal theory grew out of the interaction between Salisbury's journalistic career and his membership in the house of commons from 1854 to 1868. In this time period he was writing for the *Saturday Review* (after 1856) and the *Quarterly Review* (after 1860). The dates are the more meaningful because by 1861 he was engaged in a public quarrel with Gladstone over the Paper Duties Bill, which involved the powers of the house of lords; and the line of thought expounded by Salisbury on this occasion presaged the referendal theory to a remarkable degree. Three years later he stated that "power in these days is not with those who interpret opinion but those who

---

6. Hatfield House 3M/CC, chap. 1, p. 16. This is vol. 5 (unpublished) of Lady Gwendolen Cecil's *Life of Robert Marquis of Salisbury*, 4 vols. (1921–32).

7. *Salisbury: the man and his policies*, ed. Blake and Cecil, 105–7, 155–6, 162–3, 230. Smith, *Lord Salisbury on politics*, 124–6.

8. Corinne C. Weston, "Salisbury and the lords, 1868–1895," *Historical Journal*, 25, 1(1982), 107, note 13; 120, note 60. See also Viscount Cecil, *A great experiment* (New York, 1941), 13.

form it," and in 1867 he commented knowingly on "the class by whom *public opinion is manufactured* [italics added]–the journalists, the literary men, the professors, the advanced thinkers of the day."[9] It is notable that journalists topped the list.

There is the further point that Salisbury in this period could also have been influenced by what he knew about the parliamentary debates over the repeal of the Corn Laws in 1846, a traumatic episode that splintered families, old friendships, and political alliances. It will be necessary to consider in some detail the nature of these debates, but it should be noted for the moment that by 1872 Salisbury had made his decision to adopt the referendal theory as the best means of resurrecting the powers of the lords and making the Victorian world safe for conservatism.

That Salisbury in taking up the referendal theory departed sharply from conventional political thought may be seen by noting the very different outlook of the usual member of parliament. Influenced by the Westminster-centered writings of the third Earl Grey and in particular those of Walter Bagehot, he was likely to think in terms of a political system in which the house of commons had the deciding role. Such a system was known to contemporaries as "parliamentary government"–terminology with a precise, technical meaning. From Earl Grey's *Parliamentary government* (1858, 2nd edn. 1864) Victorian Englishmen learned that the concept of ministerial responsibility was the distinguishing principle in their government. According to Grey, the Crown's powers were exercised through ministers, who were members of parliament and held office only so long as they possessed the confidence of parliament, which was, to all intents and purposes, the house of commons. Political parties were indigenous to the system.[10]

This emphasis also distinguishes Bagehot's *English constitution* (1867, 2nd edn. 1872), which appeared initially in the *Fortnightly Review* of 1865 as a series of articles. Following out the same line of thought as Grey, Bagehot concluded that the commons'

---

9. *Lord Salisbury on politics*, ed. Smith, 289. *Saturday Review* 17 (May 1864), 547.

10. H. J. Hanham, *The nineteenth century constitution 1815–1914* (Cambridge, 1969), 13. See also the discussion in Angus Hawkins, "'Parliamentary government' and Victorian political parties," *English Historical Review*, CIV (July 1989), 638–9, passim, but especially, 657–62.

primary function was "the executive management of the whole state." This was exercised when the commons determined who was to be prime minister, and the latter then chose his cabinet. Next in importance was that house's "expressive function." This was "its office to express the mind of the English people on all matters which come before it." A related function was "to teach the nation what it does not know." Though Bagehot writes at one point as if the nation were sovereign and judge, he also refers to the commons as ruling the nation and conveys the overall impression that the electorate had at best a passive role, the commons acting upon it and not conversely.[11]

Since Bagehot treats the commons as the dominant force in the legislature, while assigning the lords very limited power, he presumably had only the commons in mind when he referred to the "accordance of parliament with public opinion." This interpretation draws support from William Sharp McKechnie, an authority in his day on constitutional history. He wrote in 1912 that "upon no aspect of the constitution was Bagehot more emphatic than on the dominating position occupied by the house of commons in deciding all questions of national policy, whether domestic or foreign, legislative or administrative."[12]

The key paragraph in the *English constitution*, on which McKechnie based his judgment, was as follows:

> The ultimate authority in the English constitution is a newly-elected house of commons. No matter whether the question upon which it decides be administrative or legislative; no matter whether it concerns high matters of the essential constitution or small matters of daily detail; no matter whether it be a question of making a war or continuing a war; no matter whether it be the imposing a tax or the issuing a paper currency; no matter whether it be a question relating to India, or Ireland, or London–a new house of commons can despotically and finally resolve.[13]

As for the lords, their legislative function was essentially confined to minor matters of little interest to the commons.

---

11. *The English constitution.* Introduction by R.H.S. Crossman (Ithaca, New York, 1966), 72, 151–3, 158.

12. *The new democracy and the constitution* (1912), 68.

13. *English constitution*, 219–20.

"When sure of the popular assent, and when freshly elected," the house of commons in Bagehot's view was "absolute": it could rule and decide as it liked.[14] Moreover, its position was equally strong when it came to the cabinet. If the latter were recalcitrant, it could be replaced. In short, the constitution was "framed on the principle of choosing a single sovereign authority, and making it good," and that sovereign authority was the commons.[15] Although Bagehot's remarks seemed to refer to a newly elected house of commons, at other times he abandoned the qualification.

Nowhere in Grey or Bagehot is there the conception of a public opinion independent of Westminster that arbitrated with binding authority when the two houses disagreed. Nor did the idea of parliamentary government allow the lords a position of consequence. Thus Bagehot, who found "the ruling influence—the deciding faculty" in the commons,[16] left little to the lords. That house was subordinate as a legislative chamber to the commons even before the Great Reform Bill of 1832; and since then its subordination had become ever more pronounced. Like the Crown it was a dignified part of the constitution, inspiring a reverence that attached people to the government; but the efficient part of the constitution was the house of commons. As the representative house, it was the centerpiece of the system.[17]

Not that the prevailing theory of the constitution recognized this constitutional change. It was a literary theory of mixed government remote from political reality, which treated the lords as an estate of the realm equal to the commons. This was not the case: a capital excellence of the English constitution was its provision for an upper house with less authority than the house of commons. The lords should possess some authority but not so much as the commons. The flaw in a system of two co-ordinate houses was that a single house might stop legislation and bring the machine of government to a standstill. Fortunately, this was not a real danger since the cabinet, its position based on the powerful house of commons, could make final decisions. "There

---

14. Ibid., 220. See also 20.

15. Ibid., 220.

16. Ibid., 67.

17. Ibid., 66, 121, 125–6, 150, 155, 157.

ought to be in every constitution an available authority somewhere," wrote Bagehot, and this "sovereign power must be come-at-able."[18] That the English government possessed this salient characteristic was demonstrated for all to see in 1832 when the Grey cabinet, in concert with the king and commons, compelled the lords' acceptance of the Great Reform Bill. Since then that house's function had altered. Earlier, "if not a directing chamber, at least a chamber of directors" it was now "a revising and suspending house." But it was no more than that:

> It can alter bills; it can reject bills on which the house of commons is not yet thoroughly in earnest–upon which the nation is not yet determined. Their veto is a sort of hypothetical veto. They say, "We reject your bill for this once or these twice, or even these thrice: but if you keep on sending it up, at last we won't reject it."[19]

A revising and leisured house of this type was very useful, if not quite necessary.[20]

To this description was added an account of Wellington as the politician-statesman who had presided over the constitutional change with minimal damage to the country. The *English constitution* gave wide circulation to the duke's celebrated letter of February 19, 1846 to Lord Stanley (later fourteenth earl of Derby and prime minister), relating how he had persuaded hostile peers to stay away from their house so the Reform Bill could become law and in the years 1835–41 had worked to lessen friction between the lords and the reformed house of commons. Wellington had guided the peers to what Bagehot considered their true position. Under his tutelage the lords had become "a chamber with (in most cases) a veto of delay with (in most cases) a power of revision, but with no other rights or powers."[21]

There was, then, no place in parliamentary government for a strong house of lords armed with an independent legislative veto, and Wellington was the great exemplar of a Conservative

---

18. Ibid., 126–7.

19. Ibid., 128.

20. Ibid., 134.

21. Ibid., 128–31. It should be noted that in the introduction to the second edition of the *English constitution* there is a sign that Bagehot knew of the new set of ideas associated with Salisbury. His central topic in both editions, however, is the Palmerstonian constitution of 1865 and 1866. Ibid., 267, 280.

leader who had realistically accommodated to the changed political world after 1832. Until the early 1880s, when the lords became more assertive,[22] Liberals and Conservatives alike accepted the maxims of parliamentary government as expounded by Grey and Bagehot; and the Liberals continued to do so thereafter, acting on its premises in passing the Parliament Act (1911).[23] But long before this Salisbury had converted his party to the populist ideology that is the subject of this study.

He developed the referendal theory in a series of speeches, delivered over a generation of politics, sometimes at Westminster but at other times before large audiences in the industrial cities. The style of his argument appears from his speech of July 8, 1884 in the house of lords, recommending the rejection of the Third Reform Bill ostensibly on the ground that Gladstone had failed to couple the extension of the franchise with a redistribution of seats in the house of commons. The issue should go to the electorate for settlement. To the peers he declared:

> In the presence of such vast proposals we appeal to the people...If it is their judgment that there should be enfranchisement without redistribution, I should be very much surprised: but I should not attempt to dispute their decision. But now that the people have in no real sense been consulted, when they had, at the last general election [in 1880], no notion of what was coming upon them, I feel that we are bound, as guardians of their interests, to call upon the government to appeal to the people, and by the result of that appeal we will abide.[24]

Such a house of lords was unknown to Wellington and Bagehot.

This is not to ascribe democratic convictions to Salisbury though the concept of direct democracy led him eventually to the referendum.[25] His interest was above all to elevate the power and authority of the house of lords in the post-1867 system; and his speeches and writings reveal no interest, for example, in the democratic device of the initiative, which is often found in the

---

22. Hanham, *The nineteenth century constitution*, 173.

23. Weston, "Salisbury and the lords," 105; 105, note 8.

24. Ibid., 106, note 11. See also note 8 and G.H.L. Le May, *The Victorian constitution: conventions, usages and contingencies* (1979) 133–45.

25. See J. L. Garvin, *The life of Joseph Chamberlain* (1933), ii, 577.

company of the referendum. But there was no need for him to be democratic in outlook for his sponsorship of the referendal theory to be richly rewarding to the house of lords and the Conservative party, so long as he was its head. His advocacy was no less radical in its effects and no less effective because he valued direct democracy as a means of promoting the lords' independent veto rather than as an ideology to be pursued in its own right. After all, it was hardly necessary for him to believe in the value of equal electoral districts for his acceptance of that principle in 1884 to have a profound effect on Victorian politics.[26] Similarly, despite the undoubted partisan use to which he put the referendal theory and his lack of interest in the initiative, Salisbury's sponsorship of direct democracy helped shape the ideological climate of late Victorian England while encouraging in the Conservative party an alienation from the parliamentary government described by Grey and Bagehot, that would be displayed so conspicuously in the years from 1910 to 1914.

By the early twentieth century Salisbury was gone from the political scene and the Conservative (also termed Unionist) party leadership had passed to his nephew, Arthur Balfour. Despite the Liberal landslide of 1906, which might have been expected to render Conservatives more cautious in their policy for the lords, they continued to evoke the referendal theory to justify that house's legislative veto. Another clear signal that the Conservatives had turned their backs on parliamentary government came with the party's adoption of the referendum as its alternative to the Parliament Bill. This action was the logical outgrowth of the referendal theory, and it will be seen that Salisbury on several occasions in the early 1890s indicated his willingness to go this route. Making the referendum the center of party policy demonstrated dramatically that the Conservatives had indeed parted company with parliamentary government. An avowedly antiparty system, it was directly opposed to the idea of representative and parliamentary government and the ascendancy of the house of commons. The referendum entered the realm of practical politics after the general election of 1906, when the Conser-

26. James Cornford, "The transformation of conservatism in the late nineteenth century," *Victorian Studies*, 7 (1963–4), 35–66.

vative leadership finally recognized that the house of lords could no longer be depended upon to checkmate a Liberal house of commons. Even then there were Conservatives unwilling to make so radical a departure from the existing system; and Conservatives as prominent as Lord Curzon and Austen Chamberlain, for their individual reasons, displayed a marked antipathy to the referendum.

The most active proponent of the referendum was the second Lord Selborne (1859–1942),[27] who began political life as a Liberal Unionist but in the course of events married Salisbury's older daughter and became an ardent imperialist, best known for his career as a proconsul in South Africa in the wake of the Boer War. He was in cardinal respects Salisbury's ideological heir in the events leading to the Parliament Act, though this statement is not meant to imply that Salisbury would have necessarily employed the same political tactics. Selborne, who was Lord Wolmer with a seat in the commons until his father's death in 1895, very early adopted the referendum and stayed with it until very late. His vigorous advocacy contributed importantly to the Unionist decision to adopt the referendum before 1914. He surpassed Salisbury in his zeal for the referendum, and his motivation was much more affected by imperialist considerations, granted the impact of Irish home rule on Salisbury. Selborne worked closely with his brother-in-law, the fourth marquis of Salisbury, usually known as "Jem," and the latter shared Selborne's strong interest in empire and was likewise receptive to the referendum though not on the same scale.

In summary, the Conservative party at Salisbury's behest turned away in the late nineteenth century from the parliamentary government defined and eulogized by Grey and Bagehot and carried forward by Wellington as leader of the lords. In its place Salisbury inserted a new theory of direct democracy in the guise of a referendal theory of the house of lords that in its main premises was hostile to parliamentary government as it had developed between the first two Reform Acts. The logic of Salisbury's

---

27. Selborne's attachment to the referendum can be seen in *The crisis of British Unionism: Lord Selborne's domestic political papers, 1885–1922* (1987), ed. George Boyce, 44–5, 51–6.

position was pushed to its limits when his party, responding in Edwardian England to Selborne's insistence, made the referendum a vital part of its policy.

Even though Salisbury was an unrivalled spokesman for the lords' referendal function, elements of the referendal theory, justifying that function, were on display before and after he made his contribution. In the earlier period Conservatives used it to oppose what they viewed as the radical measures of their leaders, and it was only after Salisbury took it up that the theory became a weapon in partisan controversy. The theory can be dated from the Corn Law crisis of 1846, and it endured thereafter without a major setback until the Parliament Act of 1911 brought it to an abrupt end. The year 1922 is the terminating point of this study, however, because at that time Liberals and Conservatives agreed that the Paliament Act was permanent, not to be disturbed whichever party was in power.

Two

The Emergent Theory, 1846–68

I

The referendal theory was very much in evidence as early as Catholic Emancipation in 1829 but was used for the first time on a broad scale in 1846 when repeal of the Corn Laws was at issue. The political quarrel on both occasions was between factions of the Tory or Conservative party. In 1829 Wellington was prime minister with Sir Robert Peel in the cabinet as a trusted ally; in 1846 the roles were reversed. The atmosphere in which they advanced their controversial policies was so highly charged with emotion that with Peel as spokesman they felt compelled to justify their course of action in constitutional terms by calling on the accepted doctrine of parliamentary sovereignty.[1] Another pertinent parallel between the two episodes requires mention. Conspicuous in the opposition of 1829 and again in 1846 was the spirited Charles Lennox, fifth duke of Richmond, one of the greatest landlords of the kingdom, experienced parliamentarian, and trusted spokesman for the Protestant constitution and the agricultural interest. In both instances his attack on Wellington drew on the political ideas that became the referendal theory; and his support, more than any other single factor, explains its prevalence in 1846.

According to Michael Brock, Richmond and his associates denied in 1829 that Wellington's government could rightfully enact the Emancipation Bill in the unreformed house of commons without a previous referral of the Catholic question to the electorate. Otherwise there would be an outcry for parliamentary

---

1. See for example Peel in 1829. *Hansard's parliamentary debates*, new series, xx, 1287–8 Cited hereafter as *Parl. debs.*.

reform within the year.[2] Although Richmond asserted that his reasons for pressing for a dissolution in 1846 were the same as in 1829, his speeches against Catholic Emancipation do not reflect the referendal theory. But his activities at that time suggest that he was thinking in these terms when he presented a series of anti-Catholic petitions to parliament with the aim of portraying Wellington and Peel as ignoring the country's will. Other Ultra Tories were more articulate on the subject. To Michael Sadler, the doctrine of parliamentary sovereignty was a legal fiction,[3] while others described Emancipation as "against the will of a Protestant country because of a pack of unprincipled borough owners" and denounced the house of commons as a machine for thwarting the popular will.[4] Some Ultra Tories, including Richmond, became parliamentary reformers. He served as postmaster general in Lord Grey's Reform Cabinet; and it was said at the time that he was considered for a place on the committee that prepared the Reform Bill. The rumor is a tribute to his influence, but none of the Ultra Tories was named.

In 1846 Richmond took the lead in demanding that Peel consult the electorate before proceeding with a Corn Bill to repeal the Corn Laws. He spoke from a position of strength as one of a very small number of leading Conservatives willing to oppose Peel. Richmond had moved gradually in this direction after Peel carried into law the Corn Bill of 1842. Although it was thought that he would make no further inroads on the Corn Laws, as early as 1843 he sponsored a Canada Corn Bill that put in doubt his further intentions. This doubt was nourished by the agitation of the Anti-Corn Law League, to which Peel was deemed to be especially susceptible. At this juncture Richmond "explicitly took up the defensive and potentially aggressive position which he and the leaders of the agricultural interest [in both houses] were to occupy during the following two years," urging his fellow agriculturists "to stand firm on the common ground of determination to resist any further changes."[5]

---

2. *The great reform act* (1973), 57.
3. *Parl debs.*, 3rd series, lxxxiii, 20 Ibid., new series, xx, 1170.
4. Brock, *Great reform act,* 55.
5. For Richmond's growing resistance to Peel, see David Robert Fisher, "The opposition to Sir Robert Peel in the Conservative party, 1841–1846." Ph.D. dissertation 6948, University of London, Jan. 29, 1970, pp. 93, 152–3. This dissertation has been used in this study with the author's permission.

Other factors besides Richmond's leadership explain the willingness to use the referendal theory in 1846. For one thing, recognition was general that Peel with Whig support had the needed majority to carry his Corn Bill in the house of commons. If rejection were to come, it would have to be in the lords, who were ill-prepared to oppose the government. The confidence of the lords had been badly shaken by the events of 1832 when Grey, with the king's reluctant consent, threatened to swamp that house with a large peerage creation if its assent were not forthcoming to the Reform Bill. A sufficient number of peers under Wellington's leadership stayed away on the final vote for the Bill to become law. In a private letter before the year was out the duke described what had occurred, writing:

> ...there is no reflecting man who in looking at the transactions of that time will not see that the Reform Bill was carried by the ministers and the house of commons against the king and the house of lords. It is true that the king and the house of lords were saved at that moment, the former from disgrace and the latter from being swamped. But I cannot consider either at present in a state of independence.[6]

Caution was also needed because a house dominated by great landlords ran the risk of being charged with self-interest if it refused to repeal a tax on food after the house of commons had voted to do just this. In these circumstances, a house of lords bent on rejecting Peel's Corn Bill proved willing to take a democratic path.

Moreover, a precedent was set during the general election of 1831 that supported the referendal theory when William IV, prior to dissolving parliament, asked for a mandate for parliamentary reform. Lord John Russell, at the time the Whig leader in the house of commons, explained: the electors were being called upon "not merely to select men the best fitted to defend their rights and interests but to answer by their conduct this question put to the electors...by his majesty in dissolving parliament: 'Do you approve–ay or no–of the principle of a reform in the representation?' "[7]

Finally, the idea of carrying repeal in a five-year old parliament, elected in 1841 to maintain the Corn Laws, proved of-

---

6. Quoted in Robert Livingston Schuyler and Corinne Comstock Weston, *British constitutional history since 1832* (Princeton, New Jersey, 1957), 29.

7. Quoted in C.S. Emden, *The people and the constitution* (2nd edn., 1956, repr. 1959), 199.

fensive to many. So ardent an advocate of repeal as Richard Cobden, leader of the Anti-Corn Law League, doubted that a commons "elected to maintain protection should abandon its pledges and do the very reverse."[8] And Russell, whose support was essential for repeal, was probably thinking in the same terms when he announced in accordance with the 1831 precedent that he favored dissolving parliament and providing the country with an opportunity to give its verdict on so momentous a question.[9]

II

It appeared for a time that Peel would not be the one to repeal the Corn Laws. In early December 1845 he resigned, only to resume the prime ministership when Russell, who had declared publicly for free trade, failed to form a government. Returning with Peel were all the members of his cabinet with the notable exception of Lord Stanley, soon to become earl of Derby and Peel's successor as leader of a much-changed Conservative party.

A conspicuous figure in the lords, Stanley seemed from the first the natural leader of the protectionists; but to refuse to rejoin Peel was not to oppose the Corn Bill publicly, and many months elapsed before Stanley emerged as the opposition leader. If the interim situation was too murky to decide exactly when he took the plunge, his main contribution to the protectionist cause is nevertheless easily identified. This was his statement of the referendal theory in a famous speech of May 25, 1846. Hailed on all sides as "one of the very finest ever made in parliament" it was remembered admiringly forty years later by a contemporary who had heard it. The theory could have had no better sendoff, but there was no substantial followup during the rest of his career. Nor at the time did he display any energy in carrying forward the campaign against Peel's Corn Bill. Observe this verdict from an historian of the Conservative party: "However loudly men might proclaim him as their leader, he persisted in not tak-

8. John Morley, *The life of Richard Cobden* (1881), i, 348 Ian Newbould, "Sir Robert Peel and the Conservative party, 1832–1841; a Study in failure?," *English Historical Review*, XCVIII (July, 1983), 529–57, especially, 549, 551.

9. Spencer Walpole, *The life of Lord John Russell* (1891), i, 424.

ing on the job."[10]

The situation in the commons was no better. There the vacuum in the leadership lasted until April, at which time Lord George Bentinck emerged as the protectionist leader. Apparently it was his intention to do so at the beginning of the session, but this was known only to a few intimates such as Stanley and Richmond. A political amateur and the subject of an admiring and influential biography by his political adviser, Benjamin Disraeli, Bentinck possessed charismatic qualities that make it easy to overestimate his role in the opposition to Peel. Yet he brought a certain cachet to protectionism as the younger son of the duke of Portland and a man of wealth in his own right with a notable record as a sportsman and racetrack reformer. Stanley was his close personal friend and admired political leader; and there subsisted between them, Disraeli writes, "warm personal as well as political sympathies."[11]

While Stanley pondered his course, Richmond filled the leadership void in the lords. Norman Gash writes of his "leading the attack on the second reading of the Corn Bill."[12] It will be remembered that he was an Ultra Tory capable of unexpectedly embracing large new principles, as in the years 1829–1832. He was also an intimate friend of Stanley, with whom his career was intertwined. Both members of Grey's Reform Cabinet, they left the Whigs in 1834 and joined the Conservatives, as the Tories under Peel were now being called. But Stanley soon outdistanced Richmond. After serving in Peel's second cabinet (1841–6), he became the Conservative party leader and was subsequently

---

10. Lady Katherine Clarendon, "Diaries," e.2092, fo. 57 These are in the Bodleian Library. See also *Duke of Argyll: autobiography and memoirs*, ed. Dowager Duchess (New York 1906), i, 276. The speech was published at the time by the Agricultural Protection Society, discussed below as the Anti-League and also as the Central Society. Richmond headed it. For the pertinent portions see *Parl. debs.*, third series, lxxxvi, 1174–5. Recognizing that the speech was important, Robert Stewart quotes from it in his *Politics of protection* (Cambridge, 1971), 69–70. Describing the speech as "an eloquent plea for aristocratic government," he overlooks its important populist aspect. The comment on Stanley's leadership is on p. 69 See also William Sharp McKechnie, *The reform of the house of lords* (Glasgow, 1909), 19–20.

11. *Lord George Bentinck: a political biography* (1852), 174 This influential book, a standard source for the protectionists in 1846, was republished in 1872 and again in 1895. It went through at least 4 editions in 1852.

12. *Reaction and reconstruction in English politics* (Oxford, 1964), 50 See also Gash, *Sir Robert Peel* (1972), 581.

thrice prime minister. Richmond and Bentinck were also firm friends; indeed, the latter's racehorses were stabled at Goodwood. Described as Richmond's household companion and racing partner, Bentinck corresponded regularly with him in 1845 and 1846.[13]

Perhaps because he is often viewed as a political leader of secondary importance, Richmond receives little attention in most scholarly accounts of the Corn Law crisis. The tendency is to neglect him completely or else subordinate him to Stanley, Bentinck and Disraeli. That this assessment requires revision is suggested by Mary Lawson-Tancred's influential article on the Corn Law crisis, which was reinforced and supplemented in D.R. Fisher's doctoral dissertation "The Opposition to Sir Robert Peel in the Conservative Party, 1841–1846." A revised assessment might run like this. Since Stanley shunned the political battle for many months, either refusing to assume the leadership or failing to exercise it vigorously after he assumed it, the role of protectionist leader fell by default to Richmond throughout much of the crisis. Though Bentinck was also an agriculturist, he was not Richmond's equal in this regard and could not claim to speak for the agricultural interest. Moreover, Bentinck like Stanley was slow to take the leadership; and when he did he displayed serious deficiencies. Finally, if Disraeli's colorful slashing attacks on Peel helped unify the opposition, the bulk of the protectionists distrusted him as an independent adventurer.[14]

Richmond stands out in this quartet for his prescience and enterprise in organizing the agricultural interest that explain so much about the changed scene when the protectionist parliament met to consider repeal of the Corn Laws. A liberal landlord and an established figure in the agricultural world, he was from 1845 until his death in 1860 president of the Royal Agricultural Soci-

---

13. *The Goodwood Estates Archives*, iii (Chichester, 1984). 75 There are for example in the Goodwood papers letters from Bentinck to Richmond as follows: MS 1669, fo. 219 (Mar. 14, 1845); ibid., fo. 221 (Mar. 19, 1845); MS 1681, fo. 132 (Jan. 30, 1846); ibid., fo. 133 (Jan. 31, 1846); MS 1681, fo. 138 (Feb. 8, 1846). This letter, ten pages long, has Bentinck telling Richmond at great length how the latter's son Henry should campaign in Sussex. See also MS 1681, fo. 159 (Mar. 23, 1846).

14. Fisher, "Opposition to ...Peel," 255–6, 435–6, 465–6, 472 Lawson-Tancred, "The Anti-league and the Corn Law crisis of 1846," *Historical Journal*, 3, 2(1960), 167–8; 168, note 30; 169; 170–1, etc. See also Gash, *The Conservatives*, ed. Butler, 100–2, 115.

ety. In 1846 he was as emotionally upset at the prospect of repeal as Bentinck, whose undisguised anger at Peel receives frequent mention in scholarly accounts of the Corn Law crisis. Richmond even made a parliamentary speech warning the Anti-Corn Law League that industrial machines were as combustible as haystacks, a remark that shocked fellow protectionists.[15] He was moreover a seasoned parliamentary leader, with lengthy experience in building support among fellow parliamentarians, a skill with a carry-over value in 1846. Despite the failure of his efforts to prevent the passage of Peel's Corn Bill, which was introduced on January 27, the thoroughgoing manner in which he aired the referendal theory before a national audience goes far to explain why Salisbury, with a very different purpose in mind, turned to that theory in the early 1860s.

That Richmond had this kind of influence was due to the network of local protectionist societies known as the Anti-League that arose during the winter of 1843–4. Its founding is usually attributed to a tenant farmer, Robert Baker of Writtle; but from the beginning Richmond, too, was involved. In London in December 1843 for the Smithfield Show, which attracted agriculturists from all over the world, a restless Richmond, by this time ready to oppose Peel if it seemed necessary, attended a meeting that Baker called to consider how best to deal with the Anti-Corn Law League. Afterwards Baker founded the Essex Protectionist Society, the model for subsequent societies; and about the same time there appeared a protectionist society in Sussex, where Richmond's influence was paramount.[16] It is important to stress that the Anti-League became not Baker's but Richmond's political instrument,[17] enabling him to bring formidable pressure to bear on Peel.

This was especially true after the formation of the Metropolitan Society of landlords and MPs under Richmond's auspices. After it met at his London House in Portland Place, it was only a question of time until his forces coalesced with Baker's. The Port-

---

15. Clarendon, "Diaries," e.2091, fos.1–2, 64 The speech was on Feb. 16 and Richmond is quoted as stating that "machinery could be burnt as well as stacks.".

16. Lawson-Tancred, "The Anti-League," 168.

17. Fisher, "Opposition to…Peel," 158–9.

land Place meeting, reported in *The Times* of February 19, 1844, was followed two days later by a tenant farmers' meeting, with Baker in charge, at the Freemason's Tavern in London. With 250 present from nine counties and also two emissaries from Portland Place (George Darby, MP for East Sussex and William Miles, MP for East Somerset), the meeting decided to organize a central organization for the Anti-League representative of both groups. A provisional committee of 22 delegates then met at Richmond's London House with Richmond, the duke of Buckingham, the duke of Leeds, and some 40 or 50 landlords. Out of this discussion came a new body of major importance, the Central Agricultural Protection Society, usually referred to as the Central Society. Richmond is said to have favored a very full representation for the tenant farmers in its management, and this was achieved. The governing group consisted of a president (Richmond), a vice-president (Buckingham), and a management committee composed of 20 members of parliament, of which two were to be peers; 20 tenant farmers; and the chairmen or vice-chairman of the protectionist societies. The Central Society's primary function was to coordinate the activities of the local protectionist societies, and this was accomplished by establishing a meeting place in Old Bond Street with a secretary and regular office hours.[18]

If the accession of the tenant farmers was essential to the Anti-League's success, so too was the support of the landlords, as Richmond's own elevation reveals. Disputing G L Mosse's assertion that tenant farmers actually supplied the leadership of the new organization, Lawson-Tancred, offers a telling rebuttal when she asserts that support from the landlords was indispensable if there were to be a movement at all. Robert Baker and his associates assured their followers that the landlords not only approved their meetings but also would be ready to assist "in purse and in person" if need be. It was usually farmers who arranged for the first meetings and then appealed successfully to landowners "for

18. Ibid., 157 Travis L. Crosby, *English farmers and the politics of protection 1815–1852* (Hassocks, Sussex 1977), 132–3 Lawson-Tancred, "The Anti-League," 168, 170–1.

that support, assistance, and cordial union without which success is not to be expected." Although the Anti-League was described as a farmers' movement, it combined country gentlemen, clergymen and the more important farmers.[19] The political figure whom Lawson-Tancred most frequently mentions is Richmond.

Moreover, she places the leadership of the Anti-League squarely in Richmond and a very able and experienced group of protectionist MPs. This means that he was strategically placed to influence proceedings in parliament and hence the ideological tone of the debates. The protectionist MPs with whom he acted included August Stafford O'Brien (Northamptonshire); Philip Miles (Bristol); his brother, William Miles, who, as was earlier noted, represented East Somerset; J G Heathcote (Rutland); Charles Newdegate (Warwickshire); George Bankes (Dorsetshire). William Miles, who had a long record of opposition to Peel before 1846, led the anti-League MPs in parliament; and also conspicuous in their ranks was Bankes. He, too, had opposed Peel before the Corn Law crisis; and he was a vigorous spokesman for the referendal theory in 1846.[20]

Despite a more centralized structure, the Anti-League was less effective for some time than one might anticipate because of Richmond's reluctance to engage in extra-parliamentary activity. He thought it unconstitutional to bring pressure to bear on parliament as the Anti-Corn Law League was doing, but it was apparent by December 1845 that a change was coming when Richmond exhorted the protectionist societies against compromise. At a time when other agriculturists waited for Peel to make public the details of his Corn Bill, Richmond, perhaps in response to a letter from his close associate, Lord Malmesbury, took a decisive step. Responding to his call for action the Central Society on January 12 amended its constitution to allow the protectionist societies to organize opinion for political purposes; and an early fruit of the new policy was the strong pressure now applied to

---

19. Ibid., 168.

20. Ibid., 168, note 30; 171 Fisher agrees with Lawson-Tancred about the leadership of the Anti-League. "Opposition to...Peel," 159–61. For Miles and Bankes, see ibid., 53, 97–8, 117–8, 164, 191, 436.

members of parliament. Talk even began of setting up a new protectionist party independent of Peel.[21]

The Anti-League sponsored widespread public meetings, which were "combined with a large number of petitions to parliament and followed by a concerted move in the house of commons." Add to this activity its influence on by-elections and the conclusion follows that "it formed the indispensable basis of the protectionist party and was thus essential to the maintenance of any serious opposition to Peel."[22] Though Disraeli slights the Anti-League's activity in his biography of Bentinck, Robert Blake writes in his *Disraeli* (1967): "It is probably true to say that the parliamentary organization of the protectionist party was largely made possible by the Anti-League and that without some such basis Disraeli and Bentinck could never have carried on such a long struggle against the repeal of the Corn Laws."[23] Yet this comment makes no reference to Richmond and while glancing at the Anti-League leaves Disraeli and Bentinck at center stage in a struggle where no organized opposition was possible without Richmond. With much reason Fisher concludes: "The `Anti-League' campaign certainly provided the impetus for and guaranteed the appearance of numerically large and protracted opposition to repeal before Bentinck and Disraeli came forward." In his view this sustained opposition, combined with the strong emotional reaction to Peel as party leader that had developed since 1841, might well have led to a permanent rupture of the party without a Disraeli or Bentinck. But in any case, "certain

21. Malmesbury to Richmond, Jan. 4, 1846, West Sussex Record Office, Goodwood MS 1690, fo. 1513. Crosby, *English farmers*, 136–9. Lawson-Tancred, "The Anti-League," 168–9; 177–81. See also Fisher, "Opposition to...Peel," 420–6, 442–50. Peel's attitude towards the Central Society's change in its rules can be seen in Gash, *Sir Robert Peel*, 574–5. He considered that the Anti-League would now be fighting the Anti-Corn Law league with its own methods, with an end result telling "in favour of democracy." His impatient description of Richmond at this time as "that great goose" probably reflects this concern. Ibid., 583. For Peel's more positive view of Richmond on another occasion, see ibid., 313–4.

22. Lawson-Tancred, "The Anti-League," 165–6, 176. Fisher, "Opposition to ...Peel," 434–6, 438–9, 442, 451.

23. Disraeli, *Bentinck*, 47–8, 77–81 Blake, *Disraeli*, 225, 758 Lawson-Tancred, "The Anti-League," 163–4 But see Stewart, *The politics of protection*, 56–7; Fisher's review of this book in the *Historical Journal*, 15, 2(1972), 371–3; and Derek Beales' comment on the Anti-League's importance in ibid., 21, 3(1978), 705 Consult also Fisher, "Opposition to...Peel," 471, note 4; 472.

facts militate against a simple interpretation of the split in terms of the emergence of viable leadership for a group of disgruntled Conservative backbenchers." Finally, he notes, only 73 Conservatives of the 252 who had voted against repeal later "joined Disraeli and Bentinck in toppling Peel on the Irish Coercion Bill."[24]

Early in January Richmond and Bentinck met at the Central Society's Bond Street headquarters to plot strategy for the coming parliamentary session. Following Peel's disclosure of the details of his Corn Bill on January 27, Bentinck then attended for the first time a meeting of the Central Society, which accepted the tactics that he and Richmond favored. The plan was to prolong the repeal debate as much as possible, agitate issues at by-elections, and stir up the country before the Corn Bill reached the lords. In this way, it was hoped, that the lords would enjoy a greater freedom of action than was possible in the commons. According to Disraeli,

> calculations were made of those who might be fairly counted on to take a part in debate; some discussion even ensued as to who should venture to reply late at night to the minister; a committee was appointed to communicate with all members on either side supposed to be favorable to the principle of protection to the labour of the country; a parliamentary staff was organised, not only to secure the attendance of members but to guard over the elections; finally, the form of the amendment to the government measure was discussed and settled, and it was agreed that if possible it should be moved by Mr Philip Miles, the member for the city of Bristol.[25]

Sir William Heathcote, the much-respected member for Hampshire, was to be the seconder; and on February 9 Miles, assisted by Heathcote, introduced a motion to postpone debate for six months.[26] It touched off the bitter and protracted opposition to Peel that, as earlier noted, owed so much to the Anti-League.

---

24. Ibid., 472–3.

25. Disraeli, *Bentinck*, 80–1 See Stewart, *Foundation of the Conservative party*, 213 for the meeting between Richmond and Bentinck at the Central Society's office to plan strategy. They were assisted by such leading members of the Central Society as George Bankes, William Beresford, Philip Miles, Charles Newdegate, and Stafford O'Brien.

26. *Parl. debs.*, 3rd series, lxxxiii, 549, 559 Disraeli, *Bentinck*, 81.

The purpose of the amendment to which Disraeli alluded and Philip Miles introduced was to allow time for consulting the country before Peel could proceed with repeal. This appears from the Central Society meetings of January 12 and 26. At the first Lord Beaumont, whose record of distrust of Peel was as long as Richmond's, suggested that if the queen's address displayed any intention of altering the Corn Laws, an amendment be moved that no such step be taken without a previous appeal to the country; and shortly afterwards Richmond signified his approval. Then there was the meeting of the management committee of the Central Society on January 26. Lord March (Richmond's son), the two Mileses, Bankes, O'Brien and Newdegate among others met to "concert action and create a skeleton organization." Although Bentinck did not attend, it appeared that he had heard from Lord Stanley that he doubted a third party could be formed at this time and consequently would not agree to head the protectionists. This did not prevent those in attendance from moving ahead. Fisher writes: "Newdegate was made `a sort of whipper-in', [William] Miles was to lead in the commons, and it was decided to wait until after Peel's statement [giving details of his Corn Bill] to divide, *putatively on the issue that the country be allowed time to consider the question.*"[27] This interpretation is not incompatible with Disraeli's account, and it is supported by the tenor of the parliamentary debates when Richmond and his associates insisted on the need to consult the country.

It should be noticed, however, that Disraeli's speeches at this time point to political ideas fundamentally different from Richmond's and the Anti-League's. By making the electorate the decision-maker with regard to the Corn Laws, Richmond took the more populist and radical position. Disraeli, on the other hand, anticipates Grey and Bagehot in their discussions of parliamentary government in that he, too, places the house of commons at the center of the political system. To Disraeli, Peel's great sin was not his refusal to consult the electorate before proceeding with repeal, as Richmond and his associates contended, but the prime minister's willingness to ignore the Conservative majority that had been returned to parliament in 1841. The elector-

---

27. Fisher, "Opposition to...Peel," 104, 106, 158, 433, 436 See note 25 above.

ate had already spoken; and the Conservative majority in parliament, pledged to protection, was the embodiment of public opinion.

The party had brought Peel to power only to find that imbued with his own ideas of his authority, which he saw as independent of party, he was pursuing an essentially authoritarian path in deciding the country's commercial policy. That is, he was defying the doctrine that executive authority rested ultimately on party support in parliament. As Disraeli observed in December 1845: "Peel...wants to figure in history as the settler of all great questions [which included the Corn Laws]; but a parliamentary constitution is not favorable to such ambitions: things must be done by parties, not by persons using parties as tools."[28] Only by maintaining the independence of party could one maintain the integrity of public men and the power and influence of parliament itself.[29] The charge against Peel was that he had prevented the legitimate action of public opinion, expressed through the party majority in parliament; he had therefore reached a conclusion and would probably achieve a result which would not be satisfactory to the community because of his approach. "We say, and say with reason," Disraeli continued, "that by the aid of that great mass of public opinion which we represent the right honourable baronet was raised into power; and that a parliament was elected to give effect to that opinion *which we represent*, and the right hon. baronet has disregarded."[30]

In Peel, Disraeli, and Richmond are to be found, then, three ideological streams. Disregarding Peel's ideas, because these represented the government, it is possible to see from the debates that the ideological line taken by the opposition emanated on the whole from Richmond rather than Disraeli. And

28. Hawkins, "'Parliamentary government' and Victorian political parties," 654–5 See also 647, 652–5 Blake, *Disraeli*, 223.

29. Ibid., 227 Hawkins, "'Parliamentary government' and Victorian political parties," 654.

30. *Parl. debs.*, 3rd series, lxxxiii, 1320 Travis Crosby reports that Disraeli reproached Peel not only for proposing the repeal of the Corn Laws without regard for the role of party but also for doing so "without consulting the electorate." In fact Disraeli was dealing only with Peel's failure to consult his parliamentary majority, which "embodied public opinion." See *English farmers*, 141–2 The speech was on Feb. 20, 1846.

this means that at the least Richmond has to be deemed on ideological grounds as important as either Disraeli or Bentinck, who are more commonly described as the key opposition figures in the repeal parliament. But it is time now to turn to the debates to see the degree to which the ideology identified with Richmond held sway in the opposition camp.

III

Before the session began on January 22, rumor had it that the protectionists would rely on a novel argument in making their case. Fresh from a party meeting on January 19, a leading Whig, Lord Clarendon, thought a small majority in the commons for the Corn Bill would permit the lords to argue that the vote did not "truly represent public opinion upon the subject" and insist accordingly on a dissolution. This was the least foolish argument available to them, "it being something of a principle," if they were not wise enough to pass the measure.[31] On the opening day Richmond set the tone for his forces, attributing this sentiment to the agricultural interest: "You, the present government, came into office pledged to protection: you have thought fit...to propose an alteration in the Corn Laws: but we say to you, you ought not to carry out such a measure without again appealing to the country." Peel should "appeal to the country and let the country decide."[32] Malmesbury echoed him: the lords should force an "appeal to the people."[33]

The seriousness with which the challenge was greeted appears from the knowledgeable diarist, Charles Greville, clerk to the privy council, Bentinck's cousin, and at one time his racing partner. He was also intimate with such prominent political leaders as Wellington, Clarendon, and Lord Palmerston. Well situated to report on gossip in high circles, Greville wrote in a pri-

---

31. Clarendon, "Diaries," e.2091, fo. 22.

32. *Parl. debs.*, 3rd series, lxxxiii, 22 See also his comment on May 18 where he stated that Peel should have recommended a dissolution. "As it is," he continued, "the people of this country have no voice in these great changes which he proposes." Ibid., lxxxvi, 729.

33. Ibid., lxxxiii, 42–3.

vate letter of January 23, the day after Richmond and Malmesbury spoke, that the lords were showing a tendency to take up a strong position which could be defended by "arguments it is not easy to answer." "They demand a dissolution," he continued, "They say (at least may say) that the country elected this house of commons to protect agriculture, that last year there was a majority of 204 against a motion of precisely the tendency of Peel's measure, and *they have a right to require that the country shall be appealed to, to say whether they confirm the vote of last year's or the determination of this.*" Nothing could be more constitutional than this course, Greville concluded; and he expected it to be followed if the Bill passed the house of commons–"very likely, if by a large majority, certainly, if by a small one."[34]

The call for a dissolution became more insistent after Peel outlined his plan. Protection of grain would end in three years, but until then temporary duties would be put on a sliding scale with the duty varying from 4 to 10 shillings, depending on the domestic price. A month later Bankes, a stout protectionist, influential leader in the Central Society, and in Disraeli's words "the popular and much esteemed member for Dorsetshire,"[35] attacked Peel's failure to advise a dissolution in a speech so severe in tone that the latter would feel compelled to justify at length his chosen course. According to Bankes, England profoundly disliked coalitions, especially when men of opposite principles, as in the eighteenth-century Fox-North coalition, combined to prevent the appeal to the people for which the constitution provided. If Peel and Russell were not working against the people's voice, they would not fear appealing to the country. Should the commons ignore his words, Bankes would look to the lords. His invitation to that house to reject the Corn Bill conveyed the essence of the referendal theory. "Whatever may be the result here," he declared, "we trust that in another place...a delay will happen which shall give an opportunity to the people to declare their opinions and feelings on the subject." The lords should use their prerogative "of counselling the crown to apply to the people to know

---

34. *Letters of Charles Greville and Henry Reeves*, ed. A.H.Johnson (1924), 145. See Sir Llewellyn Woodward, *The age of reform* (Oxford, 2nd edition, 1962), 20, note 1; pp. 639–40.

35. Disraeli, *Bentinck*, 179.

whether they are or are not willing to become parties to this great, extra-ordinary, and extravagant change."[36]

Bankes is a shadowy figure in historical accounts of the Corn Law crisis, but his importance ought not to be under-estimated. A personal friend of Richmond and Bentinck, he served at the beginning of 1846 as the unofficial leader of the protectionist MPs. He zealously pressed Bentinck to assume the leadership in the commons; and following a large protectionist meeting at his house in Palace Yard, Bentinck for the first time met his friends in the commons as their leader. After the Corn Bill passed the second reading in the lords, a meeting of June 9, likewise at Bankes' house, adopted the resolution to vote against the Irish Coercion Bill that drove Peel from office and effectually out of public life. Before Bentinck became leader, a small committee composed of Bankes, William Miles, and O'Brien and advised by Disraeli, guided the protectionists in the commons. Except for Disraeli, they belonged to Richmond's Central Society; and Miles and O'Brien, at least, belonged to its management committee. The small committee mentioned above, continuing after Bentinck undertook the leadership, acted as "a sort of shadow cabinet." When he resigned his post in December 1847, he placed his resignation in Bankes' hands.[37]

Bankes violated parliamentary practice by addressing his remarks directly to Peel rather than to the speaker–an action that attests his high emotion. Just as clearly his bitter charge found its target. Peel's response at the time was a lengthy apologia for his conduct, to which he later reverted in his *Memoirs*[38] and again in

36. *Parl. debs.*, 3rd series, lxxxiv, 253–4, 261–2 For other calls for a dissolution see ibid., lxxxiii, 124–5 (William Miles), 158 (Bankes), 285 (O'Brien), 552–3 (Philip Miles).

37. Disraeli, *Bentinck*, 141, 179, 193, 514–5 Gash, *Sir Robert Peel*, 594. Blake, *The Conservative party from Peel to Churchill* (1970), 64.

38. *Memoirs by ...Sir Robert Peel*, pub. Lord Mahon and Edward Cardwell (1857), ii, 166. Peel wrote: "It appeared to me also that there were grave objections to the proposal that we should notify to the constituent body on the eve of a general election the intention to repeal the Corn Laws for the express purpose of inviting an expression of their opinion on that particular subject. I thought such an appeal would ensure a bitter conflict between different classes of society, and would preclude the possibility of dispassionate consideration by a parliament, the members of which would have probably committed themselves by explicit declarations and pledges, and would approach a discussion which could not be deferred, with all the heat and animosity engendered by severe contests at the hustings.".

his *Letter to the electors of Tamsworth* (1847).[39] Though Peel spoke at first only in terms of the commons, he was actually defending the doctrine of parliamentary sovereignty. A dissolution, he stressed, must create a dangerous precedent since this implied that the house of commons in being was incompetent to deal in the first instance with repeal. He would never sanction "the view that any house of commons is incompetent to entertain a measure which is necessary for the well-being of the community."[40] Such a doctrine, which must shake the best laws in their foundation, had been put forward at the time of the Act of Union; and Peel now quoted Pitt's dictum on that memorable occasion:

> If this principle of the incompetency of parliament to the decision of the measure be admitted, or if it be contended that parliament has no legitimate authority to discuss and decide upon it, you will be driven to the necessity of recognizing a principle the most dangerous that ever was adopted in any civilized state–I mean the principle that parliament cannot adopt any measure new in its nature and of great importance, without appealing to the constituent and delegating authority for directions.[41]

Since parliament was competent to alter the succession to the throne, to incorporate the Irish parliament with that at Westminster, and to disfranchise its constituents through parliamentary reform, he considered it strange to hear that he should advise a dissolution before proceeding with the repeal of the Corn Laws.[42] The suggestion was the more unacceptable because of its democratic overtones, a stand that Cobden also took. It was impossible to find, in Peel's words, "a more dangerous example, a more purely democratical precedent" than that "this parliament should be dissolved on the ground of its incompetence to decide upon any question of this nature."[43]

---

39. Ibid., 106 He wrote: "I could not admit the incompetency of the present parliament to deal with this as with every other question of public concern.".

40. *Parl. debs.*, 3rd series, lxxxv, 224.

41. Ibid., col. 225.

42. Ibid., cols. 225–6.

43. Ibid., col. 226. For Cobden's comment, see ibid., lxxxiv, 278 and see Bruce Coleman, *Conservatism and the Conservative party in nineteenth century Britain* (1988), 77, note for comment on Peel as a traditionalist on this question.

The demand for a dissolution was as vigorous in the lords. When the Corn Bill reached that house in May, it encountered Stanley's stiff resistance. As earlier noted, he had stood aside for some time, hesitating to repudiate his former colleagues by acting with their political enemies. He had not joined in the demand for a dissolution, put forward on January 22 by Richmond and Malmesbury; and almost a month passed before he clarified his position. Then he followed their lead. "There could be no doubt that on a subject of such vast importance," he declared on February 6, "the sense of the country as well as of the parliament should be taken."[44] Two days later, after a conversation with Wellington at Apsley House, Stanley wrote to him that Peel's proposed legislation had completely dislocated and shattered the Conservative party in both houses. Even Wellington's great name and influence was unlikely to induce the lords to sanction the Corn Bill, and in Stanley's view Peel could never reunite the party under his guidance. Apparently the duke had suggested that Stanley act as unifier; but the latter considered that unity was now possible only in opposition. He himself might vote against the Corn Bill but would not head a movement for its rejection.[45]

Wellington's response was the letter of February 19 that Bagehot printed. The duke stated that in a recent letter to the queen he had put an end to his connection with party whenever it opposed her government. Describing himself as "the servant of the crown and people," he would have Stanley exercise the influence in the lords that had been his and in doing so guide the lords' opinion, not just follow it. In the present situation the lords should avoid a position that reflected a personal interest, and Wellington pointed out that in his opinion protection was out of the question.[46]

Stanley was not to be dissuaded, however, from the course foreshadowed on February 16 and on March 9 protectionist peers assembled at Richmond's London House heard a letter read from him in which he advised the course to be pursued in opposing Peel's Corn Bill and promised support for the protectionist cause.

---

44. *Parl. debs.*, 3rd series, lxxxiii, 941.

45. G.R. Gleig, *History of the life of Arthur Duke of Wellington* (1860), iv, 133–7.

46. Ibid., 138–45, especially 142–4.

The group then recognized him as its leader and named two whips, Malmesbury and Lord Eglinton, to assist him.[47] Yet Stanley, as the protectionist party was taking shape under Richmond's leadership, continued to pursue his tortuous path. Lady Clarendon, though willing to forecast that Stanley would be the opposition leader, reported a second speech of his on March 20 in which he continued to deny that he held the post. Much later, on May 19, she recorded that "Lord Stanley was elected as head of the protectionists by the duke of Richmond appealing to him as such in the house of lords and Lord Stanley not denying it."[48]

It appeared for a time as if the Corn Bill would be defeated without a full-scale debate in the lords. With Richmond in the lead and Stanley's approval protectionist peers planned to join anti-free trade whig peers in supporting a small fixed duty on grain hostile in principle to Peel's policy. "Peel, who goes for the total abolition, will then be obliged to go out or dissolve parliament," wrote Malmesbury.[49] On May 15 the commons approved the Corn Bill by a majority of 98, and Cobden reported the rumor that on its arrival in the lords it would be altered in committee either by a fixed duty compromise or else a perpetuation of the reduced scale.[50]

Russell scotched the rebellion. On May 23, two days before the second reading began in the lords, he informed a meeting of Whig peers at Lansdowne House that he would resist any attempt to alter the Bill. Clarendon, deeply hostile to a coalition of Whigs and protectionists, provided Russell with powerful support. He had earlier conferred with Lord Chancellor Lyndhurst; and he informed his listeners, on Lyndhurst's authority, that the government intended to call for proxies before bringing up the committee's report if the wrecking amendment carried. Since proxies could not be used in committee, Clarendon was telling

---

47. Stewart, *Politics of protection*, 66 Earl of Malmesbury, *Memoirs of an ex-minister* (1884), 1, 169–70.

48. Clarendon, "Diaries," e.2092, entry of May 19, fo. 44.

49. Malmesbury, *Memoirs*, i, 171–2 Gash, *Sir Robert Peel*, 591 According to Gash, a great protectionist meeting of May 21 with Richmond in the chair, heard that Stanley was now the protectionist leader. Ibid., 592. See also the accounts in Morley, *Cobden*, i, 370; G.M.Trevelyan, *The life of John Bright* (Boston, 1913), 149; and Herbert C. Bell, *Lord Palmerston* (1936), i, 363, 368. Palmerston would be prime minister if the coalition produced Peel's downfall.

50. Morley, *Cobden*, i, 382.

protectionist peers and their allies among the Whig peers that any success in committee would be undone when their report reached the house, where proxies could be used.[51] Lord Palmerston, the intended beneficiary of the scheme, announced the meeting's results to a friend: "All unanimous against the Bill, and all unanimous not to oppose it."[52] How seriously the setback was viewed can be seen from Malmesbury's comment soon after the meeting: "We shall…be completely beaten if they do not vote for the fixed duty."[53]

The Corn Bill was out of danger, then, when the second reading began in the lords on May 25. Aware that this was the situation, protectionist peers nonetheless made repeated use of the referendal theory in a continuing demand for a dissolution. Thus Stanley, in his widely acclaimed speech on that day, took this course, thereby giving the theory an éclat which goes far to explain its subsequent success in Victorian England. If the lords were to accept the Corn Bill without approving its contents, he warned, their house could be viewed as no more than a subordinate branch of the constitution, "the registrars of the edicts of the house of commons." It was their duty to oppose hasty legislation, to be sure, but also "to protect the people…against the treachery of those whom they have chosen to be their representatives." From this dichotomy between the commons' views and those of the electorate, which Stanley professed publicly to discern and Salisbury would later so successfully and repeatedly exploit, the referendal theory grew and prospered. If the lords were to arrest the progress of this hasty measure, he continued, giving "time for the intelligence of the country to act upon the public mind," they would receive a grateful nation's approbation. What they would not do, however, was set their will against that of the nation. As he said, in words echoing into the early twentieth century, it had never been "the course of this house to resist a continued and deliberately formed public opinion." Their lordships "always have bowed, and always will bow, to the expression of such an opinion."[54]

---

51. Clarendon, "Diaries," e.2092, fos. 48–52.

52. Lord Broughton, *Recollections of a long life*, ed. Lady Dorchester (1911), vi, 173.

53. Malmesbury, *Memoirs*, i, 172. See also the conclusion in a lead article in *The Times*, May 25, 1846.

54. *Parl debs.*, 3rd series, lxxxvi, 1174–6 At one point Stanley referred to the lords as "the trustees for the constitution of the empire." Ibid., col. 1174 See also William Sharp McKechnie, *The reform of the house of lords* (Glasgow, 1909), 19–20.

Other protectionist peers embroidered on the theme. During the last general election, Malmesbury declared, the country had given its verdict for protection as opposed to free trade. Now it was being deceived and betrayed by its representatives. If he were mistaken in making this charge, he said, "the real opinion of the people was easily ascertained; and it was their lordships' duty to ascertain it." If the new house of commons had a "clean" majority, for the bill rather than the existing "clear" majority, Malmesbury would "bow to the decision of an undoubted and indubitable majority of the English people."[55] Eglinton called upon the peers as "the hereditary guardians of the people, to reject this measure,"[56] and the ultra-conservative earl of Winchilsea was equally democratic. The lords ought not "to sanction a measure which might be attended with such disastrous results, until the people had a full and a fair opportunity of recording their free, unfettered opinions upon the change."[57]

The impact of Stanley's argument was lessened, though not erased, when Wellington on May 28 wound up the debate on the second reading by placing his great name and authority squarely in opposition to the emergent referendal theory. Clearly he continued to believe, in accordance with his letter of February 19, that conflicts between the houses ought to be avoided; and he now implied that Stanley's line of reasoning of May 25 would provoke such conflicts. Granted that the lords had the duty of protecting the people from the commons' rash measures, still they ought not to enquire into the relationship between the commons and their constituents. It was really none of their business. Noting that Stanley had found the commons' vote of May 15 for the Corn Bill "inconsistent with the original vote given by the same house of commons on this same question, and inconsistent with the supposed views of the constituents by whom they were elected," Wellington emphasized that this was no subject for the lords to consider. They could have no accurate knowledge of the fact; and whether or not it was the fact, they knew that it was the commons who had sent them the Corn Bill.[58] The more impor-

55. *Parl. debs.*, 3rd series, lxxxvi, 1265.

56. Ibid., 1359.

57. Ibid., 1226.

58. Ibid., 1404–5.

tant fact was that it had come to them with the crown's and the commons' approval: in these circumstances the lords were entirely powerless. If they rejected the Corn Bill, it would come to them again; and in any case they should wait until the normal course of events brought a dissolution rather than insist on consulting the country.[59]

Not even Wellington could speak this way without raising suspicion of being hostile to the popular will and clinging to outmoded political theories. He was abruptly informed that the peers would be well-advised to look to the people for direction when an anonymous writer in *The Times*, who also believed that the Corn Bill should pass, strongly criticized Wellington's constitutional theory. Without the people's support,the duke was advised, a vague speech from the crown and the lords' approval held little meaning. The anonymous writer pointed out: "His grace contrives to elude this fact. The views of the constituency cannot be ascertained he says, and whatever they are to have nothing to do with them. He has more to do with them than he chooses to confess." Said *The Times*, referring directly to Wellington: 'he studiously blinked the people."[60] The duke's experience illustrates the difficulties inherent in condemning the referendal theory. To oppose it squarely was to risk being charged with an anti-democratic or anti-populist mindset; and if the risk carried few penalties in 1846, these would increase as the century went on.

From the standpoint of constitutional theory Lord Brougham's was a more telling riposte. Responding on January 22 to Richmond and Malmesbury, he revealed his grasp of the new theory's implications for parliamentary government or, as

---

59. Ibid., 1404–5. Wellington warned that rejection of the Corn Bill could lead to a dissolution with possible injurious effect on the royal prerogative.

60. *The Times* (June 1, 1846), 4. But in the crisis over the Third Reform Bill *The Times* (July 24, 1884) quoted Wellington's doctrine approvingly. To Lady Clarendon, Wellington's speech was "curious." He had failed to advance any argument for the measure while speaking to the peers as if they were engaged in a "military movement to retreat in time." "Diaries," e.2092, fos. 62–3 Disraeli's comment was caustic. "After a discussion of three nights, closed by the Duke of Wellington in a speech in which he informed the house of lords, that 'the bill...had already been agreed to by the other two branches of the legislature' " and that, under these circumstances,"there was an end of the functions of the house of lords, and that they had only to comply with the projects sent up to them; a sentiment the bearing of which seems not easy to distinguish from the vote of the long parliament which openly abrogated those functions, the lords passed the second reading...." *Bentinck*, 229.

he termed it, representative government. In much of his comment Brougham sounded like Peel, and the subject is of course closely related to the idea of parliamentary sovereignty. He returned to it on June 12, two weeks before the Corn Bill became law. The very essence of representative government, the greatest political discovery of modern times, was that government should be in the hands of representatives. Constituents ought not to settle questions that should properly be left to representatives, a line of argument suggesting an attack on the Anti-Corn Law League and the Anti-League. Nor was an appeal to the people any more acceptable. "If, because a question was called a paramount question, parliament must be dissolved, and an appeal made to the people, there was an end to the representative system." He then combed the past for examples of great questions settled without such appeals. There had been no demand for a dissolution at the time of the Union with Ireland, nor in 1829 when Catholic emancipation was the issue, nor over the Maynooth question; and he invoked Charles James Fox's authority at the time of the Union. The latter had insisted on the rule that parliament was chosen for general purposes. Should it fail to legislate without a prior appeal to the people because it was said that a particular measure was important, successive questions would be described in these terms with the result that representative government would be ended. Not that dissolutions were never justified. If ministers differed from parliament or the two houses from each other, the proper course was a dissolution.[61]

Although the arguments during the debates seem at times jejeune, this was not the contemporary view. Thus Brougham, after the conflict cooled, considered the referendal theory in his influential work on the constitution;[62] and Peel's concern was no-

---

61. *Parl. debs.*, 3rd series, lxxxiii, 33–4. Brougham was mistaken about 1829. Richmond would agree that there was mischief in sending delegates to parliament but noted that protection or free trade had been an issue in 1841. While he did not like pledges, he also disliked their being broken. Richmond thought that the Conservative ministers' course would lead to more members being made delegates since constituents would have reason to question the honesty of their representatives. Ibid., lxxxvii, 366–7.

62. A comparison of the two editions of Brougham's *The British constitution: its history, structure and working*, one published in 1844, the other about 1860 (it carries no publication date but the dedication is dated Dec. 11, 1860), suggests that the debates on the Corn Laws had led him to consider carefully the theory of representation. He

ticeable when he answered Bankes. This appeared not only from his speeches and later writings but also from the close attention that he devoted to procedural matters in repealing the Corn Laws. The very fact that the crisis did not seem a matter of constitutional importance was alarming to him; without precautions the door might inadvertently open to constitutional change. According to Betty Kemp, who has written perceptively about Peel's viewpoint in these months–but without reference to the ideological tone of the Corn Law debates that sheds so much light on Peel's attitude–the crisis "might easily, and to some extent unperceived, have produced precedents enough to push the constitution decisively along the road to democracy." She considered this outcome the more possible because the events of 1845–6 could have reinforced the democratic implications of 1831–2. Thanks to Peel's awareness, this did not happen. His fear that the manner of repeal might undermine the constitution was very real, and she writes that it "is the key to his conduct throughout the crisis, and because of his steadfastness and his ability, it is the key also to the course of events."[63]

Peel's attitude was evinced in a number of ways. By returning to office after Russell failed to form a government, he had ensured that parliament, not the electorate, would decide the issue of free trade. Similarly motivated, he made provision for repeal of the Corn Laws to extend over three years and by so doing reduced friction between the houses to a minimum and thus the possibility of a dissolution and a general election that might produce a mandate. In Peel's opinion, the purpose in holding a general election was to choose a house of commons, not as in 1831 to decide a policy or designate a government. Kemp writes:

---

does not deal with the subject in the first edition; but in the second he praised representative government and laid down canons for its operation. They began: "The deputy chosen represents the people of the whole community, exercises his own judgment upon all measures, receives freely the communications of his constituents, is not bound by their instructions, though liable to be dismissed by not being reelected, in case the difference of opinion between him and them is irreconcilable and important." *The British constitution*, 2nd edition, p. 94.

63. "Reflections on the repeal of the Corn Laws," *Victorian Studies*, V, (Mar., 1962), 189–90, 195–6, 200–4.

> The alternative view, that the people should make the decision–that, in this case, there should be a general election held specifically on the question of repeal and the continuance of Peel's government–was Disraeli's [in 1868] and had been [William] Cobbett's. It was a view encouraged by the Reform Act, and by the circumstances of its passing, but by no means firmly established.[64]

Finally, Peel resigned in June 1846, after defeat on an Irish Coercion Bill, doing so on the constitutional ground that defeat in the commons should lead to resignation. Urged to seek a dissolution, he refused. By resigning he would take his dismissal from the commons, not the electorate.[65]

In summary, Peel in the midst of a social and economic crisis discerned an important constitutional and ideological principle and acted consistently to maintain it. Contrary to the precedent of 1831, when the general election provided the Grey ministry with a mandate for parliamentary reform, Peel and Wellington in 1846 railed off the constituencies from the political arena. Had they not done so, Kemp points out, the crisis could have produced precedents that would tilt the constitution decisively towards democracy. An incident of greater constitutional importance than casual consideration suggests, it was one that Peel and Salisbury viewed very differently.

Salisbury's opinion was expressed in a speech of 1884 defending the lords' rejection of Gladstone's Third Home Rule Bill on the ground that a redistribution bill should have accompanied it. When a Liberal spokesman (Sir William Harcourt) asserted that it was for the house of commons, not the lords, to decide upon the franchise and redistribution, he turned to the precedent of 1831. At the time the Great Reform Bill was before parliament; and Harcourt, so Salisbury related, insisted that the Grey government, basing its action on the commons' vote, overawed the lords. Why had they yielded in 1831? According to Salisbury, these were the salient facts. A dissolution had taken place after the Bill was introduced, and the general election that

---

64. Kemp, "Reflections on...the Corn Laws," 201.

65. Ibid., 202–4.

66. *Speeches of the Marquis of Salisbury*, ed. Henry W Lucy (1885), 140.

followed plainly revealed the nation's desire. At this juncture the house of lords was right to yield, and he wished that it had done so sooner–indeed, at "the moment the voice of the nation was clearly pronounced."[66]

The Corn Bill received a final reading in the lords on June 25, 1846 after five months of debate that wounded family relations and disrupted long-standing political alignments. Its passage has often been discussed in terms of its economic and social effects as well as its impact on party; but it is urged here that its ideological impact is also worthy of consideration. Protectionists in both houses had called for a parliamentary dissolution as the necessary preliminary to legislating free trade, and Stanley had insisted that the lords would honor the electoral verdict when it was returned. These political arguments gave rise to the referendal theory, and Stanley's provided the classic statement. The theory was expounded in the commons by such leading members of the Anti-League as Bankes, William and Philip Miles, and O'Brien; and in the lords by Richmond, Stanley, Malmesbury and their associates. And it drew alarmed responses from Peel, Wellington, and Brougham. To Peel, the opposition argument violated the doctrine of parliamentary sovereignty and, in particular, put in question the competence of the commons to handle public issues without the electorate's prior approval. Wellington had relied on a view of the constitution that contemporaries thought strange. And Brougham, while his argument resembled Peel's, stressed the constitutional relationship between the constituencies and the members of parliament and the danger to representative government that the demand for a dissolution posed. Three major speakers–Peel, Cobden, and Brougham–stigmatized the demand for a dissolution as democratic in nature and hostile in its tendencies to the existing constitutional system.

IV

Despite a marked resemblance between the protectionist attitude in 1846 and that of the late Victorian house of lords, no attempt seems to have been made to use the referendal theory for some years after the repeal of the Corn Laws. That theory was the product of a particular set of circumstances; and, as these receded, the lords reverted to the more traditional path. Nor did any important Conservative leader emerge with a powerful and persistent interest in the theory, a negative fact of considerable consequence. To be sure Stanley, now Derby, brought the theory forward once more in 1869, when the Irish Church Bill was under consideration; but not in the interim. Yet Derby's influence in this regard was much more important than this summary comment suggests. The protectionist argument in 1846, of which his speech on May 25 provides the shining example, in all probability sparked Salisbury's decision to take up the referendal theory. In doing so, he, too, stressed that the lords would accept the nation's will though not that of the commons if the houses fell out; and his parliamentary activity gave this important tenet a credibility that stood the lords in good stead during the remainder of the century.

Not until 1868 did the theory return to center stage, doing so when the lords rejected Gladstone's Suspensory Bill, the prelude to the Irish Church Bill. Once more political circumstances combined to produce this result, and once more it appeared as if the referendal theory would be abandoned on the morrow of the political struggle that had produced it. That the outcome was different was largely due to Salisbury, newly arrived in the lords. Presumably he brought with him the ideas broached during the Corn Law crisis though the evidence is scanty and circumstantial.

It would be surprising if he had not since the household in which he grew to maturity was saturated with memories of 1846. His father, who had voted with Richmond and Stanley at that time, was lord privy seal in the latter's first cabinet and lord president of the council in his second. Salisbury was himself protectionist during his undergraduate days at Oxford University (1847–9), and in the course of a debate in the Oxford Union, he spoke forcefully of the need to reunite the Conservative party. Prior to his return to the commons from Stamford, Salisbury is supposed to have said on the hustings that reform is seldom an improvement and referred to "the unhappy policy of the late Sir Robert Peel," which had brought free trade. There were other strong familial ties that could have made him aware of the events of 1846. His father was Wellington's cousin; and his first wife,

Salisbury's mother, corresponded regularly with the duke. So, too, did his second wife, Salisbury's stepmother. One of the signs of the close links between the Salisbury family and Wellington was the latter's willingness to act as godfather to the children of the second marriage. Often asked to serve in this capacity, Wellington took the obligations seriously, and was conscientious in discharging them. Finally there was also a familial link with the Derbys. Two years after Salisbury's father died, his widow married Stanley's son, the fifteenth earl of Derby.[67]

The beginnings of Salisbury's own political career coincided with the period in which the Conservative party discarded the protectionist policy with which it had been associated since Peel's fall from power in 1846. It had clung tenaciously to the idea of restoring the Corn Laws until the Derby government defeat in the summer of 1852. A few months later Salisbury, a reluctant convert to free trade, issued an electoral address promising to abide by their abolition; and by this time, too, Disraeli, so conspicuous in the Corn Law crisis, was foremost in urging this course on his party. Paradoxically, his much-reprinted *Bentinck* was instrumental at this time in keeping alive the ghosts of yester years. Very likely, Salisbury, a voracious reader, was familiar with it, especially given the subject matter; and he may well have seen the passage in the biography responding to Wellington's insistence that the lords subordinate their judgment to that of the crown and the commons. Disraeli, who disliked the duke's position, equated his language with the long parliament's vote in 1649 to abolish the house of lords, an analogy so striking that it would have commanded a reader's attention.[68]

Other reminders of the Corn Law crisis abounded in the 1850s and 1860s. For one thing, the reading public, with every

---

67. *A great man's friendship: letters of the Duke of Wellington to Mary, Marchioness of Salisbury, 1850–1852*, ed. Lady Burghclerc (1927), 4, 14, 80, 89 F.S. Pulling, *The life and speeches of the Marquis of Salisbury* (1885), i, 6–7 "The Marquis of Salisbury: A personal and political sketch," a paper read before the Hackney Young Men's Liberal Association, Oct. 6, 1882, 4–5.

68. *Bentinck*, 229 See also ibid., 215 Wellington's speech and Disraeli's response in *Bentinck* are noticed in such works as Sheldon Amos, *Fifty years of the English constitution* (Boston, 1880), 32. See also Salisbury's reference to the Corn Law crisis in May 1864, which reflected an opinion much like Wellington's in 1846. *Saturday Review*, xvii, 547. Gleig, *History of the life of ... Wellington*, iv, 143.

opportunity to become acquainted with the February exchange of letters between Stanley and Wellington, may have followed them up by reading their May speeches. The prominence of the two political leaders guaranteed a large audience. It has been noticed that Stanley was for some time leader of the Conservatives, and Wellington had become a living legend in his own lifetime. Conqueror of Napoleon, British envoy to the Congress of Vienna, and prime minister (1828–30), he occupied a position unique not only in England but also in Europe. Despite his high Tory opinions, he was somehow seen as above politics, a "fourth estate"; and his death in 1852 released a flood of biographies, chief among them those of A.H. Brialmont and George Gleig. Brialmont's work appeared in French in 1856 and between 1858 and 1860 in Gleig's translation. In 1862 Gleig published his own study of Wellington, which went through a people's edition. The translation of 1860 and the people's edition contained the exchange of letters between Stanley and Wellington. Finally, the duke's speech of May 28, 1846 was reprinted in 1854 in a collection of his speeches.[69]

Little wonder that in a review of a popular life of Wellington Salisbury declared: "Every event in the duke's public life has been described and re-described till it is as familiar as the Bible to the English eye." Further, "every record of expressed opinions has been collected, abstracted, and abridged, till no more remains for the most diligent labourer to undertake."[70] Given the personal relations between Wellington and Salisbury's family, Salisbury had a surprisingly adverse view of the duke's policies. Peel, in his opinion, ought not to have carried the Corn Bill; and he attributed to the duke the decision to proceed with it. Moreover, Wellington had demonstrated repeatedly in 1829, 1832, and 1846 that he did not appreciate the importance of consistency in public men.[71] For this quality in Wellington Salisbury had neither sympathy nor respect, as his own political career reveals.

---

69. *The speeches of the Duke of Wellington, collected and arranged by...Colonel John Gurwood* (1854), 665–9.

70. *Saturday Review*, ix, 215.

71. Ibid., 216.

In later years Salisbury displayed keen resentment when reproached for not emulating Wellington as leader of the lords. Quite naturally, after the experience of 1832 and 1846 and the publication of Bagehot's *English constitution*, the Liberals held out Wellington as the received model of such a leader. Thus Gladstone, in referring in 1871 to the lords' rejection of the Ballot Bill regretted the rise of an anti-lords movement but pointed out that the lords themselves were not without fault. They had been imprudent in their treatment of the Ballot Bill and the abolition of army purchase, both measures to which Salisbury was hostile. "There is no Duke of Wellington in these days," Gladstone continued; and he followed Bagehot–or even perhaps Wellington's letter to Stanley on February 19, 1846–when he added: "His reputation as a domestic statesman seems to me to rest almost entirely on his leadership of the peers between 1832 and 1841."[72] However, he stopped short of noting Wellington's stand in 1846 though it was the logical continuation of the duke's earlier policy. But Salisbury's outlook when he recalled Wellington's example was very different. Assigning to Lord Granville, the Liberal leader in the lords, the doctrine that it was the house's whole duty to obey the commons, Salisbury held Wellington responsible for what he regarded as an unfortunate outcome. The duke's course, he declared sarcastically in 1871, had "raised this house to its present high pitch of authority."[73]

If Salisbury early in his career became familiar with the protectionist ideology of 1846, he was attuned to the potential value of the referendal theory to his party well before the Irish Church Bill became a prime object of controversy. The second son of a peer with little prospect of inheriting the title and a limited income, Salisbury took his seat for Stamford in 1854; and

72. John Morley, *The life of William Ewart Gladstone* (New York, 1903), ii, 369.

73. *Parl. debs.*, 3rd series, ccviii, 479 See also Salisbury's reference to Wellington reported in *Speeches*, ed. Lucy, p. 120 His attitude may have been reflected in Selborne's comment on Wellington and Peel in 1912, quoted in Alan Sykes, *Tariff reform in British politics 1903–1913* (Oxford, 1979), 289. Given Selborne's devotion to the referendal theory, he could have had the theory in mind, as well as free trade, when he ascribed his party's lack of moral courage at this time to "the disastrous leadership of the duke of Wellington and Sir Robert Peel, which taught the party to conform to the motives of its opponents and to turn its back on its most cherished convictions.".

for the next fourteen years he was its MP before he went, reluctantly, to the lords. In these years which were critical in formulating his political credo, he reached the iconoclastic position that public opinion was the logical and appropriate arbiter when the two houses disagreed. He recognized the possibilities in "inciting and exploiting the power of public opinion" at much the same time as Gladstone, but the latter was adamantly opposed to ideas of the kind ascribed here to Salisbury. Of the two political leaders, Salisbury was the more radical on this point. The matter was put out of doubt, or so it seemed, when Gladstone in 1867 protested earnestly in the commons against any "circumstance by which the business of governing this country is taken from within the walls of this house and transferred to places beyond them."[74]

Salisbury was sensitive to the changed atmosphere of the 1850s, a decade marked by frequent discussion of the relationship between public opinion and parliament. The Crimean War had highlighted the Aberdeen coalition's failure to meet new demands on governmental machinery; and the press, in particular *The Times*, seemed to exert an unusual influence on government and public policy. As confidence faltered in the conduct of the war, it was increasingly considered that the army in the Crimea had been saved primarily by the press. The thundering of *The Times* and W.H. Russell's Crimean reports seemed to push ministerial policy "away from parliamentary government and towards a kind of direct democracy." In this heated atmosphere the *Saturday Review* was founded with the express aim of deflating *The Times.*

Following the Crimean War Salisbury contributed for a decade to the *Saturday Review*, his great activity coming in the years 1861–4. This was a seminal period for him, and the ideas to which he now subscribed stayed with him for the remainder of his public life. At a time when memories of 1846 were still vivid and signs of a growing interaction between public opinion and

---

74. *Parl. debs.*, 3rd series, clxxxvii, 719 For critical comment on Gladstone and his view of public opinion see T.A.Jenkins, *Gladstone, whiggery and the Liberal party, 1874–1886* (Oxford, 1988), 24–28 Cp. Lawrence Goldman, "The social science association, 1857–1886: a context for mid-Victorian liberalism," *English Historical Review*, ci (Jan., 1986), 95–134, passim.

politics were plentiful, a parliamentary episode had a cataclysmic effect on his thinking. Part of a celebrated quarrel between the lords and Gladstone, chancellor of the exchequer and a political leader of national stature, it occurred about three months after Salisbury's review of Wellington's biography. The quarrel grew out of the lords' rejection of Gladstone's Paper Duties Bill on May 21, 1860–to an exultant Salisbury an unexpected display of spirit. The lords had rediscovered in rejecting Gladstone's Bill that they had "a living power, wielded freely by themselves and recognized instinctively by the people."[75]

This outcome was completely unacceptable to Gladstone, a Peelite engaged in completing the movement towards free trade inspired by the Anti-Corn Law League. By the 1860s its leaders, Cobden and Bright, were working very closely with Gladstone; and the group was convinced that the lords' action would have to be reversed. Salisbury's sentiments were equally strong on the other side. Not opposed to free trade, he was angered by Gladstone's increase in the income tax as a means of offsetting the revenue loss that his Bill entailed. In Salisbury's opinion, the action signalled an intention of replacing a financial system dependent on indirect taxation with one based on direct taxation. The result would be the transferral of taxes from one class in the community (the manual laborers) to another (the propertied), with whose interests Salisbury identified himself. His forebodings were increased because he considered democracy on the march. Parliamentary reform, supported by Russell in the Palmerston government and Bright outside it, would encourage Gladstonian finance; and it was ominous for the future that as recently as 1860 Russelll had brought in a reform bill. "This question of the incidence of taxation" was, in Salisbury's words, "in truth the vital question of modern politics." It was "the field upon which the contending classes of this generation" would "do battle."[76]

Salisbury expounded his views at some length in two important articles in the *Quarterly Review*, the first of these "The Budget and the Reform Bill" in the April 1860 issue; the second, the

---

75. Quoted by Robert Stewart in *Salisbury: the man and his policies* ed. Blake and Cecil (1987), 91. See also Olive Anderson, *A liberal state at war* (New York, 1967), 43, 49, 50, 71–2, 78, 85, 88 Michael Pinto-Duschinsky, *The political thought of Lord Salisbury 1854–68* (1967), 39.

76. *Lord Salisbury on politics*, ed. Smith, 112–3; 124–6.

extraordinary "Democracy on its Trial," published in July 1861. In the latter, which was aimed at Gladstone and Bright, Salisbury related democratic institutions in the United States to the coming of the Civil War. The American experience provided the first modern instance of the application of the democratic theory to a large state, and the breakup into chaos and bloodshed was inevitable. There were lessons here for domestic politics. Gladstone and Bright were working to Americanize English institutions, and the former was actively tearing down the only two barriers between them and "the uncurbed dominion of the multitude." The barriers were a limited franchise and the lords' independence, both indispensable in Salisbury's opinion.[77]

So far as the lords were concerned, he had in mind their humiliation at Gladstone's hands after the rejection of the Paper Duties Bill. A pragmatic Palmerston would not have pursued the quarrel, but this was not Gladstone. He was determined to settle in the government's favor "the great question now depending between the lords and the English nation," and his most recent biographer reveals his zeal in pursuing his objective.[78] What Gladstone did was put all taxation measures, including repeal of the paper duties, into a single budget, and carry it through parliament. It passed the commons in late May and the lords on June 7 in 1861. Gladstone's action angered Salisbury, and so did his political alliance with Bright and other Radicals. On March 31 Salisbury had written to his friend, Lord Carnarvon: "My idea of angelic behaviour consists of supporting Palmerston and opposing Bright on all possible occasions–at all events the latter."[79]

In these circumstances Salisbury turned to the electorate as the counterweight required to do battle with Gladstone and the Liberal house of commons. Without the impetus supplied by these irritants, it is unlikely that he would have broken the mold of contemporary political thought at so early a stage in his career. Registering his public protest on May 6, 1861 Salisbury insisted that Bright and others who had taken a strong stand against the lords had mistaken the question of the previous year. They seemed to consider it "one of jurisdiction"; further, that

77. "Democracy on its trial" *Quarterly Review* (July, 1861), 286. The article itself is paged 247–88.

78. Richard Shannon, *Gladstone* (1982), 417 and passim.

79. Salisbury Papers D/30/3.

"the two houses were fighting in the arena by themselves, and that there was no one else whose behests they ought to consider and obey." As for the government, it seemed to think it was "a fight of procedure, and forms, and precedent, and parchment."[80]

At this point Salisbury adopted a distinctive ideological argument that certainly bore traces of 1846 but just as certainly in key respects went beyond Lord Stanley. In retrospect it can be seen that he took a giant step forward in formulating his later policy for the lords. What he did was to call upon public opinion to arbitrate between the houses. A simple formulation, to be sure, it was nevertheless revolutionary for the time in which it appeared. This was Salisbury's argument. Gladstone and his allies had failed to perceive that "behind and acting through the house of lords, there was the great educated public opinion of the country," of which the two houses were "merely the vehicles and instruments." They seemed to conceive of a struggle between the houses, in which the action of the lords could be fettered by an ingenious device. Not so. The outcome would depend on whether that house had the country with it. If it did, those hostile to the lords must submit.[81] Salisbury's comments on May 13 were equally germane: the lords and commons were the "servants of a common master–the nation, which watched their proceedings, and judged between their disputes." If the commons considered last year that their privileges were being disregarded by the lords, they should not have taken refuge in vague and ambiguous resolutions. Why did they "not dare in an open and manly way to appeal to the common master?"[82]

The same note sounded a few months later in the *Saturday Review*, but this time in the form of a spirited challenge to the lords. That house ought first to change its practices and then compete in the marketplace of ideas with the commons. Decrying the lack of attendance in the lords and the want of vigor in

---

80. *Parl. debs.*, 3rd series, clxii, 1582.

81. Ibid. Salisbury repeated some of these ideas in the *Saturday Review*, xvii (May, 1864), 547.

82. *Parl. debs.*, 3rd series, clxii, 2031 The quarrel between Gladstone and the lords is discussed in Richard Shannon, *Gladstone* (1982). Pinto-Duschinsky relates Salisbury's attitude towards repeal of the paper duties to his view of taxation. *The political thought of Lord Salisbury*, 146. See also 141.

their debates, Salisbury faulted the house for having "too many marks of an institution from which the life is departing." Nor was it any excuse to speak of events moving out of the lords' control. In a word, it was "idle to say that the spirit of the day is against them and that they dare not exercise the powers which the constitution has placed in their hands." They had never genuinely tried, had "never ascertained by experiment what amount of trust the public would place in a body doing its duties with as much zeal as an elective assembly." The issue should be brought to a test, and Salisbury now enunciated a theme that became a favorite with him. How much more pernicious to have a sham second chamber with only a perfunctory role in legislation, its very presence excluding a more efficient substitute! There would be time enough to find such a substitute when the house of lords had "shown by actual experiment that public opinion does not trust it to exercise a vigorous and effective control over legislation."[83]

Five years later, in January 1866, Salisbury made yet another pronouncement on the role of public opinion in the political system that revealed the direction that his thoughts were taking. His comments appeared in the *Quarterly Review* about the time when Bagehot in the *Fortnightly Review* was describing the predominance of the commons and the enfeeblement of the lords, with no more than a glance at public opinion. Salisbury wrote:

> *Our system is constructed to carry out in the policy of the government the actual opinion, at the moment, of the million and a quarter of electors by whom the nation is ruled.* It is a machine of the most exquisite delicacy. *The conduction from the electors, who are the source of power, to the ministers, is so perfect that while parliament is sitting they cannot govern for ten days in opposition to the public will.*[84]

---

83. *Saturday Review*, xii, 113–4 (Aug. 3, 1861) See also Lady Gwendolen Cecil, *Biographical studies of the life and political character of Robert, third Marquis of Salisbury* (1953?), 30–1. For Salisbury's abhorrence of anything that he saw as a sham, see, in particular, Lady Gwendolen's *Life of Robert Marquis of Salisbury* (1921), ii, 5, where she describes the practice at Hatfield House of referring to him as "Citizen Salisbury," because he objected to his title as a "sham." It maintained the rank without the original power. Also pertinent are Salisbury's denunciations of Liberal intentions to create a sham house of lords in 1884 and 1895. *Speeches of the Marquis of Salisbury*, ed. Sir Henry Lucy (1885), 142 *Parl. debs.*, 5th series, i, 33–4.

84. Cited in Cecil, *Life of ... Salisbury* (1921), i, 139.

The stands of two highly intelligent observers on this cardinal point, writing about the political system at approximately the same time, could hardly have been more different.

In sum, very early in a long political career Salisbury embraced the idea that the lords in a quarrel with the commons could safely turn to the electorate for support. At the least, he was saying, the experiment was worth a try. This approach, which he may well have inherited from the Corn Law crisis, was more congenial to him than one would suppose, given his much-publicized reputation for hostility to democracy. That reputation had arisen from his anger when the Derby-Disraeli government "shot Niagara" by passing the Second Reform Act (1867) with its provision for household suffrage in the boroughs. Although he had resigned in protest, along with Carnarvon and General Peel, rather than be party to the measure, his attitude at this time is no index to his later activity. If his reason told him that a particular outcome was determined, he did not look back in anger, so his daughter and biographer affirms. In Lady Gwendolen's words, he displayed no "tendency towards sullen or disheartened inaction"; indeed, he could be very aggressive and combative.[85] By the time he evoked the referendal theory on a consistent basis, he had long been a member of the house of lords; and the Second Reform Act was behind him.

His devotion to the lords was expressed in the *Saturday Review* and also in the *Quarterly Review* of July 1861. As he said, "it is generally admitted that the testpoint of Conservatism is the desire to uphold–in opposition to American theories–an hereditary second chamber."[86] That he made much headway in converting other Conservatives to this viewpoint, or holding them to it, appears from Lord Randolph Churchill's language in the *Fortnightly Review* (May 1883). Finding in the lords the nucleus of the party whenever the Conservatives were in opposition, he treated this as a sound reason for preferring Salisbury to Northcote as party leader in the period of dual leadership af-

---

85. Cecil, *Biographical studies*, 76–7. See also Stewart, "The conservative reaction," *Salisbury*, ed. Blake and Cecil, 112–3.

86. *Quarterly Review* (July, 1861), 281.

ter Disraeli's death. As Churchill stated: "Under present circumstances, it is to the house of lords alone that the Conservatives in the commons and in the country look for the maintenance of their principles, for the rejection or modification of existing legislation, and for an effective control of a government which is believed to aim at great constitutional changes." And it was in the lords that the genius and experience of his party were concentrated. He wrote: "The large Tory majority in the upper house, well and wisely handled by a statesman possessing the full confidence of the entire party in and out of parliament can fulfill these duties with safety and success." Since these duties were in many respects delicate, at times full of political danger, requiring for their discharge both tact and courage, nothing could be more destructive than a leader in the commons possessed of "co-ordinate authority with the statesman who may be leading the lords."[87]

More than twenty years passed before Salisbury held the high position that would tempt Churchill to employ such terms in discussing the party situation after Disraeli. Meanwhile, Salisbury went much further in building on his intuitive realization in the early 1860s that the house of lords could be plausibly associated with public opinion in a way that would protect it against political enemies while advancing the goal of legislative equality for that house. The critical occasion came very early in the post–1867 period, at a time when he had barely caught his breath after Disraeli passed the Second Reform Act. As early as 1868–9, when the Irish Church Bill was at the center of controversy, Salisbury underwent a political experience that alerted him more fully to the possibilities of the position that he had adopted in opposing Gladstone's repeal of the paper duties. But more than the Irish Church Bill sent Salisbury in this direction: his experience in the lords during Gladstone's great ministry as a whole contributed to his taking up the referendal theory on a systematic basis. That he did so had inestimable effects on the lords and parliamentary government too.

---

87. "Elijah's Mantle," *The Fortnightly Review*, no. cxcvii, new series–May 1, 1883, 619. See also R.E. Quinault, "Lord Randolph Churchill and tory democracy, 1880–1885," *Historical Journal*, 22 (Mar., 1979), 152–5, 158, 160, 162.

Three

Salisbury and the Irish Church Bill

I

The personality, temperament, and intellect that made Salisbury so formidable a figure in late Victorian England go far to explain his taking up the referendal theory. A strong will, an intense emotional commitment to the lords extending over many years, a deeply conservative yet combative temperament verging on recklessness, at least early in his career, a high intelligence, critical in nature, and a fertile and inventive political mind–these qualities made it impossible for him, after fourteen years in the commons, to sit in the elegant and empty house of lords without a strenuous effort to strengthen its power and authority. At the same time, Gladstone's mastery of the commons, in contemporary esteem so much the more powerful house, rankled with Salisbury and accelerated his drive to elevate the lords' position.[1]

---

1. As earlier noted, Blake saw Salisbury as "the most formidable intellectual figure that the Conservative party has ever produced." *Disraeli*, 499. Smith considers that Salisbury's combative instincts at times exceeded reasonable bounds, *Lord Salisbury on politics*, 8. For Salisbury's longstanding distrust of Gladstone, see L. P. Curtis, *Coercion and conciliation in Ireland* (Princeton, 1963), 67–8. Also to be noted is Salisbury's attitude towards the house of commons, which he left reluctantly in 1868 on the death of his father, and proceeded thereafter to treat with an air of great contempt. According to Henry Lucy, "whenever in debate he was compelled to allude to it, he managed to throw into his tone a note of contempt that greatly amused commoners thronging the bar, or privy councilors standing on the steps of the throne." Lucy thought this attitude one of pure affectation. *Memories of eight parliaments* (1908), 121. But this was not the opinion of Sir Michael Hicks Beach, an experienced politician with ample opportunity to observe Salisbury. He considered that the latter had "small respect for the opinions of the house of commons, and constantly chafed against his obligation as prime minister to support in the lords proposals to which his colleagues in the commons had been obliged to agree." Cited in Hanham, *The nineteenth century constitution*, 68. Another contemporary, Lord Stanley, later fifteenth earl of Derby, wrote of Salisbury shortly after he entered the house of lords that he "seems to feel himself at home in the lords, which he never did altogether in the commons." *Disraeli, Derby and the Conservative party: Journals and memoirs of Edward Henry, Lord Stanley 1849–1869*, ed. John Vincent (New York, 1978), 335. There is also relevant comment in A. L. Kennedy, *Salisbury, 1830–1903: Portrait of a statesman* (1953), 75. But Kennedy's statement that Salisbury had no desire to strengthen the house of lords in relationship to the house of commons is mistaken, as is his comment that Salisbury was willing to accept the will of the house of commons as supreme. Ibid. Contemporaries dated a change in the house of lords from Salisbury's entrance. *The Times*, June 9, 1869, p. 9; *Saturday Review*, 27 (June 26, 1869), 829.

Salisbury's determination to uphold the lords' power and authority was sustained by his interpretation of history. Like his contemporary Karl Marx, he discerned a continuing class struggle through the centuries. Here was the underlying reality in politics, even its driving force. According to Paul Smith, Salisbury considered most political issues to be "at bottom matters of property."[2] "The struggle for property," he wrote in 1862, "lies not between crown and people, or between a caste of nobles and a bourgeoisie" but "between classes who have property and the classes who have none."[3] The struggle had made methods of taxation "in truth the vital question of modern politics"[4]–"an engine which may be used almost without limit for the transfer of property from one class to another."[5] Salisbury would align himself with the classes of education and property against those of ignorance and poverty, the latter made more threatening by the Second Reform Act.[6]

An instructive example of how his view of the class struggle underlay his exposition of the referendal theory is provided by his famous article entitled "Disintegration," published in the *Quarterly Review* in 1883. *The Times*, construing it rightly as an attack on parliamentary government, pointed out that though Salisbury posed as champion of the constitution "his principles, logically developed, would be quite as fatal to the constitution as any that he attributes to the Radical party."[7] Explaining that the nation, but not the house of commons, must arbitrate between classes, Salisbury writes:

> Undoubtedly, in a modern state, the only arbitration possible between classes is the judgment–the cool and deliberate judgment–of the generality of the nation. At the best it may not be an ideal form of arbitration; in ordinary circumstances its genuine decisions are hard to obtain: but it is the only one available under modern conditions of political life. The reproach to which the house of commons acting for the nation is liable is

---

2. Smith, *Lord Salisbury on politics*, 26–7.
3. Cited ibid., 26. See also 33.
4. *Salisbury: the man and his policies*, ed. Blake and Cecil, 105.
5. Smith, *Lord Salisbury on politics*, 125.
6. Ibid., 27–9.
7. Cited ibid., 338.

> that it does not in its dealing between classes, even approximately, represent this deliberate judgment. If its policy is unstable, and its action is watched from year to year with uncertainty and dread, it is because its mode of procedure is ill-fitted to ascertain or faithfully to transmit the decisions of the nation in the issues submitted to it–because it suffers them to be dictated by impulse or falsified by sectional bias [that is, too much subservience to the interests of sections of the United Kingdom]. If it ever forfeits completely...the confidence of large classes of the community over which its authority extends, the cause must be sought partly in the unexampled extent of its powers, which permits hastiness of decision, partly in the peculiar play of parties within its walls, which vitiates the fidelity of its action as an exponent of national opinion.[8]

Nor should it be overlooked that the Victorian house of commons differed markedly from its predecessors. Since 1867 it had been in the hands of a democracy, a system awarding practical supremacy to the lower classes and making it necessary for the prime minister, if he were to retain power, to manipulate contending groups in the commons. In this situation it was "a transparent mockery to tell the classes whose great litigation it is the supreme function of legislation to determine, that the verdict of their countrymen is expressed in the decisions which in any parliamentary crisis may be dictated to the ministry by the exigency of tactics in the house of commons."[9] This was not the parliamentary government of the eighteenth century, when a strong minister's position was secure from sudden shifts of feeling in that house though the power of the king and aristocracy still controlled his action.[10]

The final decision to rely on the referendal theory as the ideological mainstay of the lords' veto came during Gladstone's great ministry (1868–74), which coincided with Salisbury's first years in the lords. Successive defeats in opposition, writes Lady Gwendolen, "convinced him anew of his isolated impotence,"[11] and Donald Southgate, an historian of the Conservative party,

---

8. Ibid., 346. See also 33.
9. Ibid., 347.
10. Ibid., 346–7.
11. Cecil, *Salisbury*, ii, 27.

writes of Salisbury's "elephant moods" in this stressful period as he opposed, year after year, without success the major items in Gladstone's reform program.[12] His anger and frustration boiled over in a sharp exchange (June 8, 1869) with the duke of Argyll during debates on the Life Peerages Bill of 1869. The latter, Salisbury charged, seemed to be "compelled by an irresistible desire to profess the absolute subordination of this house to the house of commons." He could not accept this description. Salisbury declared: "I am not prepared to have any part in an assembly which should make such an unrestricted profession of subserviency to the other branch of the legislature." Then came his own definition of that relationship. The lords were "subordinate to the nation" but not "to the house of commons."[13] To this definition he clung steadfastly in the late nineteenth century.

II

Salisbury's attempt to strengthen the house of lords gained momentum after 1880, especially when home rule for Ireland became the leading question in politics. But the particular form that his attempt would take was determined much earlier in his career, as early in fact as his experience at Westminster in the immediate years after the Derby-Disraeli government, to his deep displeasure, passed the Reform Act of 1867. In the post–1867 era—at a time when Salisbury was at odds with the leadership of his party—Gladstone sponsored two controversial measures: the Suspensory Bill of 1868, which did not become law; and the Irish

---

12. *The Conservatives: a history from their origins to 1965*, ed. Lord Butler (1977), 171.

13. *Parl. debs.*, 3rd series, cxcvi, 1377. At this time Salisbury indicated that, in his view, adding a limited number of life peers from commerce and industry would make clearer the representative character of the lords. He favored the reform; and although it was not enacted in his lifetime, he followed the principle when peers were created during his tenure of office. On this point see Ralph E. Pumphrey, "The introduction of industrialists into the British peerage: A study in adaptation of a social institution," *The American Historical Review*, 65, 1 (Oct. 1959), 8–13. Discussing the appearance in the Victorian house of lords of individuals with industrial and commercial connections but without links to the aristocracy, Pumphrey finds the turning point in Salisbury's first ministry (1885–6) and explains the phenomenon in terms of the impulse provided by the Second Reform Act. It is just as possible that the explanation lies in Salisbury's policy for the lords; that is, in the exigencies of the referendal theory.

Church Bill, based on the Suspensory Bill, which disestablished the Irish church in 1869. The Irish church question set the stage for a more complex and extended conflict between the houses than that of 1846; and from the party struggles, in which Salisbury figured large, came the full-blown referendal theory that distinguished the late Victorian house of lords. When at this juncture he made a decisive and important contribution not only to its formulation but also to its credibility, he made that theory his own.

The antecedents of the Suspensory Bill, which throw much light on the theory, are in the months between the passing of the Second Reform Bill into law in August 1867 and the general election of November 1868.[14] Midway through the period Derby resigned as prime minister and was replaced by Disraeli, his faithful lieutenant, as head of what was essentially a caretaker government. Weakened by having only minority support in the commons, he was determined nevertheless to persist in office until a general election could be held under the new electoral arrangements. The Second Reform Act applied only to England, and similar legislation still pended for Ireland and Scotland. Once this was enacted and the voting registers prepared, the Conservatives planned to brave the electoral waters and learn who would govern England. Meanwhile, its labors incomplete, the Disraeli government clung to office.

From this unusual situation came the Suspensory Bill and not long afterwards the referendal theory. In fact, the whole sequence of events is pertinent. A few days after Disraeli took office, an Irish member moved to draw attention to the state of Ireland; and Disraeli, playing for time, responded with the denial that the present house of commons was morally competent–a softened version of what was said in 1846–to settle a question not before the electorate in 1865. He had been a leading participant in the events of 1846 but at the time was more interested in Peel's betrayal of his party than in his obligations to the electorate.[15] In 1868 Disraeli sounded more like Richmond and his as-

---

14. The following account is derived from Weston, "Salisbury and the lords," *The Historical Journal*, 25, 1(1982), 103–29.

15. Ibid., 108–9.

sociates. Sir Erskine May notes that Disraeli's objection to the Suspensory Bill raised an important issue. "By a singular inversion of parts," May writes, he "now appeared as the champion of the democratic theory of the mandate, while Mr. Gladstone, perceiving an obstacle in his path and eager to overthrow it, maintained with his customary passionate eagerness, the uncontrolled right of parliament to deal with what subjects it pleased."[16] After Gladstone introduced several resolutions preparatory to disestablishing the Irish church, including a resolution affirming the desirability of an immediate disestablishment, Disraeli sponsored a temporizing amendment, known as the Stanley amendment, to the effect that the house of commons, while admitting that considerable modifications in the temporalities of the Irish church might after the impending enquiry appear to be expedient, was "of the opinion that any proposition tending to the disestablishment or disendowment of that church ought to be reserved for the decision of a new parliament."[17]

Gladstone, however, not Disraeli, shaped the course of events. Rejecting the Stanley amendment in favor of Gladstone's resolutions, the commons opened the way for the Suspensory Bill, which suspended appointments to the Irish church for a year. As political defeat once more loomed, while the need to gain time remained imperative, Disraeli decided to leave rejection to the lords. After clearing the house of commons with impressive majorities, the Suspensory Bill went to the lords; and that house, basing itself on the democratic rationale so conveniently supplied by Disraeli, now fulfilled its assigned role. It rejected the Suspensory Bill, doing so after numerous speakers spoke in terms of a referendal function in the lords.

Salisbury took the lead. In a famous speech of June 26, 1868, which was printed and circulated, he had crisp advice for the lords. They should disregard the majorities in the commons and reject this crude and violent measure. This was the proper

---

16. *May's constitutional history of England*, ed. and cont. to 1911 by Francis Holland (1911), iii, 206–7. For Salisbury's action in 1892 and an explanation of it, see Marsh, *Discipline*, 222. Although he does not suggest this, one suspects that Salisbury's interpretation of Gladstone's majority, for which see chapter 5 of this study, explains his failure to follow the Disraelian precedent. To do so would be to legitimize that majority.

17. *Parl. debs.*, 3rd series, cxci, 507.

course despite Clarendon's warning that they should give closer attention to public opinion and those majorities. Salisbury proceeded to separate the commons from the country, as had been done in 1846, and to advance the iconoclastic proposition that the lords on a given occasion might be more representative of public opinion than the commons. Dismissing Clarendon's warning contemptuously, Salisbury wondered aloud whether the Liberal leader had ever considered the purpose for which the lords existed. To become "a mere echo and tool of the house of commons was slavery." To be sure, the lords must yield their opinions when the sustained convictions of the country clearly favored a particular course, but this was very different from simply echoing the commons. Although it was not easy to ascertain the country's opinion, the lords might be better at it than the commons. And Salisbury now recalled how thirty years earlier, with the tide running against the Irish church, the commons had sent anti-Irish church measures to the lords. But when the lords rejected them, the nation became apathetic on the question. "In course of time it turned out that you were right," Salisbury told the peers triumphantly. "You knew the opinion of the nation better than the house of commons." This example demonstrated the necessity of determining the nation's opinion before acting in favor of the Bill, and it was the lords' duty to take a course marked no less by firmness than by prudence.[18]

The last speaker for the Conservatives was Lord Chancellor Cairns, intimate friend of Disraeli's and Conservative leader in the lords during the parliamentary session of 1869. An Ulsterman, who had earlier sat for Belfast in the commons, he defended the Irish church and attacked the Suspensory Bill in a lengthy speech that was printed, widely distributed, and much admired. Urging the rejection of the Suspensory Bill as an attack on property, supremacy of the Crown, Protestant interests, and peace in Ireland, Cairns concluded on this significant note:

---

18. Ibid., cxciii, 88–90. Writing in the *Central Literary Magazine* (1903–4), 150. Isaac Bradley described the part of Salisbury's speech where it was said the peers would yield their opinion when the country's sustained convictions favored a course as "the celebrated statement, now accepted, practically, by all parties, as to the true position of the upper house." The speech, printed in the *Standard* (June 27 1868), was reprinted for the National Union of Conservative and Constitutional Associations, in that year. There is a copy in the British Library.

> My lords, these are the vast issues involved in this Bill. These are the issues involved in your lordships' decision now, and they are the issues yet to be presented to the country in the great appeal to its enlarged constituencies... In that appeal...the government will stand as the defenders of all that this Bill and the policy of its promoters would seek to overthrow.

By the result of the appeal to the constituencies the government would abide.[19]

On June 29, 1868, the lords sent the Suspensory Bill to the country with generously worded pledges to accept the electoral results. According to *The Times*, that house had remitted "the question of the Irish church to the constituencies of the kingdom."[20] Little wonder that late Victorian Englishmen, harking back to this episode, considered that the lords had deliberately and self-consciously acted out the tenets of the referendal theory in rejecting the Suspensory Bill.[21] Yet the use of the theory at this time was no more than the product of a fortuitous combination of circumstances rising out of the minority position of the Conservative party in the post–1867 house of commons and the politics of improvisation as Disraeli sought to lengthen his tenure of office and enhance his party's electoral prospects.

The only important issue in the election was the disestablishment of the Irish church. Gladstone won a ringing endorsement from the newly enlarged electorate when the Liberals were returned to Westminster with the impressive majority of 112. Recognizing the significance of the electoral result and fully aware of his government's choice of language before the general election,[22] Disraeli resigned before parliament met, taking his dismissal as it were from the electorate rather than the commons and thus inaugurating a new era in politics. According to May, it was "the first open acknowledgment of the truth that a ministry in reality

---

19. *Parl. debs.*, 3rd series, cxciii, 288.

20. *The Times*, June 30, 1868, p. 11. "The defenders as well as the opponents of the Irish establishment...appeal to the nation," ran another passage.

21. Bradley, *The Central Literary Magazine*, 149–50. There is a Victorian interpretation of the events of 1868–9, published between the Third Reform Act and the First Home Rule Bill, in F. S. Pulling, *The life and speeches of the marquis of Salisbury* (1885), 125–9.

22. Alfred Erskine Gathorne-Hardy, *Gathorne Hardy, first earl of Cranbrook* (1910), i, 286.

derives its commission from the electorate."[23] Gladstone now acted swiftly to carry out the electoral commitment. The Irish Church Bill, based on the Suspensory Bill, passed early in the session with remarkable celerity and by large majorities through the commons; and on June 14, 1869 the second reading began in the lords. Words must now be matched with deeds, but it was no easy matter to muster the self-discipline needed to carry out the pledges so freely given before the general election. In the *Spectator*'s words, "the great vote was on the very subject on which of all others average Conservative peers felt most strongly."[24]

Whatever their misgivings, the lords, if they expected to use this particular language again in dealing with the commons, could ill afford the luxury of yielding to them. Should the Irish Church Bill fail the second reading in the lords, after profuse promises to respect the results of the general election, they must wreck the referendal theory just as it matured. Conversely, reading the Bill a second time, as was done on June 19, constituted a milestone in the history of the lords. Self-restraint and discipline under the most trying circumstances provided convincing evidence that the lords would respect the nation's will once it was expressed at the polls, regardless of the manner in which that house dealt with the commons.[25] That is, the celebrated case of the Irish Church Bill could be used thereafter to legitimate a leading tenet of the referendal theory, indeed its most important tenet. If it were accepted, it was more likely that another would carry conviction.

The passage of the Irish Church Bill was, then, a testing time for the theory. Yet it appeared for some time as if the Bill would fail the second reading, and it even seemed as if Salisbury would play no part in the outcome. Meetings were underway to determine Conservative policy before the Bill reached the lords; and major obstacles to passage were evident as early as the meet-

---

23. *May's constitutional history of England*, iii, 75. See *The Conservatives*, ed. Butler, 169, for the statement that Disraeli's action was "far more democratic than his acceptance of Hodgkinson's amendment."

24. The *Spectator*, xlii, (June 26, 1869), 753.

25. Leonard Courtney, *The working constitution of the United Kingdom* (New York, 1901), 101–2.

ing of May 8 at Lambeth palace, arranged at Disraeli's suggestion by the archbishop of Canterbury, Archibald Campbell Tait.[26] When Tait proposed that the peers vote for the second reading, to be followed by amendments in committee, Lord Grey–the only Liberal peer present–was amenable; but Salisbury seems to have been non-committal, as was Cairns, who held the balance of power in the party.[27] Derby, the ex-premier, to whom the peers had long looked for leadership, was not even present. A zealous champion of Protestant ascendancy throughout the United Kingdom, he is said to have asserted at this time that no consideration on earth could induce him to compromise on the Irish Church Bill,[28] a position to which he steadily adhered.

Meanwhile Disraeli had retired to the sidelines: he was very quiet during this session and the two following sessions. The Liberal victory in 1868 had weakened his position by suggesting that the Conservative sponsorship of parliamentary reform in the preceding year had brought the party no political gain; and it is by no means clear that he was in any position to influence events in the house of lords.[29] His place as a possible mediator passed to Queen Victoria, who was impressed by the electoral verdict of 1868 and by the large majorities for the Irish Church Bill in the newly elected house of commons. She was soon in close touch with the principals, with important consequences.[30] As early as June 4 she urged Tait to exercise a moderating influence; two days later he reported that Derby had apparently won the support of the Conservative rank and file.[31] A meeting of 140 peers, on June

---

26. Randall Thomas Davidson and William Benham, *Life of Archibald Campbell Tait, archbishop of Canterbury* (1891), ii, 18–9.

27. Cairns felt very strongly on the Irish church question, saying at one point that if the Irish church went, the English would follow suit in twenty years. Yet as late as Apr. 8, 1869, he told the shadow cabinet that the lords would not throw out the Irish Church Bill on the second reading though they might amend it in detail. *Disraeli, Derby and the Conservative party*, 328, 331, 340. See also note 30, below.

28. Wilbur Devereux Jones, *Lord Derby and Victorian conservatism* (Oxford, 1956), 345, note. P.M.H. Bell, *Disestablishment in Ireland and Wales* (Church Historical Society 90, 1969), 143. Cp. John D. Fair, "The Irish disestablishment conference of 1869," *The Journal of Ecclesiastical History*, 26, 4 (Oct. 1975), 385.

29. Blake, *Disraeli*, 516, 520–21. E. J. Feuchtwanger, *Disraeli, democracy and the Tory party* (Oxford, 1968), 1–16.

30. Fair, "The Irish disestablishment conference," 383–7.

31. *Tait*, ii, 25.

5, at the duke of Marlborough's house, had voted for rejection; and this time Cairns had joined forces with Derby, making a long speech against giving the Bill a second reading. One of the few peers to resist was Salisbury. Considering the passage of the Irish Church Bill only a question of time and pressure, he would not vote for rejection; nor would his close friend and ally, Lord Carnarvon. But they were in the minority. When Derby denounced the Irish Church Bill as "revolutionary and abominable," he spoke for the meeting.[32]

Even Salisbury's position was by no means firm. On June 3, before the meeting at Marlborough's house, Lord Granville–the Liberal leader of the lords and Gladstone's chief political associate–reported a conversation with Lord Grey. "Grey told me," he wrote, "that he was afraid there was a chance of the rejection, & that Salisbury to his surprise, had become shaky."[33] Six days later, on June 9, Granville wrote of another conversation, this one with Carnarvon. It appeared that Salisbury would refrain from voting on the Irish Church Bill. "He [Carnarvon]," wrote Granville, "has still some hopes of getting Salisbury to vote, and of persuading other peers, but he is always over sanguine in this matter."[34] Yet Carnarvon had it right. While Salisbury hesitated, Tait wrote optimistically, on June 7, to the queen that the majority against the Bill had dwindled to twenty. He considered this too small a margin for rejection and forecast that the Conservative majority would allow a second reading and insist on amendments later.[35] He then asked Disraeli to advise his friends to adopt this policy.[36] By this time the Liberals, responding to the queen, were more conciliatory; and as the debate began Granville announced the government's willingness to consider alterations in

---

32. *The Times*, June 7, 1869, p. 5. Fair, "The Irish disestablishment conference," 386–7. Sir Arthur Hardinge, *The life of ...Earl of Carnarvon* (1925), ii, 9–10. According to *The Times*, however, Salisbury was undecided about the best course to be followed. Cairns' attitude is explained in Fair, "The Irish disestablishment conference," 386, note 2 and in Bell, *Disestablishment in Ireland*, 143. See also note 27 above.

33. *The political correspondence of Mr. Gladstone and Lord Granville, 1868–1876*, ed. Agatha Ramm (1952), i, 26.

34. Ibid., i, 27.

35. Davidson and Benham, *Tait*, ii, 26–7. Carnarvon to Salisbury, June 7, 1869; Hatfield MSS 3M/Class E.

36. Davidson and Benham, *Tait*, ii, 27–8.

the Bill's details.[37]

To *The Times* the Irish Church Bill was now safe,[38] but other observers found the turning point in Salisbury's speech on the night of June 17. They agreed with the *Spectator* that it was "the main influence which induced the conservatives to desert their leader, Lord Cairns, and their ex-leader, Lord Derby, and sustain the government."[39] Derby spoke in debate before Salisbury. Pale and ill, his voice feeble, he disappointed an attentive audience despite a strenuous attempt to justify his unwillingness to accept the results of the general election. Urging the rejection of the Irish Church Bill, he denied that the question of disestablishment had been adequately submitted to the voters. "The Bill now before [the house of lords] never was before the country," he declared. Indeed, it appeared that the ministers and their chief supporters had studiously held back many provisions in their declarations.[40]

Disagreeing with Derby, Salisbury recommended reading the Bill a second time and amending it later; and he now offered a discourse on the constitution, destined to have much influence, that would allow the peers to vote gracefully for the second reading. He found the position of the house of lords to be high, indeed the equal of the commons, but stressed that both houses were subordinate to the nation. But what of the widespread assumption that the house of commons as the representative of the nation was supreme in law-making? That proposition was completely unacceptable to Salisbury. Granted that in 99 cases out of 100, the house of commons theoretically represented the nation, this was so only in theory. In an equal number of cases the nation took no interest in politics, following out its usual avocations and

37. Fair, "The Irish disestablishment conference," 387.

38. *The Times*, June 14, 1869, 8. The *Spectator* noted, however, that until the night of June 14 it was believed that Derby held the house in his hand. Ibid., 42 (June 26, 1869), 753.

39. Ibid., July 17, 1869, 387. Lord Granville to Queen Victoria, June 17, 1869, *Letters of Queen Victoria*, ed. G. E. Buckle (1926), 2nd series, i, 610–1. Lord Edmond Fitzmaurice, *The life of ...second Earl of Granville* (1905), ii, 10. Pulling, *Salisbury*, i, 128–9. "The nature of democracy," *The Quarterly Review* (Oct. 1884), 329, note. The author is said to have been Sir Henry Maine. See also P. T. Marsh, *The Victorian church in decline* (1969), 35. Bell, *Disestablishment in Ireland*, 116–7. Bell implies that Disraeli, with Cairns, opposed a second reading of the Irish Church Bill in the house of lords.

40. *Parl. debs.*, 3rd series, cxcvii, 37.

viewing the political scene with detachment. When the nation was not directly concerned, the house of lords was equal in all essentials to the house of commons. In fact, the two houses were co-ordinate in law-making. In all of these cases there were absolutely no distinctions between the prerogatives of the two houses.

Yet a few cases existed where the voices of the two houses were less important–where "the nation must be called into council and must decide the policy of the government." That is, direct democracy must operate. This happened when grounds existed for believing that the commons were misinterpreting the opinion of the nation. On such occasions the lords must insist on consulting the nation. How were they to know when intervention was required? Salisbury's advice was more general at this time than later in the century: it was "a matter of feeling and judgment." The lords must decide by all they saw around them and by events. Each must decide for himself upon his conscience and to the best of his judgment in exercising "that tremendous responsibility which at such a time each member of this house bears–whether the house of commons does or does not represent the full, the deliberate, the sustained convictions of the nation."[41] If the lords decided that commons and the nation were one, their vocation, except in very exceptional cases, passed away. That house must devolve the responsibility upon the nation and accept its conclusion. In so acting the lords would not be accepting the commons' verdict, not at all, but rather that of the nation acting as the arbiter of the issue. The nation had decided in the general election against the Protestant ascendancy in Ireland–the opinion of Scotland, Ireland, and Wales was passionately in favor of this measure of disestablishment, and England, too, favored it though more doubtfully and languidly–and Salisbury was certain that "this house would not be doing its duty if it opposed itself further against the will of the nation."[42]

Two days later he was as good as his word when he, and Carnarvon too, took the extreme step of voting for the second reading alongside the Liberals in the house of lords.[43] He did so

---

41. Ibid., cols. 83–4.

42. Ibid., col. 85. Le May, *The Victorian constitution*, 135–6.

43. *Parl. debs.*, 3rd series, cxcvii, 305.

despite strong personal piety, deep attachment to traditional institutions, devotion to the principle of establishment–that is, with sympathies much like Derby's. When the momentous vote was taken at three o'clock in the morning of June 19, in the fullest house in living memory and before crowded galleries, 36 conservative peers voted with the government, providing a winning margin of 33 in the vote of 179 to 146. Salisbury had even led the contingent of Conservative peers into the lobby in favor of the second reading, while Cairns and Derby voted with the minority.[44]

It was a remarkable performance. So conservative in his political opinions as to elicit from the liberals the witty epithet "Young Sarum" and described variously in his lifetime as a "feudal baron," a "capital fossil," even an "Elizabethan relic," Salisbury was sufficiently self-controlled to avoid a conflict with the newly elected house of commons that could jeopardize the future usefulness of the lords. Perhaps he considered it but a question of time and pressure before the Irish Church Bill became law, the position maintained at Marlborough's house, or perhaps felt bound by the peers' promise to accept Irish disestablishment if the electors voted for it in the general election.

But his motivation may have been more complex. This was not the first occasion on which Salisbury publicly defied the party leadership, and his biographers agree that he was not as yet recovered from the trauma of 1867. At that time he and Carnarvon (with General Peel) had resigned from the Derby-Disraeli government rather than accept household suffrage; and as recently as March 1868, while still in the house of commons as Lord Cranborne, he had refused to follow his party's lead on the Stanley amendment, urging instead a forthright rejection of Gladstone's resolutions regarding the Irish church. Salisbury's anger was so great that he would not sit on the opposition front bench beside Cairns, who had recommended it, and after Cairns gave way to the sixth duke of Richmond as Conservative leader in the lords, Salisbury, although willing to sit beside him, still refused to participate in party counsels. With this defiance of party leadership went a vitriolic personal attack on Disraeli for his role

---

44. Fitzmaurice, *Granville*, ii, 10. *Parl. debs.*, 3rd series, cxcvii, 304–7.

in carrying the Second Reform Act.[45] Earlier that month Salisbury had written to Carnarvon of his mistrust of Disraeli as a leader; he enjoyed "the old game of talking green in the house and orange in the lobby."[46] The comments of Disraeli's supporters are equally revealing. Writing to Gathorne Hardy, on April 1–after Salisbury's attack on Disraeli in the commons–Cairns remarked: "Cranborne's ardour for the Irish church has remained dormant until he found he could use it as a means of expressing his hatred to D."[47]

Now, a year after refusing to support the Stanley amendment, Salisbury broke publicly with Cairns and Derby on the course to be adopted on the second reading of the Irish Church Bill. While Disraeli's position at this point is by no means clear, Salisbury, in adopting a different policy from Cairns, could have been striking at Disraeli. After all, the latter was Disraeli's choice as Conservative leader in the house of lords, though he could not select him for the post; and he was not only a colleague whom Disraeli thoroughly trusted but also an intimate friend and close political associate.[48] Disraeli had made Cairns lord chancellor in 1868. And Derby was of course the prime minister who presided over the passing of the Second Reform Act. In his famous article in the *Quarterly Review*, describing what he saw as the Conservative surrender to the pressure for parliamentary reform, Salisbury censured Derby, as well as Disraeli, though in his view the latter's influence was paramount in what was done.[49]

The course adopted was consequential for the lords. Salisbury's speech of June 17, coupled with his earlier speech recommending the rejection of the Suspensory Bill, supplied major tenets of the referendal theory in late Victorian England, while

---

45. Ibid., cxci, 532–41. The speech was given on Mar. 30, 1868. *The Conservatives*, ed. Butler, 167–8. See the comment in Blake, *Disraeli*, 498–500 and in Jeyes, *The life and times of...Salisbury* (1895), i, 119. Lord Stanley considered Salisbury more conciliatory after he went to the lords but still unwilling to act with Disraeli. *Disraeli, Derby and the Conservative party*, 335, 340, 345.

46. Cited in Curtis, *Coercion and conciliation*, 8. The letter is dated Mar. 6, 1868.

47. Gathorne-Hardy, *Cranbrook*, i, 268. See also ibid., 266.

48. Ibid., i, 281. Feuchtwanger, *Disraeli, democracy and the Tory party*, 5. Blake, *Disraeli*, 544. William F. Monypenny and George E. Buckle, *The life of Benjamin Disraeli, Earl of Beaconsfield* (New York, 1929), ii, 378, 427, 434, 451–2, 513.

49. Smith, *Lord Salisbury on politics*, 256–7, 263–6, 272–3, 276, 277, etc.

his response to the general election of 1868, made independently of Cairns and Derby, gave that theory viability for the future. Thanks to Salisbury's leadership, the lords, if they chose to act again on such a theory, must enjoy a large measure of credibility. In fact, though this was not apparent for some time, the speech of June 17 provided the lords with an astonishing propaganda victory. This is to say a great deal since that house had in effect lost the general election of 1868 and as a consequence had to swallow the bitter medicine of the Irish Church Bill. But no defeated house, in the wake of a political disaster, ever received a more effective ideological gloss than Salisbury imparted in 1869. His argument for giving the Irish Church Bill a second reading was remembered as long as the referendal theory was associated with the lords.[50] Salisbury himself recalled it to the public in 1895 in a letter to *The Times*, and in 1906 Lord Lansdowne (Conservative leader in the lords during the debates on the Parliament Act) reminded the peers of Salisbury's words. The latter had once described the lords "as an instrument for reserving on all great and vital questions a voice for the electors and the people of this country."[51] In the following year the duke of Devonshire–formerly leader of the Conservative party in the lords and one of the most respected men in public life–quoted at length from Salisbury's speech, telling his fellow peers: "So long as this house accepts that canon for its conduct I do not believe it can go far wrong."[52]

The lords' conduct in 1869 seemed to contemporaries to

---

50. C.H.K. Marten, "The marquess of Salisbury," *The political principles of some notable prime ministers of the nineteenth century*, ed. F.J.C. Hearnshaw (1926), 280. Cecil, *Salisbury*, ii, 24–6. See also the *Dictionary of national biography* article on Salisbury, written by his nephew, Algernon Cecil. The latter refers to Salisbury's speech of June 26, 1868, as laying down, in words often quoted since, what he considered the function of the peers in the modern state. And he adds that Salisbury reaffirmed the doctrine in an impressive speech after the general election of 1868, advising the peers to pass the second reading of the Irish Church Bill.

51. *Parl. debs.*, (lords) 4th series, clxvi, 702. See also Weston, "Salisbury and the Lords," 127–8.

52. *Parl. debs.* (lords), 4th series, clxxiv, 15–6. This portion of Devonshire's speech was quoted by Bernard Henry Holland in a political biography of the duke published in 1911, the year of the Parliament Act. *The life of Spencer Compton, eighth duke of Devonshire*, ii, 406–7. In Devonshire's view, the lords' action in 1869 provided convincing proof that they did not hesitate to defer to the will of the electorate even when that will was contrary to their own. Ibid., 406. See also the speech of Lord Robertson, about the same time, in *Parl. debs.* (lords), 4th series, clxxiii, 1264. Robertson was a law lord and faithful member of the Conservative (Unionist) party.

introduce a new era in their history. In September 1893, as the second reading of the Second Home Rule Bill for Ireland got underway in the lords, *The Times* urged rejection on the ground that the electorate should give the verdict. Should a general election take place on the issue, the peers would accept the outcome. To be sure, their course of action had been very different in 1832 when they defied the electoral verdict for the Reform Bill in the general election of the preceding year and brought the country to the brink of revolution. But this constitutional mistake had been corrected a generation later. The opportunity came after the lords rejected Gladstone's Suspensory Bill, despite its having been carried by a majority of 65 in the commons. When the appeal to the electorate revealed the nation's mind on the issue, they had accepted the disestablishment of the Irish Church.[53] Here was the illustration *par excellence* of the relationship between the lords and the post-1867 electorate.[54] But if they bowed to the nation, there was much less necessity to do so in dealing with the commons, so many an observer reckoned.

III

With the passage of the Irish Church Bill into law, the circumstances vanished that had spawned the referendal theory; and it looked for a time as if no more would be heard of it. Its abandonment was probably due to its association with failure. The peers' rhetoric had led to a statute for which they had no sympathy, and they must have seen in the reference to the people a dangerous policy that would not bear repetition. Not even Salisbury was ready at this point to make systematic use of the referendal theory. Yet by February 1872 he had brushed aside his doubts and was seeking a consistent principle to govern the acceptance or rejection of legislative measures by the lords–such a principle, it must be understood, as would permit them to exercise their legislative power with a minimum of risk to that house and to its freedom of action. Mindful of the events of 1868–9, he turned to the

---

53. *The Times*, Sept. 5, 1893, 7.

54. Jeyes, *Salisbury*, i, 120. Jeyes wrote: "The Irish church was emphatically a case in point." See also Earl Cadogan's speech on July 7, 1884. *Parl. debs.*, 3rd series, ccxc, 185.

referendal theory that had been so conspicuous in the controversy over the Irish church.

His doing so was crucial for the Victorian house of lords. There were earlier parliamentary episodes in which questions were raised about the competence of parliament to handle a given question and the cry raised that there must be an appeal to the constituencies for a decision, notably during the crisis over Catholic Emancipation in 1829 and again in 1846 when the repeal of the Corn Laws was before parliament. But in their wake no political leader of Salisbury's stature came forward, determined to use such a theory persistently to elevate the lords. That the aftermath of the Irish church controversy was different in this respect is still another reason for stressing its distinctive role in developing the referendal theory. At this time Salisbury's personal qualities assumed a particular importance. He was too proud, too spirited, too combative, too pugnacious to stand by passively as evidence mounted that the house of which he was a leading member was incapable of dealing effectively with Gladstone. Depressed by the lords' failure to stanch Liberal reform legislation and angered at their situation, he wrote to Carnarvon on June 20, 1870:

> I send you a leader of Maguire's [in the *Cork Examiner*] which will illustrate what I mean in saying, that in point of power and public weight, the h. of lords is dying of rapid decline. I give only one instance of observations that I have heard in every direction. I feel convinced that if we make any substantial retreat from the very moderate position we have taken up, our future position in the constitution will be purely decorative.[55]

One year later that house's weakness was publicly exhibited in a dispute with Gladstone over abolishing the purchase of army commissions. The manner in which he handled the dispute proved more than ordinarily humiliating to the lords, and very probably the episode led a thoroughly resentful Salisbury to make the referendal theory the core of his policy in dealing with Liberal legislation.

The Gladstonian maneuver that ended army purchase

---

55. Hatfield MSS 3M/D31/22. Typescript copy. See Salisbury to Carnarvon as late as Jan. 1, 1882. Ibid., 3M/D31/81; and Jan. 19, 1883, ibid., 3M/D31/88. Cecil, *Salisbury*, iii, 27.

came after the peers voted, July 17, 1871, by a margin of twenty-five votes, to set aside the Army Regulation Bill until a larger reform scheme was produced. The action was tantamount to rejection and the vote so close as to suggest a divided house, and in fact much soul-searching had preceded the adoption of this course. But not on Salisbury's part. He early insisted on rejection and carried other members of his party with him. "He was evidently influenced by the old feeling of irritation at the humiliating position in which he thought the house of lords was placed, and was by no means averse to a conflict with the house of commons," so Lord Carnarvon's biographer concluded.[56] Both Carnarvon and Cairns, who favored a more pacific course, waived their objections in deference to strong opinions within the party. As tension mounted after the rejection, Gladstone announced that a royal warrant, signed by Queen Victoria on ministerial advice, had ended army purchase. If army officers were to receive compensation for their losses, the peers would have to reverse their action on the Army Regulation Bill; and this was what happened. Liberal insistence that the queen had acted, not on the basis of her prerogative but of power conferred by a statute of George III, met with skepticism; and in the commons Disraeli denounced Gladstone's action as "part of an avowed and shameful conspiracy against the undoubted privileges of the other house of parliament."[57]

An angry house of lords censured the Gladstone government for what was deemed an abuse of power and breach of faith. In a supportive speech, described by Argyll as one of the bitterest and narrowest party speeches in his memory,[58] Salisbury reproached the government for bringing forward the abolition of purchase as a question subject to parliamentary jurisdiction, only to withdraw it in the face of a hostile reaction. It was as if the Liberals had said: "We snap our fingers in your face against your decision, and will decide for ourselves in spite of you." The government had treated the lords in a way that no private individual

---

56. Hardinge, *Carnarvon*, ii, 24.

57. *Annual Register*, N.S., 1871, 77. Hardinge, *Carnarvon*, ii, 24. The episode was remembered in Conservative circles in 1914 when the amendment of the Army Act was under consideration.

58. Described in the *Annual Register*, N.S., 1871, 79.

would treat another. When Salisbury now asserted that the government had acted emotionally because it was being thwarted by the lords, Granville cheered; and Salisbury responded with a cutting statement: "I can sympathize with the noble earl who thus cheers me," he said, "for he has been the instrument–I have no doubt the most reluctant instrument–of insulting the order to which he belongs."

Assigning to Granville the doctrine that it was the whole duty of the lords to obey the commons, Salisbury, as was earlier noted, traced that doctrine to Wellington. Rejecting it scornfully, he now foreshadowed the position he would take in February 1872 and thereafter. He recognized, he stated, that the lords ought to pay earnest attention to the party in power and opinion current in the country; but these considerations were by no means paramount. For example, the vote in the commons deserved to be taken less seriously when extremism was ascendant among the Liberals. If the majority was used to enforce the opinion of a radical element, the lords "must reserve for the opinion of the constituencies measures passed by the house of commons under that pressure."[59]

Before summer was over, Salisbury was encouraged by a visible sign that the country was tiring of Gladstone's reforming zeal. A by-election in East Surrey, on August 24, administered to the government its first serious setback when a Conservative was victorious by 1,163 votes. The Liberal majority in 1868 had been 384.[60] Less than six months later Salisbury wrote an extremely important letter to Carnarvon, urging the need for a consistent principle to govern the acceptance or rejection of bills and recommending for this purpose the referendal theory. It would give the lords a genuine legislative independence, whatever the outward appearance. If the letter's tone suggests expediency, the elements of the theory he was advocating were discernible as early as his dispute with Gladstone over the Paper Duties Bill; and on public occasions he had often asserted an independent legislative power in the lords. Urging the rejection of the Ballot Bill on

---

59. *Parl. debs.*, 3rd series, ccviii, 475–80.

60. Smith, *Lord Salisbury on politics*, 339.

the second reading, Salisbury explained his position at length, writing:

> I am strongly for rejecting the Bill on the second reading, for this reason. It appears to me of vital necessity that our acceptance of bills to which we are opposed should be regulated on some principle. If we listen to the Liberals we should accept all important bills which had passed the house of commons by a large majority. But that in effect would be to efface the house of lords. Another principle–which is, so far as I can gather, what commends itself to Derby [the fifteenth earl]–is to watch newspapers, public meetings and so forth, and only to reject when "public opinion" thus ascertained, growls very loud. This plan gives a premium to bluster and will bring the house into contempt. The plan which I prefer is frankly to acknowledge that the nation is our master, though the house of commons is not, and to yield our own opinion only when the judgment of the nation has been challenged at the polls and decidedly expressed.

This doctrine, he continued, had a number of advantages. It was "(1) theoretically sound, (2) popular, (3) safe against agitation, and (4) so rarely applicable as practically to place little fetter upon our independence." Not that he was so hostile to the ballot, though he plainly disliked it, but that he favored resistance as "part of a general principle." On this ground he was urging Richmond to resist the second reading even though Disraeli favored acquiescence. A postscript to the letter harked back to the last general election, often in Salisbury's mind when he thought of politics. "I forgot to note–as to ballot," he wrote, "that at the election of 1868 the chief of the present ministry appeared as anti-ballot man: so that the nation has not been consulted."[61]

Salisbury's speech on the Ballot Bill (June 10, 1872) is a suitable companion piece to his speeches on the Suspensory Bill and the Irish Church Bill from which so much of the political language of the referendal theory sprang. By 1872 he was more exact. Thus the word "mandate" has crept in; and there is an insistence, as in the letter to Carnarvon, that the house of lords in

---

61. The letter is published without the postscript in Cecil, *Salisbury*, ii, 25–6. A typescript of the complete letter is at Hatfield House. Salisbury to Carnarvon, Feb. 20, 1872, Hatfield MSS 3M/D31/23.

deciding on a given measure, look directly to the results of a general election if its members were to learn the nation's wishes. Although the general election of 1868 was foremost in his mind on the night of June 17, 1869, he had not at that time singled out the electorate as the source of authority, saying only: "We must decide each for himself, upon our consciences and to the best of our judgment."

Otherwise his speech on the Ballot Bill bears a marked resemblance to the speeches of 1868 and 1869. This time, too, he carefully distinguished between the house of commons and the nation: for the most part they were separate entities, and it was to the nation alone that lords should look for direction when important questions arose. "I draw the widest possible distinction between the opinions of the house of commons and the opinions of the nation," he asserted, as he excoriated the view that the commons represented the nation. This was a constitutional fiction convenient for practical purposes to respect but literally true only on certain occasions and subjects, as when a question was being discussed on which the commons had been elected. At other times that house represented the nation only in theory. As he said, when four years had elapsed and the memory of all the questions on which the commons was elected had passed away and when change had overtaken many opinions of the government, which the commons were elected to support, that house represented only theoretically and not literally the nation's opinion. If reason existed for believing that a measure before the house of lords lacked a mandate, it was the lords' duty to reject the measure until the electorate gave its verdict. This was such an occasion: there was no mandate for the Ballot Bill. Those now advocating the ballot had been non-ballot politicians in the general election of 1868. That is, "the country has never had a fair opportunity of considering whether it likes the ballot or not." Under these circumstances the lords must act as the agents of the nation, seeing to it that the house of commons "in thus tampering with the laws under which it was itself elected, has not transgressed the mandate it received."[62]

Yet Salisbury did not take up the referendal theory steadily

---

62. *Parl. debs.*, 3rd series, ccxi, 1493–5.

until 1880, when a new chapter began in the history of the theory. The need to do so had disappeared after the passage of the Ballot Act. There was no legislation of major importance in 1873, and as by-elections turned against the Liberals it became apparent that Gladstone's government was in its last stage. When the lords rejected measures, they did so without referring to such a theory. After 1874 the Conservatives had six years of power. Salisbury and Disraeli reconciled; and the former entered the government, first as secretary of state for India and then, in April 1878, as foreign secretary. There was underway by this time a startling development, replete with far-reaching implications for parliamentary government. Gladstone's populist crusade known as the Bulgarian agitation against the Conservatives' eastern policy provided the pattern for the great Midlothian campaigns; and Gladstone's oratory and the manner of its delivery inevitably gave an impulse towards direct democracy.

In two periods, from November 24 to December 8, 1879, and again from March 12 to April 8, 1880, he addressed vast crowds in Midlothian, the country district around Edinburgh. The spectacle fascinated the country. Members of parliament, candidates for election, clergymen–indeed everyone with an interest in politics–hung on his words, which became "the principal news of the day."[63] For the first time a major political figure campaigned in the American presidential style, stumping the country and addressing meetings in railway stations, public halls, and out of doors with fireworks and bonfires lighting the skies. During the first Midlothian campaign Gladstone addressed in person some 75,000 people and in one way or another reached vast crowds whose numbers approached a quarter of a million.[64]

Gladstone's first use of the new methods was in South Lancashire during the campaign for the disestablishment of the Irish church, and they secured a broad moral basis in the agita-

---

63. M.R.D. Foot, "Introduction," *Midlothian speeches: 1879* (Leicester, 1971), 11. See also M. Ostrogorski, *Democracy and the organization of political parties* (New York, 1970), i, 179. This was originally published in 1902. Subsequent citations of this work refer to volume i.

64. Jephson, *The platform*, ii, 519. Blake attributes much of the technique used to Lord Rosebery, who had attended a Democratic convention in New York. *Disraeli*, 700. See also Hanham, *Elections and party management*, 202.

tion against Bulgarian atrocities when he condemned the evil practices of the Turks and their misrule of Christian minorities. During the agitation he discovered in public opinion a life of its own, "independent of parliaments and politicians";[65] and the conviction grew, as he recorded, that the materials existed "for forming a public opinion, and for directing it to a particular end." It was not enough simply to accept public opinion "founded upon the discernment that it has risen to a certain height needful for a given work, like a tide."[66] By this time he had concluded that the best hope of developing a righteous public opinion to sustain moral causes lay in appeals to the masses for support, not to the wealthy and well-born. He was thus led to the theme developed in his Midlothian speeches. The nation as a whole must sit in judgment on Disraeli's administration and the Conservative house of commons that supported him. According to Blake, politics for Gladstone was "a moral crusade based on the highest instincts of British democracy; or it was nothing."[67] In dispute, according to Gladstone, was "a whole system of government." The country would have to decide whether to share responsibility for the program that he excoriated as "Beaconsfieldism."

This note sounded in a speech as early as July 1878, even before Midlothian, when Gladstone declared: "It is quite time that the people of this country should, on the earliest convenient opportunity, be consulted as to the mode in which they are being governed."[68] A similar note sounded at Greenwich in the following November. At the next general election the people would have to deal with the question of how the country was to be governed, and this meant that they would have to decide on their attitude towards the Afghan war. Responsibility for that war was at present with the cabinet, soon to be divided with parliament;

---

65. R. T. Shannon, *Gladstone and the Bulgarian agitation 1876* (Sussex, 1975), 100, 111. This was first published in 1963.

66. Ibid., 111. Both views were expressed in a famous memorandum that Gladstone wrote in 1896, a few years before he died. For Shannon's skepticism about their validity as an index to Gladstone's leadership of his party, see ibid., 111–2 and, at greater length, T. A. Jenkins, *Gladstone, Whiggery and the Liberal party 1874–1886* (Oxford, 1988), 24–8. It is a curious paradox, given the usual historical judgments of Gladstone and Salisbury, that Gladstone's description of himself, now under fire, is genuinely applicable to Salisbury.

67. *Disraeli*, 600.

68. Quoted in Jephson, *The platform*, ii, 509.

and if the English people were willing to assume the responsibility, they should realize that theirs would be the largest share. For they were "the tribunal of final appeal." On whoever sanctioned an unjust war would lie the shame and guilt.[69] Gladstone developed these ideas on a large scale in a speech of November 25, 1879, that launched the first Midlothian campaign.

His indictment centered on foreign affairs. The Conservatives had augmented the power and influence of the Russian empire while alienating its population and had involved England in an unjust war in Afghanistan, that was full of danger to India. Moreover, their use of the Crown's powers of war and peace had abridged parliamentary rights and presented the royal prerogative in a harsh light to the nation. A house of commons that supported such policies must share responsibility for them, and the question to be resolved was whether or not the nation would support such a government. Gladstone's choice of language pointed to a force in the nation superior to parliament and ultimately its arbiter when he declared:

> If faith has been broken, if blood has been needlessly shed, if the name of England has been discredited and lowered from that lofty standard which it ought to exhibit to the whole world, if the country has been needlessly distressed, if finance has been thrown into confusion, if the foundations of the Indian empire have been impaired, all these things as yet are the work of an administration and a parliament; but the day is coming, and is near at hand, when that event will take place which will lead the historian to declare whether or not they are the work, not of an administration and not of a parliament, but the work of a great and a free people. If this great and free and powerful people is disposed to associate itself with such transactions, if it is disposed to assume upon itself what some of us would call the guilt, and many of us must declare to be the heavy burden of all those events that have been passing before our eyes, it rests with them to do it. But, gentlemen, let every one of us resolve in his inner conscience, before God and before man, let him resolve that he at least will have no share in such a proceeding.[70]

This was the issue the country must face.

---

69. Ibid., 509–10.

70. Ibid., 516.

As the campaign was closing, Gladstone placed the issue once more before a large audience, this one in Glasgow. Would the people, he asked, "ratify the deeds that have been done, and assume themselves that tremendous responsibility?" The whole aim of his proceedings was to bring home this great question to the mind and conscience of the community at large.[71] He repeated the message in the second Midlothian campaign. Treating the next general election as a great state trial, Gladstone asked the constituencies to find the Disraeli government "guilty."[72] Little wonder that the first Lord Selborne, lord chancellor under Gladstone and later a Liberal Unionist, described the first Midlothian campaign as a landmark in moving the political center of gravity from parliament to the constituencies. And he quoted Gladstone as declaring that the statesman was every day becoming "more the delegate, and less the leader of the people."[73] But the statement is misleading if it creates the assumption that Gladstone was willing for the people to share in the business of governing the state to the degree contemplated in Salisbury's referendal theory. Richard Shannon, Gladstone's biographer, writes of him that he never envisaged at any stage of his career that the people "would make decisions about what was to be the great business of the state. All his politics consisted in his deciding what that business was to be, and in his giving the appropriate lead."[74]

Gladstone's record majority in the general election of 1880 has been variously explained. His party was said to be the beneficiary of such factors as the swing of the pendulum, the great depression in agriculture that became prominent in the late 1870s, the new extraparliamentary organization headed by the National Liberal Federation and wielded as a political weapon by Joseph Chamberlain and Francis Schnadhorst. There were also strong moral overtones to the Liberal victory, related intimately to the Midlothian campaigns; and Gladstone himself believed he had won because he had aroused the country's moral sense against

---

71. Ibid., 518.

72. Philip Magnus, *Gladstone: a biography* (New York, 1954), 269.

73. Roundell Palmer, earl of Selborne, *Memorials* (1896–8), i, 470.

74. Shannon's remarks are in *The Times Literary Supplement*, Oct. 2, 1992, p. 6.

Beaconsfieldism.[75] Salisbury, who as Disraeli's foreign secretary was Gladstone's target only less than the prime minister, considered the electoral verdict "as...delivered primarily against the policy of his own department."[76] As a peer he could not electioneer, and he left for the south of France in this period. But it will be seen that he read the Midlothian speeches, and the campaigns affected him deeply.

Lady Gwendolen attributed a change in Salisbury to the notable impetus to "stump oratory" that came out of the campaigns. "Up to the last year of the previous parliament," she wrote, "a few speeches in the smaller London halls or in the neighborhood of his own country home represented all Lord Salisbury's non-parliamentary output." Then came the change. "During the years from 1880 to 1886 he spoke on more than 70 public platforms in all parts of the kingdom, to audiences which in the majority of instances had to be counted by thousands."[77] At the beginning of this period Salisbury wrote to his son: "Power is more and more leaving parliament and going to the platform."[78] From this time on Salisbury was associated with this kind of appeal to the people and the same may be said of the lords.

IV

Salisbury's speech to the Hackney Conservative Club on November 19, 1880 (reported in *The Times* on November 20) inaugurated a new era. It is best treated as his studied response to Gladstone's Midlothian campaigns, and coming from a political leader about to enter a new stage in his political career, it has a special importance. He spoke in the shadow of the general election of the previous spring but also in the twilight of the career of Disraeli, for

75. *Disraeli*, 719.

76. Cecil, *Biographic studies*, 31.

77. *Salisbury*, ii, 369; iii, 2–3. Smith, *Lord Salisbury on politics*, 338. See also *The Conservative leadership*, ed. Donald Southgate (1974), 108–9. In 1887 Salisbury wrote to Queen Victoria that the duty of making political speeches, which aggravated her ministers' labors, was due entirely to Gladstone. *Letters of Queen Victoria*, ed. G. E. Buckle (1930–2), 3rd series, i, 365.

78. Quoted in *Salisbury: the man and his policies*, ed. Blake and Cecil, 200.

whom time was now running out. At Hackney Salisbury reverted to ideas that he had put forward in 1868, 1869, and 1872, but this time emphasis was on the lords as a representative house in a manner setting it apart from the commons. The lords' main function was to represent "the durable and continued current of feeling and opinion in this country." Indeed, their duty was "to represent the permanent as opposed to the passing feelings of the English nation."[79]

The faithful performance of this duty was the more necessary because the nation would be governed by a new Liberal party, not that of Palmerston but that of Gladstone; and under the Gladstonian regime the energizing force came from Radicals, who had no respect for individual property rights. This could be seen from the Liberal attitude towards Ireland. Not only did Gladstone and his party hold up Irish landlords to opprobrium; they also lost no opportunity to treat individual property rights with contempt. According to Salisbury, many who had voted for the Liberals for their individual reasons would become disillusioned: they were "not prepared to sanction lawlessness that brings to an issue the very foundations of the social community." They would come to see that the lords were justified in much of what they had done in the past and would do in the future. Once more Salisbury's main theme emerged: the lords' duty was "to represent the more enduring rather than the transient interests of the English people."[80] In an equally important speech at Liverpool (April 12, 1882) Salisbury added the corollary that the lords must ensure that no permanent and irrevocable change took place in political institutions until the people had the opportunity to learn about it and form a mature, solemn decision on the subject.[81]

In summary, the Midlothian campaigns established that Salisbury, once in a position to determine party policy, would make the referendal theory the ideological mainstay of the Conservative position whenever his party was in opposition. At the

---

79. Salisbury at a meeting of the Hackney Conservative Club, reported in *The Times*, Nov. 20, 1880.

80. Ibid.

81. For this speech see Pulling, *Salisbury*, ii, 116–8; *The Times*, Apr. 13, 1882. Arthur Leach discusses the speeches at Hackney and Liverpool in the *Fortnightly Review*, old series, 38; new series, 32, 358–60. He was seeking the theory on which the lords were acting.

same time he adopted a radically new method, patterned on Gladstone's, of delivering his message to the country. He could hardly have missed the campaigns' impact. Not only had Gladstone enthralled the country; there is also the very considerable point that Salisbury had seen himself and his department as a major object of attack. Further, in a speech at Sheffield on July 23, 1884, he referred to his thorough search of the Midlothian speeches to learn whether parliamentary reform had been an issue in 1880. His conclusion was that the commons' majority coming out of that election may have "been put together by false promises or...accidental circumstances."[82]

The change in his electioneering style signalled Salisbury's recognition that he must act boldly and aggressively to renovate the lords in public esteem. As earlier stated, his strategy called for a hard and fast alliance between that house and public opinion in an effort to limit the commons' power, perhaps even to wrest political leadership from that house; and he considered that only by aligning the lords with the rising strength of public opinion could he hope to give his own house a new direction. His political performance is the more striking because Gladstone's campaigning style was so repugnant to him. A scion of the aristocratic Cecil family, with Lord Burghley and the first earl of Salisbury as forebears, he looked out at the world through the windows of Hatfield House–hardly the most helpful training ground for a popular leader with a campaign style shaped by the Midlothian campaigns. The transition was doubly difficult because as a frail, highly sensitive boy at Eton, Salisbury had lived in such dread of meeting classmates during holidays that he travelled the passages and alleys in the neighborhood of his London home to avoid chance encounters. As Lady Gwendolen notes, he was afraid of injury; and she adds: "This burden of prolonged mental oppression probably inflicted lasting mischief both upon the boy's physical nerves and, at the least, upon his superficial relations with his fellowmen in after life."[83] Paul Smith, too, writes of Salisbury's nervous illness and almost morbid diffidence.[84]

How far advanced the transformation was by the early

---

82. The speech is reported in *The Times*, July 23, 1884, 10.

83. Cecil, *Salisbury*, i, 15.

84. *Lord Salisbury on politics*, 9–12.

1890s appears from Salisbury's advice to his followers in 1891 to train themselves to meet the rising demand for public oratory. He stated:

> In these days, whether we like it or not, the power is with the tongue, the power is with those who can speak, whether on the platform or in parliament. I am not holding up this state of things as the ideal of political existence, but as a fact with which we are confronted now. I have known very distinguished orators who were perfectly incompetent men, and I have known very competent men who could not put two sentences–two grammatical sentences–together. But in spite of that fact, it remains true that the desire for oratory, for speaking on every platform and in every portion of the country, is intense, and seems to be growing in intensity every year.[85]

Another sign of the value he attached to communication skills appeared when he declined in 1892 to speak to the National Union of Conservative and Constitutional Associations, known as the National Union.

Neither he nor Balfour would be free at the time suggested. Furthermore, Salisbury expressed concern about their speaking too frequently to its members. "A constant recurrence to the same names" diminished the National Union's influence. He was not in favor of their doing much speaking until Gladstone brought out his Home Rule Bill. If they spoke too often, with too little to say, the electors would not listen so readily when they had a great deal to say. There was something to be learned from the circumstance that Gladstone's greatest platform achievement, the Midlothian campaigns, "followed immediately upon a period of 3 or 4 years of almost complete silence on his part."[86] This is as good testimony as one is likely to find that Salisbury and those around him knew full well that they were living in a new era where old rules no longer applied.

---

85. Quoted in Ostrogorski, *Democracy and the organization of political parties*, i, 384–5.
86. Salisbury to C. B. Stuart Wortley, Aug. 8, 1892, Secretary's Notebook, C7/475.

Four

"Legislating by Picnic"

I

As Salisbury moved to center stage in the early 1880s, so, too, did his referendal theory. After Disraeli's death he was Conservative leader in the lords and with Northcote of the party itself. The house's successful defiance of Gladstone in 1884 in an extended quarrel over the Third Reform Bill gave Salisbury primacy in his party, and that year he formed his first cabinet. For four years he had kept the referendal theory before the country, his doing so the more notable because of his skill in capitalizing on a widespread suspicion of post–1867 party organizations to undermine public confidence in the Liberal house of commons. He was playing what might today be termed a zero sum game. By lowering the house of commons in public esteem, he could hope to elevate the lords–the Conservative citadel on which he so much relied to frustrate radical Liberal legislation whenever his party was in opposition.

That Salisbury reasoned on these lines appeared when he charged the Liberals with "legislating by picnic." The reference was to the great political demonstrations, mounted by the new Liberal party organization, to show popular support for the Third Reform Bill. Salisbury was implying that the Liberal house of commons, by responding to these demonstrations, sanctioned the idea that the true source of public opinion was the streets rather than a general election. In retrospect it can be seen that Salisbury's anti-commons campaign of the early 1880s was the prelude to his notable success after Gladstone introduced his Second Home Rule Bill in 1893. Building on the foundation already laid, Salisbury in an age of expanding democracy ably defended the lords' rejection of the Bill by arguing that the lords not the commons deserved the country's trust. The fruit of his policy was his party's great electoral victory in 1895, which seemed to put this contention beyond doubt.

The necessary preliminary to discussing these matters is a brief consideration of the constitutional developments after 1867 that tell so much about Salisbury's course of action in the early 1880s. In the wake of the Second Reform Act, both political parties had founded local associations in their effort to win over the enlarged electorate. These were then banded together to form the National Liberal Federation and the National Union of Conservative and Constitutional Associations known as the National Union. Ignoring their marked similarities, Salisbury centered attention on the defects in the National Liberal Federation while obscuring with remarkable skill those in the National Union. At the beginning, the Radical Joseph Chamberlain dominated the Federation, but he soon had Gladstone at his side. Or so it appeared when Gladstone at Chamberlain's invitation attended a great demonstration at Bingley Hall, Birmingham, that launched the Federation in 1877. Seeking to associate the Federation with American machine politics, Salisbury labelled it the caucus, a term suggestive of secrecy, irresponsibility, and corruption. Its main crime, so Salisbury's rhetoric suggested, was its treatment of Liberal MPs, which according to the Conservative leader constituted a threat to independent government at Westminster. The goal was "to dictate to the men whom they had got into parliament" by binding them tightly with instructions from local Liberal associations. How different were Conservative practices: the National Union only assisted candidates during elections, kept an orderly register, and imparted Conservative principles to the electorate.[1]

Although neither the National Union nor the Federation established the dictatorship over parliament that critics feared, they had a decided impact on parliamentary government when they reversed the flow of power between cabinet and parliament. Parliamentary reform in 1867 and 1884, by creating a mass electorate, set the stage for increasing ministerial power at the expense of members of parliament. Personal resources now became

---

1. Robert Taylor, *Lord Salisbury* (1975), 77–8.

too limited to finance campaigns, and parliamentary candidates turned to party organizations for support. The beneficiaries were the party leaders, who let their backbenchers know that independence in voting had costs. They might have to fight the next election without the party label. In the end result parliamentary power diminished in the critical areas of legislating and the making and unmaking of cabinets.[2] The conservative journalist and minor historian, Sir Sidney Low–often referred to as Bagehot's intellectual successor–described the commons' changed position in his influential *Governance of England* (1904). That house's importance had been much reduced: the power to shape legislation was now in practice in "the inner ring of the cabinet." Further, "the house of commons no longer controls the executive; on the contrary, the executive controls the house of commons."[3] That is, Bagehot's exposition of a commons-centered regime at Westminster was anachronistic almost as soon as the *English constitution* was published.

Salisbury's opposition argument reflected the changed situation. The caucus was providing Gladstone with "mechanical majorities"; and if there was a threat to the Victorian constitution it came from the unholy alliance of Liberal prime minister and caucus, and not, as Liberals charged, from the hereditary house of lords. That house only performed its referendal function, seeing to it that the nation was part of the legislative process. This was the more necessary because the caucus, claiming to speak for local constituencies, was squeezing out independent opinion. According to Lady Gwendolen, Salisbury in private was skeptical of party machinery as an organ of opinion so far as both parties were concerned. She tells of his warning against equating the wirepullers' mentality with that of the electorate at large. It would be a very great mistake to do this.[4] For Salisbury there was the best of reasons to speak in this vein. To assume that the wirepullers reflected the outlook of the electorate was to undercut the lords' veto. After all, why place a high value on that house's

2. A. H. Birch, *Representative and responsible government* (1966), 74–5.

3. *Governance of England* (5th impression, rev. ed., 1914), 81. Robert Livingston Schuyler and Corinne Comstock Weston, *Cardinal documents in British history* (New York, 1961), 126–8.

4. *Salisbury*, iii, 197.

referendal function if the genuine voice of the electorate could be heard by way of the caucus and the National Union?

Although Salisbury's arguments were clearly the most influential, there were other critics of the new constitutional developments, notably the conservative Liberals known as the "old Liberals."[5] Whatever the intention, their writings broadened support for the referendal theory in audiences that he did not reach. Dismayed and alienated by Gladstone's reform legislation, his elevation of principles of moral justice in foreign and imperial policies, and the appearance of an autocratic cabinet, which they likened to the French revolutionary committee of public safety, they turned against the party system itself. Their number included Sir Henry Maine, his close friend and associate, James Fitzjames Stephen, Matthew Arnold, A. V. Dicey, John St. Loe Strachey, Low, and W.E.H. Lecky. Also supportive of Salisbury's arguments, though he was not an "old Liberal", was the noted Polish scholar, Mosei Ostrogorski, whose *Democracy and the organization of political parties* was published in 1902.

The leading figure among the "old Liberals" was Maine, with whom Salisbury had warm personal and professional relations. His extremely successful *Popular Government* (1885), initially published serially in the *Quarterly Review* in 1884–5, reflected party polemics in the summer and autumn of 1884. Lacking the scholarly qualities of Maine's earlier writings, it passed through six editions between 1885 and 1909, the year in which the lords' rejection of David Lloyd George's Finance Bill set in motion the train of events culminating in the Parliament Act. The extent of Maine's influence can be seen in the writings of Arnold, Dicey, Low and Ostrogorski; and he and Dicey were the foremost constitutional authorities in an age when appeal to the constitution was common in political discourse.

Vinerian professor of common law at Oxford and a Liberal Unionist after Gladstone adopted home rule in 1886, Dicey

---

5. The seminal article is John Roach, "Liberalism and the Victorian intelligentsia," *Cambridge Historical Journal*, 13, 1 (Cambridge, 1957), 58–81. But Roach does not know of Salisbury's importance in this context. See also George Feaver, *From status to contract: a biographical study of Sir Henry Maine, 1822–88* (1969), passim. Salisbury, Maine, and Stephen were early contributors to the *Saturday Review*, and as secretary of state for India in Disraeli's second cabinet, Salisbury had dealings with both men. Salisbury nominated Dicey for the Vinerian professorship.

was well-known in the late nineteenth and early twentieth centuries for his eloquent and persistent advocacy of the referendum as a check on party. In a letter (January 29, 1894) to Strachey, also a prominent Liberal Unionist and editor of the *Spectator*, Dicey explained his reasons for taking up the referendum, writing:

> I am sure we are right in agitating for the referendum. Wherever I go I find it popular. Personally I think that I should have preferred real parliamentary government as it existed up to 1868. But I have not the remotest doubt that under the present condition of things sham parliamentary government means a very vicious form of government by party, and from this I believe the referendum may partially save us. It has the great merit of being the only check on party management which is in perfect harmony with democratic sentiment...The only course which can be safely taken is to appeal in every shape from factions to the nation.[6]

The letter is the more interesting because a few graphic sentences tell so much about the disillusionment of the "old Liberals" with parliamentary government after 1867. Moreover, Dicey's solution was the logical offshoot of Salisbury's referendal theory and the direct product of the crisis over home rule.

II

In establishing the referendal theory Salisbury benefitted, too, from the simple fact that the lords were independent of extra-parliamentary organizations and, further, that unlike the commons after 1881 that house had no procedures for limiting debate. Their freedom of action permitted the claim that their house was a safe haven for traditional values and liberties. Salisbury's argument ran on these lines. The lords were a breed apart from the commons, who were fast sinking in public esteem, partly because of their chronic inability to deal effectively with the growing amount of public business but also because of the new party structures that had changed the commons beyond recognition when

---

6. Cited in Richard Cosgrave, *The rule of law: Albert Venn Dicey, Victorian jurist* (Chapel Hill, North Carolina, 1980), 107.

the Liberals held office. At such times the commons were subject to the influence of the caucus, their direction was determined by professional politicians, that is, "wirepullers" and "machine men," and their decisions were made by the "logrolling in which special interests, many of them sectional, delighted."[7] Given these circumstances, only the lords could protect the nation from the baleful effects of a Gladstonian dictatorship, resting on the caucus and driven by the foibles and fads of Radical Liberalism.

This harsh indictment became even more stinging after the almost complete collapse of parliamentary business on January 31, 1881 compelled a reluctant Gladstone to take up closure. On that memorable occasion Charles Stewart Parnell's Irish Nationalists kept the house in continuous session for some forty hours before the exhausted speaker pronounced the commons' legislative power paralyzed and stated that a new course of action had become imperative. In the following year the house provided for closure by a simple majority though the Conservatives favored a two-thirds vote.[8] According to an acerbic Chamberlain, the Conservative goal was to allow a minority to postpone indefinitely any proposal it found objectionable.[9]

Partisan zeal was certainly a factor, but the picture was more complex than Chamberlain allowed. Long before closure became an issue, Salisbury objected to it on principle as opposed to the absolute freedom of parliamentary speech that was a major source of English liberty and prosperity. Earlier attempts at

---

7. Cecil, *Salisbury*, iii, 197. There is a reference to wirepullers in Salisbury's article on disintegration; and though he does not use logrolling at this time as a term, he comes close to doing so when he associates a system of political bargains with the Liberals. See Smith, *Salisbury on politics*, 352–4 and Ostrogorski, 320 for a reference to logrolling and the Newcastle program and 600–1 for the Liberal tendency towards faddism and logrolling. There is pertinent material in Dicey, preface to the 8th edition of *Law and the constitution* (1915), xcviii. See also the reference to permanent majority, xciv. W.E.H.Lecky, *Democracy and liberty*, 1, 437 refers to the logrolling strategy that had of late been growing so rapidly in politics. It had been repudiated in the general election of 1895. Strachey in his *Adventure of living: a subjective autobiography* (1922) discusses the anomalies of the representative system and their correction by the referendum. One abuse was logrolling by minorities. Too often under the present system the conduct of the government was in a minority's hands; the referendum would bring majority rule.

8. Edward Hughes, "The changes in parliamentary procedure, 1880–1882," *Essays presented to Sir Lewis Namier*, ed. Richard Pares and A.J.P. Taylor (1956), 311, 316.

9. Ibid., 315–6.

limitation had failed, he explained, because "the fear of a tyrannous majority has always operated to make statesmen prefer the severest punishment which it is in the power of a bore to inflict, rather than place in the way of a majority a temptation to stifle discussion."[10] Moreover, he was deeply suspicious of any parliamentary mechanism promising to expedite the flow of legislation. Perceiving in legislation "a more unequivocal capacity for inflicting injury than for imparting benefit," Salisbury had more faith in administration as a source of improvement than in new laws. He warned Balfour not to go too far in accepting closure; but if it were adopted, he would distinguish between parliamentary functions "the performance of which is absolutely necessary to secure the working of the executive machine and those which, having no object but to change laws under which we are living quite tolerably, can be suspended without serious injury and often with great advantage." He would limit closure to the first category, which included mutiny, continuance bills, and measures for maintaining the public peace. "To grease the wheels of all legislation was not to the party's interest and might do infinite harm to Conservative classes."[11]

On another occasion Salisbury explained that Conservatives must satisfy both the classes and the masses. The former were more difficult to deal with because all legislation was "rather unwelcome to them, as tending to disturb a state of things with which they are satisfied." It followed that his party had to work "at less speed and at a lower temperature" than their opponents, their bills "tentative and cautious, not sweeping and dramatic."[12] He even contemplated with equanimity the prospect of a Conservative party in permanent opposition, a position certainly preferable, he considered, to taking office and passing as the price of power a measure like the Second Reform Act to dish the Liberals. Yet Salisbury at times did sound like the political leader that Chamberlain denounced, for example, in his stress on the Con-

---

10. Smith, *Lord Salisbury on politics*, 165–6.

11. Salisbury to Balfour, Jan. 15, 1881, cited in G.H.L. LeMay, *The Victorian constitution* (1979), 159–60. There is also pertinent comment in Lady Gwendolen Cecil, *Biographical studies*, 75, 77–83; Eric Akers-Douglas, third Viscount Chilston, *The political life and times of Aretas Akers-Douglas, 1st Viscount Chilston* (Toronto, 1962), 170.

12. *Salisbury: the man and his policies*, ed. Blake and Cecil, 230–1.

servative duty to prevent the passage of Radical legislation.[13]

The adoption of closure brought Irish obstruction to an end; but as Salisbury and others had foreseen, the new machinery tempted governments to make use of it to carry their own policies. Faced in his second government (1886–92) with large-scale obstruction on the part of both the Irish and the Liberals, Salisbury, ironically, presided over the introduction of more severe forms of cutting off debate. In 1887 he used closure against the Liberals when a new standing order transferred the initiative in moving closure from a minister to an individual member. The speaker retained a veto where it seemed that closure would be an abuse of the house's rules or an infringement of the minority's rights. There was another innovation of note when an allocation of time order, known as the guillotine, was introduced. Closure had to be invoked to obtain it. Moreover, Salisbury was willing to use it for ordinary legislation.

From the first the Liberals lagged badly in the war of words over closure and the caucus. The zeal for closure, openly professed by Radical Liberals, embarrassed Gladstone politically by strongly suggesting an intimate relationship between its introduction and the caucus; and contemporary observers often, though unfairly, traced the double development to Chamberlain, the leading Radical Liberal in Gladstone's second cabinet. According to W. T. Marriott, later a Liberal Unionist, the Birmingham caucus, sometimes referred to as the central caucus and the organizational model for Liberal associations, was more interested in imposing its program on political opponents than in curbing Irish Nationalist obstruction. In Marriott's view, there was a direct relationship between the caucus and the introduction of new rules of procedure in the commons,[14] a conclusion supported by Ostrogorski's massive study of late nineteenth-century party organization. But today the latter's own conclusions have been described as highly controversial, and *Democracy and the organization of political parties* is dismissed as "now very much a period

---

13. Ibid., 231.

14. Cited in LeMay, *Victorian constitution*, 159. See also Marriott, "The Birmingham caucus," *Nineteenth Century*, 2 (June 1882), 949–65. Ostrogorski also discusses Marriott, 214, note; 215–6.

piece."[15] This condemns the book from the viewpoint of modern historical scholarship, but not as an account of the way Salisbury made his referendal theory acceptable to large numbers of Victorian Englishmen. A debit in the first instance, it is a credit when one deals with the referendal theory. For it matters very little whether the perceptions that Ostrogorski chronicled matched political reality. Of much greater significance is the fact emerging from his study that many late Victorian Englishmen disliked both caucus and closure and viewed them as interrelated. In seizing on these developments as the political targets needed to place Liberal policies in a negative light while at the same time elevating the lords in public esteem, Salisbury displayed faultless political judgment.

Two points are worth making in this connection. The period with which Ostrogorski was concerned ran from 1867 to 1895, important years in the rise and spread of the referendal theory. And he exercised much care and an exemplary thoroughness in compiling the evidence for his conclusions. First making enquiries in both parties in a strenuous effort to elicit the truth, he then constantly verified the facts and impressions that were obtained by putting himself "in touch with men and things." He interviewed and questioned the staffs of the party organizations and such eminent figures as the Liberal James Bryce, whose *American Commonwealth* (1888) was widely seen as authoritative for the American scene. Some of his information came from Captain R.W.E. Middleton, the Conservative party's extremely capable principal agent, with whom Salisbury often conferred, and J. E. Gorst, said to be the founder of the Primrose League. One of Middleton's most competent predecessors, Gorst was a leading member of Lord Randolph Churchill's fourth party, to which Balfour also belonged.

No event had a more dramatic impact on observers of the caucus than the introduction of closure. Ostrogorski, who considers that it gave the caucus a sinister air, writes: "Among the many questions by means of which the caucus interfered in the

---

15. Hanham, *The reformed electoral system in Great Britain, 1832–1914* (The Historical Association, 1968), 37. He does see it as "a storehouse of strong opinions and of many facts."

workings of the constitution, none gave it an opportunity of appearing in so many aspects, of showing how far reaching and penetrating its intervention could become as the reform of the procedure of the house of commons in 1882." According to his account, the caucus cut in almost as soon as opposition to closure emerged in the commons. The Birmingham caucus summoned other Liberal associations to arms to ensure party support for Gladstone, and the powerful, instantaneous response led him to abandon concessions and carry closure by an almost completely Liberal vote. This was the impact.

> Rightly or wrongly, people feared that it [closure] was to be used more for paralyzing the opposition than for preventing obstruction; that in deference to the militant Radicals a whole series of measures would be placed before parliament and that they would be forced through the house by means of the closure. The idea prevailed that the latter was "part of a vast scheme of political manipulation" set on foot by the Birmingham group, that it would be the counterpart of the caucus in parliament, and that it would enable the former to control the latter and transform it into a chamber for registering the decrees of the caucus and of the press of the party.

Seeking to allay fears and quell suspicion, Gladstone denied categorically that the Liberals would treat closure as a party weapon.[16]

The prominent Radical, Henry Labouchere, took an altogether different public stand. Contradicting Gladstone, he expressed his own ideas about how to bring the country into harmony with the "spirit of the age." The government's first duty was to use closure as a party weapon and as the result of a particular process. There should be frequent elections, during which measures would be discussed before they reached parliament. After the people had reached a decision, the government must act. It "had an imperative mandate" to pass the measure in question. No parliamentary discussion was necessary since it had already taken place.[17]

---

16. Ostrogorski, *Democracy and...political parties*, 212–5.

17. *Parl. debs.*, 3rd series, cclxxiv, 678 ff. See also Patricia Kelvin, "The development and use of the concept of the electoral mandate in British politics, 1867 to 1911," Ph.D. dissertation, University College, University of London, 1977, pp. 17, 20, 60–1.

As earlier seen, not all Liberals exhibited this zeal for closure. The author of an article in the *Nineteenth Century* (October 1878)–a professed Liberal–expressed a not uncommon view when he referred to it as the opening wedge in introducing American machine politics. These were crushing out every form of individuality at home, and once in place were impossible to root out. Public opinion was no match for the machine.[18]

Only if Salisbury established that his strictures did not apply to his own party could he extract maximum advantage from the stir over closure and the caucus. Otherwise the referendal theory might be lost in a welter of charge and countercharge. Fortunately for his theme, his party's origins and operation supported the proposition that the Conservative leadership was likely to be more independent of outside pressure than its Liberal counterpart. Unlike the caucus, sprung from grassroots and hence more vulnerable to the charge of pressuring MPs from outside parliament, the National Union was subordinate from the beginning to the party leadership; and Salisbury intended to keep it that way. Yet it seemed as if this advantage would be lost when Churchill, under the banner of "Tory democracy" undertook in 1883 to give the National Union the "caucus" flavor. Capitalizing on middle-class dissatisfaction in local Conservative associations, he posed a formidable threat because he headed the fourth party in the commons and as a pungent, dynamic speaker commanded a wide audience beyond Westminster.

In the end Salisbury's settlement with Churchill did not, in Robert Blake's words, "abandon a single jot or tittle of the powers that the leadership inherently possessed." And Blake distinguished sharply between the Liberal Federation and the National Union. Whereas the first was a strong pressure group that favored Chamberlain's and the Radical Charles Dilke's policies, the National Union was subservient to the Conservative party leadership.[19] Unsurprisingly, the memorandum that supplied the basis of the settlement contained a provision that Conservative asso-

---

18. Edward Wilson, "The caucus and its consequences," *Nineteenth Century* (Oct. 1878), 708, 709.

19. Blake, *The Conservative party from Peel to Churchill* (1970, repr. 1972), 150–9. Marsh, *Discipline*, 47–9.

ciations were "to have nothing to do with direction of matters incident to the duties and policy of our members in parliament."[20]

That the difference between the two parties' organizational structures held ideological implications for Salisbury is easily seen, and so, too, are his interest and skill in taking advantage of it. Thus he told Birmingham Conservatives on March 30, 1883: "When I praise organization do not let me be supposed to have given any kind of back-handed approval to that special production and manufacture which is called the caucus. The difference between them is this, that while you organize to rally the strength of your party to bring yourselves together and induce everyone to put forward his exertions on behalf of the cause, they organize for the purpose of dominating their member when they have selected him and of making him the mere slave and creation of the organization by which he was elected."[21]

The distinction enabled Salisbury to present a strong case for the lords' referendal function. Justifying their treatment of the Third Reform Bill he skillfully established his own frame of reference for viewing the struggle with Gladstone. Voters should center their attention on a domineering prime minister whose already great power was swelled by the caucus' unswerving support. He told his audience eloquently:

> If you have any danger to fear to the free working of our institutions, it is from the growth of the power of the wirepuller, centered in the caucus under the direction of the prime minister–master of the house of commons, master of the house of lords, nay, yielding but apparent and simulated obedience to the orders of the sovereign, gathering into his own hands every power in the state, and using them so that when the time of renewal comes, his influence may be overwhelming and his powers may be renewed.[22]

---

20. Taylor, *Lord Salisbury*, 77.

21. Ibid., 77–8.

22. Salisbury at Glasgow, Sept. 30, 1884. *Speeches of the marquess of Salisbury*, ed. Henry Lucy (1885), 124–5. The speech was reprinted in *The Times*, Oct. 2. Robert T. MacKenzie, *British political parties* (2nd ed., 1964), 176, states that Salisbury gave "a classic warning of the menace of the caucus" and relates it to his quarrel with Randolph Churchill in the context of the struggle over the party leadership. But the two political leaders had come to terms in the preceding July, and Salisbury's argument is more properly related to his advocacy of the referendal theory. For the Liberal denial that Gladstone was a dictator, see Lord Askwith, *Lord James of Heresford* (1930), 135.

Here was the real danger to be feared: all power was centering in the prime minister. Even the power of dissolving parliament, nominally in the Crown, had passed to him. "Do you expect that under such a system," Salisbury asked rhetorically, "the people will have any real hold over the conduct of affairs?"[23]

There was another, more indirect, means of establishing that Conservative organizational methods were not those of the Liberals. This was to extol publicly and support formally the Primrose League, "the popular wing of the Conservative party," which had grown up "outside the orthodox organization of the party." Its facade set it apart from the Federation and the National Union. Founded "to supply the antidote of the caucus,"[24] it was not easily accused of machine politics, for despite its association with the Conservatives, the League appeared independent of party with values superior to the professional politician's. That Salisbury placed a high value on the Primrose League appears from the fact that almost his last act as prime minister before leaving office in 1902 was to address its ruling body.

The Primrose League became part of the Conservative establishment almost by accident. Founded in Disraeli's memory in 1883, it appeared in the year that the Corrupt Practices Act compelled the parties to find new sources of unpaid help for electoral purposes. A major turning point came when Salisbury and Churchill settled their differences. A clause in their agreement provided for Conservative recognition of the League. A number of MPs, including Marriott, entered the governing Grand Council; and Salisbury and Northcote became patrons. In 1885 and again in 1887 Salisbury was grand master, and Balfour served as such in 1903. Lady Salisbury and the Cecil daughters, Lady Gwendolen and Lady Beatrix Maud Cecil, later countess of Selborne, were members, as was Salisbury's son, Robert Cecil. Salisbury is said to have been at first cool to the organization on reading its statutes, only to have been influenced favorably by his wife, "an extremely clever woman."[25] But it is unlikely that a

23. *Speeches*, ed. Lucy, 125.

24. Martin Pugh, *The Tories and the people* (Oxford, 1985), 16. Ostrogorski, *Democracy and...political parties*, 514, 535.

25. Robert James Rhodes, *Lord Randolph Churchill* (1959), 128. Pugh, *The Tories and the people*, 25, 26, 65; Appendix 1. Algernon Cecil, *Queen Victoria and her prime ministers* (1953), 314. Salisbury's last speech was to the Primrose League. Donald Southgate, *Conservative leadership, 1832–1932* (1974), 149.

political leader as acute as Salisbury was slow to perceive the manifest advantage of links with the League if he were to distance his party's organization from that of the Liberals.

With more than a million members by 1891, the League was by 1914 the largest mass political organization in England. The secret of its success lies largely in the explosive impact of Gladstone's home-rule policy, beginning in 1886, but also in the policy decision to recruit without regard for sex, class, social station, even party allegiance. Founded avowedly to propagate "Tory principles," the League broadened its appeal by dropping "Tory" from the original "Tory Primrose League" and placing the words "independent of party politics" after its name. Its base was further broadened by defining its principles in general terms such as defense of religion, the fundamental institutions of the realm, and imperial ascendancy. Salisbury used this felicitous language in addressing its members at an early annual meeting: "You are not confined within rigid party lines; you are not attached to members or candidates in any locality. You are the general missionaries of the principles which you profess, and, if I may say so without irreverence, you are rather the preaching friars of the message that you have to convey than the regular clergy attached to each particular locality."[26] But Ostrogorski writes briskly of the Primrose League as a formidable "Tory militia" reaching into the recesses of the kingdom and soon after its founding surpassing the regular party organization in numbers and fighting spirit. He describes it as basically machinery for manufacturing sentiments, and a more recent observer writes of it as both a means of creating public opinion and a very valuable propaganda instrument.[27] On both scores it served Salisbury well.

The skill with which the League harnessed potent social emotions, notably social snobbery, on behalf of the Conservative party also disguised its essentially political nature. Calling attention to its slogan "the union of classes," its most recent historian, Martin Pugh, writes appreciatively of its skill in integrat-

---

26. Ostrogorski, *Democracy and...political parties*, 536. See also ibid., 535, 536, 540, 547, 551.

27. Ibid., 551. See also Quinault, "The Fourth Party and the Conservative Opposition to Bradlaugh, 1880-1888," *English Historical Review* XCI (April, 1976), 335.

ing the classes in town and country. It recruited "non-voters and voters, the apathetic as well as the political, women as well as men, children as well as adults, and the working classes as well as the middle class."[28] The union of the classes was completed, in Ostrogorski's words, "by the union of the sexes." The women, recruited from the working and middle classes, were traditionalist housewives seeking to brighten their drab routines. To them the League's political fare was more palatable than that of the Federation or National Union and infinitely more rewarding in a social sense. To bring Westminster closer to the workaday lives of voters and their families, branches, called "habitations," competed vigorously with the new music halls in arranging musical entertainments, dances, teas, summer fetes, and excursions. Equally, if not more to the point, they made it possible for elements of the lower and middle classes to mingle on a regular basis with the upper reaches of society. By paying a small prescription, Ostrogroski writes, they became the colleagues of titled or simply rich personages, obtained access to their drawing rooms and parks, made available for League meetings, and enjoyed a certain familiarity with personages whom they admired as the great ones of the earth.

The League's image was infinitely more attractive than the Federation's and the National Union's, its appeal virtually irresistible. As member of a committee, a lower- or middle-class woman might have social contact with a marchioness or duchess, perhaps helping with the tea and cutting the sandwiches. As Ostrogorski puts it, "the self-love and vanity" of members made them "fall into line behind a political party, often apart from...all political conviction." Hence the great willingness of League leaders to exhort their great ladies: "Do not argue, take them in socially." Here was the "watch-word" that summed up the strategy and tactics of the Primrose League, that most romantic and glamorous of political organizations.[29]

Pugh finds that these attributes made the Primrose League more attractive than the National Union to Salisbury on ideo-

---

28. *The Tories and the people*, 2, 16.

29. Ostrogorski, *Democracy and...political parties*, xxxiii, 538–45. Hanham, *The reformed electoral system*, 21.

logical and organizational grounds,[30] and Ostrogorski reports that Conservative leaders with Salisbury in the vanguard tirelessly extolled the Primrose League's beneficent effect on political life. The League had encouraged public spirit and "*rescued the English democracy from the domination of the professional politician.*" How had this been achieved? The answer went right to the point: "*by preventing it from sinking into the condition of a mechanically wire-pulled democracy.*"[31] That this was Salisbury's view of the Primrose League could be seen from his speeches of April 23, 1889 at Bristol, and May 20th on the occasion of the sixth annual meeting of the Grand Habitation, the national meeting of delegates.[32]

Salisbury's message was more convincing because Conservatives had no episodes comparable to those in the Liberal party involving W. E. Forster at Bradford and Joseph Cowen at Newcastle. Both arose out of attempts by Liberal associations to establish firm control over MPs elected from these constituencies. Undoubtedly Salisbury was familiar with them. They received much attention at the time, and in an article written for the *Quarterly Review* he used two of Forster's speeches as his point of departure.[33]

In short, the great difference between the beginnings of the National Union and those of the Federation, and the informal association of the Conservative party with the Primrose League, given the latter's pronounced social characteristics and seemingly non-partisan program, enabled Salisbury to defend the lords' independent veto with a minimum of embarrassment while simultaneously promoting the referendal theory. This set of political ideas, as earlier noted, won greater acceptance because proceedings in the lords were free of closure and pressure from extra-parliamentary organizations. Salisbury's practice of contrasting the commons of the 1880s with those of the past and then stressing the dire need for a second chamber strong enough to protect the people from their elected representatives imparted a novel twist to political rhetoric, achieving a success not easily

---

30. *The Tories and the people*, 15.

31. Ostrogorski, *Democracy and...political parties*, 550.

32. Ibid., 550, note 1.

33. Smith, *Lord Salisbury on politics*, 338. LeMay, *The Victorian constitution*, 177.

understood apart from the context that has been described. Thus Salisbury declared at Liverpool in April 1882, in a speech commanding national attention: "A house of commons, enslaved by the caucus, and muzzled by the cloture, would be a very different body from that which has hitherto been the glory of English history." The speech, published in newspapers with a national audience, was also circulated separately by the National Union and reprinted in a contemporary biography of Salisbury.[34] On another occasion he used memorable language in denouncing the commons as "the most servile house of commons–servile to the ministers, servile to the caucus–that the palace of Westminster has ever seen."[35]

The only solution–unsatisfactory at that–was to replace septennial parliaments with triennial or even annual parliaments if for any reason the lords failed to perform their referendal function and keep the electorate within the political process. As he put it at Liverpool, "a triennial, or even an annual parliament would be the only substitute for a second chamber."[36] The force of this Salburian argument probably explains the provision in the Parliament Act replacing septennial with quinquennial parliaments. For there seems to have been little or no advocacy of this cause before 1911. To be sure, the Parliament Act did not provide for annual or triennial parliaments, the alternatives posed by Salisbury; but the move in 1911 was certainly in this direction. This means that in an ideological sense this provision was the direct outgrowth of Salisbury's crusade for the renovation of the lords, giving mute testimony to the importance of the referendal theory in shaping English political institutions.

III

A major stumbling block to Salisbury's rehabilitation of the lords was the question of whether that house had sufficient stamina to

34. F. S. Pulling, *The life and speeches of the Marquis of Salisbury* (1885), ii, 118. *The Times*, Apr. 14, 1882.

35. Salisbury at Sheffield, ibid., July 23, 1884.

36. Pulling, *Life...of Salisbury*, ii, 118 The argument was recalled in the *Quarterly Review*, 196, (July to Oct. 1902), 652.

hold out against a determined commons in a prolonged confrontation. Despite the ring of his rhetoric, he knew, as did his fellow peers, that a conflict between the houses would put the lords at risk; and he had no illusions about that house's strength of will. At the outset of his leadership in the lords, he found the house, in Lady Gwendolen's words, "habitually and almost morbidly afraid of resisting the will of the commons' majority."[37] To Carnarvon, a close observer of the current scene, Salisbury's confrontational tactics reflected the belief that the lords must fight "to arrest the habit of compromise that was sapping the moral courage of the peers."[38]–a tacit admission that the problem of the lords was of very considerable dimensions.

Whatever Salisbury's reservations, they were cloaked under a bold exterior. A prime example of his mode of argument is supplied by his speech at the little Scottish village of Kelso in the autumn of 1884. It deserves to be known, both because it reflects the spirited quality of his leadership, which had important effects on the lords, and because this line of thought had a lasting impact on some of his followers. Its message resonated during the diehard revolt against the Parliament Bill and the Conservative leadership. In a conflict with the commons, he insisted in 1884, the only suitable policy for the lords was to go down fighting rather than lingering on as a weak, passive house. Single-chamber government was deplorable, to be sure, but not nearly so much as acquiescence in a policy leaving the lords "a mere screen and mask for any enterprise that the minister might like to undertake." If that house were to bleed to death, its power repudiated and defeated, the people would not realize how precarious their liberties had become or grasp that "the despotism of a single chamber, or of a single minister" had replaced "the old constitution of the crown, lords, and commons."[39]

The dangers facing the English people were very different from those represented by Laud and Strafford in the seventeenth century, and there was no protection against them except that provided by the lords when the Liberals held office. The

37. *Biographical studies*, 30.

38. *The life of...Carnarvon*, iii, 84.

39. *Speeches*, ed. Lucy, 142–3.

question was one of machine politics, and most to be feared was the complex party organization that left no place for individual opinion. Supreme power resided with those who controlled the electoral machine–the wirepullers. The reigning doctrine made the political problem more complex. If the lords were for any reason removed from the scene, everything would be at the mercy of the commons' majority; and to all intents and purposes, came the familiar refrain, this meant the prime minister. Armed with the power of dissolution and the caucus, he would have "all power, executive as well as legislative." Here was the real rub, and it should give pause to any move to weaken further the lords' already reduced power. That house constituted "the only control left upon an aspiring and engrossing minister." Nowhere in modern times had a single chamber without check and control disposed of both legislative and executive power. Conservatives must struggle to the end against so monstrous a combination of power.[40]

The argument was reasoned and intelligent, as one would expect from Salisbury; and it was effective. Its strength lay in striking a tender nerve, while evoking nostalgia for an earlier golden age of constitutionalism at a time of growing sensitivity to the very concerns that Salisbury was articulating. And his habit of driving his ideas home relentlessly must always be kept in mind in judging the efficacy of his arguments. Their weaknesses are obvious. That he was putting the lords to a partisan use would have been clear to a sophisticated observer, and so was the fact that the house of lords lacked the business-like characteristics of the more politically experienced house of commons. As late as 1884, the year of a prolonged struggle between Gladstone and the lords, the attendance was bad in the lords "except at the beginning and end of a debate."[41] On another occasion Salisbury informed Lord Cairns, who had been absent from a debate, that he could not be paired as no whips were available for this purpose. One of them was laid up with rheumatism, the other did not agree with the leadership in the matter.[42] A modern authority, writing on

---

40. Ibid., 143–5.

41. Salisbury to Cairns, Jan. 21, 1884, Cairns Correspondence, PRO 30/51/6, fos. 130–1.

42. Same to same, Mar. 21, 1884, ibid., fos. 138–9.

Salisbury's position during the struggle, reported that he could not carry on if Richmond and Cairns were to defect.[43]

Still certain factors favored Salisbury. Political change was erasing old landmarks too rapidly for popular acceptance; and unease in the ruling classes, for whom Salisbury was spokesman, deepened with land war in Ireland. Nor was it allayed by Gladstone's response. Many were outraged by the Liberal land legislation of 1870 and 1881–2, which was perceived as violating recognized property rights and the freedom of contract deemed essential to an advancing civilization.[44] Particularly disturbing was the changed relationship between Irish landlord and tenant, which might be extended to England. As early as 1880, before the more radical land legislation was enacted, Salisbury voiced his fears to Balfour when he described the election of that year as a hurricane–a strange and new phenomenon that would defy understanding for some time. He doubted that so much enthusiasm and unity of action proceeded from a sentimental opinion or an academic judgment. More likely, the electoral result reflected a definite desire for change and meant business. Salisbury thought it possible that it portended a serious class war; but in any case, he forecast, Gladstone would seek to give it that meaning.[45]

That others shared this distrust of Gladstone appears from a letter written on April 1, 1880 by Lady Sophia Palmer, daughter of the first Lord Selborne, lord chancellor in Gladstone's first cabinet. A Liberal, she wrote of Gladstone that half the world, including in particular most of the upper classes, had a positive hatred for him. To him they attributed "evil motives, passions, and actions, with a vigor that has never been surpassed."[46] This was six years before Gladstone introduced his First Home Rule Bill for Ireland that broke up his party. At that time Henry Sidgwick wrote: "The anti-Gladstonian feeling seems growing

---

43. Marsh, *Discipline*, 42.

44. Roach, "Liberalism and the Victorian intelligentsia," 73–8. For a statement on Salisbury's views, see L. P. Curtis, Jr., *Coercion and conciliation in Ireland, 1882–1892* (Princeton, New Jersey, 1963), 31–3.

45. Cited in Akers-Douglas, *Chilston*, 6.

46. *A political correspondence of the Gladstone era: the letters of Lady Sophia Palmer and Sir Arthur Gordon*, 1884, ed. J. K. Chapman, *Transactions of the American Philosophical Society*, new series, 61 (1971), 17. Hereafter cited as *A political correspondence*.

and hardening at least among the people I meet...I am moved to write about politics, chiefly to mark with some alarm, the extent of my alienation from current Liberalism. We are drifting on to what must be a national disaster and the forces impelling are party organization and Liberal principles."[47] If these remarks are a dependable index, Salisbury had chosen with great tactical skill the ground on which to debate his archrival.

These developments were in the future when Salisbury became Conservative leader in the lords. Disraeli had designated him as his successor in leading the party, but the objections of ex-leaders in the commons led to the dual leadership that ended when Salisbury established his superior credentials in the struggle over the Third Reform Bill. A strongly partisan biographer savored Salisbury's triumph in what must have been by this time familiar terms. He considered that the peers had successfully made a stand that ensured the country against an incomplete and unsatisfactory measure, demonstrated the caucus's impotence against the people's wishes, and broken "the prescription of ministerial despotism."[48] The language could not have been more acceptable to Salisbury had he written the passage, and the place of its appearance points to still another way in which his argument was being transmitted to the public.

That matters would take this turn was not foreseeable when the dual leadership was established. Northcote was viewed as the senior partner and as member of the commons was thought to have Queen Victoria's support. Moveover, he had a more amiable personality and benefitted from Salisbury's earned reputation for rashness and instability rising out of his public anger at Disraeli's role in passing the Second Reform Act. As late as 1874 the latter spoke of Salisbury as "not a man who measures his words" but "a great master of gibes and flouts and jeers."[49] It has been said of Salisbury that he "never entirely ceased to live up to this description."[50]

---

47. A. S. Sidgwick and E. M. Sidgwick, *Henry Sidgwick: a memoir* (1906), 436. Cited in Paul Adelman, *Victorian radicalism: the middle class experience 1830–1914* (1984), 66.

48. Pulling, *Life...of Salisbury*, ii, 236.

49. Cited in R.C.K. Ensor, *England: 1870–1914* (Oxford, 1936, rep. 1960), 34, note 3.

50. Ibid. See also *The Conservatives*, ed. Butler, 169, 171.

The first test of his leadership came with the fiasco of the Arrears Bill, which for the moment put in doubt his leadership abilities. This measure remedied a defect in the Land Act of 1881 by wiping out the poor tenant's arrears, with the state sharing the landlord's loss. The principle was anathema to Salisbury, a strong believer in landlord rights; but his course was also affected by Conservative MPs who wanted a general election on the issue. Although the lords favored an outright rejection, the MPs pressed them to strengthen safeguards against dishonest tenants. In securing a compromise between the two groups, Salisbury pledged support to two amendments prepared by the shadow cabinet; and relying on this pledge the lords gave the Bill a second reading.

He was caught flat-footed when Gladstone rejected the amendments and Conservative MPs pressed for a reversal of course. The indispensable Cairns announced his departure for Scotland, and Salisbury learned about the same time that he could no longer depend on his fellow peers. Making no attempt to conceal the party split, he announced publicly that if he had his way the Bill would be thrown out. These candid remarks told against him in contemporary opinion, but Lady Gwendolen Cecil believed his leadership was not in fact endangered. Things did not work out that way, she contends; and she notes a steady rise in his influence in the lords thereafter. Nor did she consider that he ever encountered a similar situation again.[51]

In fact, Salisbury did face a similar dilemma in 1884; but this time, profiting from experience, he adroitly papered over the cracks in party unity.[52] His guiding policy, which he was subsequently forced to abandon, was to secure a dissolution of parliament and a general election by which the Conservatives might return to office. He seized his opportunity when Gladstone introduced the Third Reform Bill in the form of a Franchise Bill extending household suffrage to the counties without an accomp-

---

51. Cecil, *Salisbury*, iii, 52–6.

52. My view of what occurred in 1884 differs sharply from that of John Fair. The pertinent political literature is as follows: Weston, "The royal mediation in 1884," *English Historical Review*, lxxxii (1967), 296–322. Fair, "Royal mediation in 1884: a reassessment," ibid., lxxxviii (1973), 100–13. Weston, "Disunity on the opposition front bench, 1884," ibid., cvi (Jan.,1991), 80–96. Fair, "The Carnarvon diaries and royal mediation in 1884", ibid., 97–116.

anying seats bill. This was to fly in the face of 1832 and 1867, and the Conservatives were ready for him. Salisbury had himself criticized Gladstone's Bill of 1866 for making no provision for a seats bill, and before his death Disraeli warned of a possible repetition of this approach when the Liberal leader brought in his measure for household suffrage in the counties. He would advise the lords to insist on dealing simultaneously with the franchise and redistribution, and he expressed the belief that the Liberals had little choice except compliance. They must either lose the Franchise Bill or give in. Resort to a dissolution was too risky: the small boroughs would oppose change and hence the Liberal program. This was the strategy employed in 1884 though unlike Disraeli Salisbury aimed for a dissolution and may have thought the end result would be the loss of the Franchise Bill. Careful not to oppose extending the franchise, the lords insisted on an accompanying seats bill. As was noted earlier, Salisbury would have the nation act as arbiter in this situation. If its judgment supported Gladstone's approach, he would be surprised but would not dispute the verdict.

An angered Selborne considered that history might be searched in vain "for so willful and unnecessary a disturbance of the balance of constitutional power in any state, as the lords, under the guidance of...Lord Salisbury, have in this case created." The matter would be different if the lords had not professed to approve the Franchise Bill, but to reach this stage over "the mere order of procedures in legislating for two objects,...both of which they profess to agree with the government in desiring" was to "encourage republicanism." The lords' rejection was "nothing short of infatuation."[53] Selborne's dislike of Salisbury's leadership in this insistence was part of a larger picture. According to Lady Sophia, her words implying that this was Selborne's view, Salisbury had given the lords a new tone. That house was "entirely altered since Lord Derby's day." Earlier the lords had supported the government of the day more or less and only in very exceptional cases had thrown out government measures. Now, she continued, everyone knew that whatever measure great or

53. Roundell Palmer, first earl of Selborne, Lord High Chancellor, *Memorials* (1898), ii, 124–5. Disraeli's strategy is described in Balfour, *Chapters of autobiography*, ed. Blanche E. Dugdale (1930), 126.

small was brought in by a Liberal government would be thrown out.[54]

Yet there was an important practical reason for the lords' resistance. According to Salisbury, a general election under the Liberal plan might result in a loss of forty-seven Conservative seats; and a majority of the peers believed that extending the vote without redistribution would result in a generation of Conservative eclipse.[55] Perhaps recalling the Arrears Bill, Salisbury this time lined up support ahead of time. The Franchise Bill reached the lords in July, and there it ran into trouble. A good omen for Salisbury was that Cairns, also speaking for Richmond, moved the amendment embodying his party's position; and supportive peers turned to the referendal theory to make their case. Earl Cadogan remembered that the lords had bowed as a result of the general election of 1868 and vowed to do the same on this occasion if this were the wish of the constituencies.[56] Others denied that parliamentary reform had been before the electorate in 1880. Lord Balfour of Burleigh, later known for his zealous advocacy of the referendum, pointed out that neither Gladstone nor Lord Hartington had given the question prominence;[57] Earl Stanhope noted that very few of the Liberal candidates "had alluded to the subject in their published election addresses";[58] and the earl of Wemyss, though willing to accept the Franchise Bill, spoke of learning from an institution in Bloomsbury called the Universal Knowledge and Information Office that fewer than one-third of the election addresses had referred to electoral reform.[59] Carnarvon, denying a mandate for the Bill, stated simply: "We appeal to Caesar."[60]

Salisbury's lead was so vigorous that he seemed to be urging a dissolution at the lords' behest, and for the first time since 1846 this issue became central. On July 8, the day that the lords

---

54. Lady Sophia Palmer to Arthur Gordon, July 2, 1884, *A political correspondence*, 22.

55. Cecil, *Salisbury*, iii, 105–6.

56. *Parl. debs.*, 3rd series, ccxc, 185(July 7, 1884).

57. Ibid., cols. 149, 153.

58. Ibid., cols. 155–6.

59. Ibid., cols. 290, 438.

60. Ibid., cols. 384–5.

rejected the Franchise Bill, he made their case in sweeping terms, declaring:

> As a mere party matter, we have no desire to force a dissolution; but we do, with reference to this great revolution in the machinery for electing the members of the house of commons—we do urge upon the government, not only the prudence, but the justice of consulting the people. We do urge upon them that they have no right to make these vast constitutional changes without formally consulting the opinions of those by whose authority they really, in the long run, make them, and whose interests will be specially affected.[61]

Any accusation that the peers were trying to keep electors off the franchise, he continued, was without merit. The issue at stake should go to the electorate for settlement. The lords were duty bound to act as guardians of the people's interest, and by the results of the general election they would abide.[62] Here was a classic exposition of the referendal theory, and it carried a special meaning for those mindful of events in 1845–6 and 1868–9. By a vote of 205 to 146, the lords refused the Franchise Bill a second reading; and a meeting of the Conservative party on July 16 heard Salisbury urge uncompromising resistance.

Gladstone was not to be outdone. There would be no general election, and the Franchise Bill would be returned to the lords in an autumn session. Addressing directly the premises on which Salisbury claimed to be acting, he denounced the Conservatives as the greatest innovators of the day. It did not 'signify a rush whether they can find in history or in the constitution a precedent for what they ask or what they do; if it suits their immediate purpose, it is demanded with the greatest gravity and coolness that can be imagined." The recent discussions had brought forward two novelties: the lords' claim "for what they call an appeal to the people" and their manifest desire to bypass the Liberal commons and "call upon the people by means of a dissolution." He and his audience ought to know something about the people. They represented constituencies of three millions. They had won their seats by labor and care and at the risk of defeat, and they had been since the time of election "in close intimate, and con-

61. Ibid., cols. 468–9.

62. Ibid.

stant correspondence" with their constituents. Not content with this, the lords wanted to ignore those who had been elected and call directly upon the people by means of a dissolution "in order, forsooth that the people may again give their opinion. They are asking that that should be done which never, in a single instance in any constitutional crisis, has been...dreamt of or thought of in this country." The usual pattern was to dissolve that house at the instance of the executive when there was suspicion that it was not in harmony with the country. The lords' claim to call upon the people by means of a dissolution was "a perfect and complete innovation." Gladstone could never accept such a position for the commons.[63]

Before the month was out Salisbury defined his position further in an address to the deputations from the various Conservative associations of London and Middlesex. F. W. Pulling, Salisbury's biographer and editor of his speeches, thought the speech a clear, unanswerable exposition of the Conservative position; and he included it verbatim in the biography on the ground that it struck a note that echoed throughout the country during the parliamentary recess. In the end, he added, it contributed in no small measure to the government's discomfiture and surrender. According to Salisbury, constitutional law held that the power of dissolving parliament resided, not in the executive as Gladstone claimed, but in the queen. Since this was one of the few cases in which the minister was being described as "in issue with the people," she could not "abandon her will absolutely to her advisers." Not that he placed a constitutional right in the lords to press for a dissolution. Still they had the right to say: "We do not approve of the measure you bring before us. If you like to accept its rejection, well and good; if you object to its rejection, your remedy is to appeal to the people." No other remedy existed under the constitution. The right was not claimed for ordi-

---

63. Reported in *The Times,* July 11, 1884, p. 10. Gladstone returned to the subject in the last years of his life. *The prime minister's papers: W. E. Gladstone, 1: autobiographica,* ed. John Brooke and Mary Sorensen (1971), 104. Hanham notes that the lords did not begin to assert themselves positively until the 1880s, and he notes that by this time, too, the Conservatives were talking boldly of forcing the government to go to the country on issues in dispute between the government and the lords. *Nineteenth century constitution,* 173. See the *Gladstone diaries,* ed. H.C.G. Matthew, xi (Oxford, 1990), 172, note 2.

nary legislation. But the question before the lords involved a revision of the constitution; and the Conservative leader then discoursed at length on constitutional revision in France and the United States. Unlike England, where a single legislative act could make fundamental changes, these countries had numerous obstacles to revision. In the circumstances the lords were upholding the true principles of English liberty.[64] *The Times*, siding with Gladstone in these years, dismissed the argument as spurious. To state that the lords were not directly demanding a dissolution was no more than a subterfuge.[65]

During the parliamentary recess (August 14-October 23) a popular agitation set in against the lords. The aged reformer, John Bright, put forward a veto plan leaving that house with a suspensory veto and no intervening general election before the lords would have to accept an objectionable bill. At that time, too, Chamberlain and John Morley coined such slogans as "the peers against the people" and "mend them or end them"–solutions much too radical for Gladstone, to say nothing of the queen, the Conservatives, and more moderate Liberals. Historical accounts of the late Victorian age frequently bring out the Radical attitude but not the novel ideas about the lords' role developed in such detail in the course of 1884 by Salisbury and his supporters. Yet the issues raised at this time by the Conservative leadership held as much meaning for the country at large–indeed probably much more–as the Radical ideas associated with Bright, Chamberlain, and Morley. They are in fact still relevant to English political problems.

IV

During the parliamentary recess the referendal theory for the first time received a thorough-going airing outside Westminster. A monster demonstration in London before the recess touched off a national demonstration against the lords, and a defiant Salisbury responded with an important speech at Sheffield on July 23.

---

64. *Life*, ii, 213 ff., but especially 225.

65. *The Times*, July 29, 1884.

Questioning the commons' right to consider itself representative, he noted that since its duration already exceeded that of the average house since 1832 it was a dying and decaying house. Nor had it been elected to legislate parliamentary reform. Moreover, it was a servile house, servile to Gladstone and the caucus; and it was for the constituencies, not the commons, to judge whether the lords erred in preventing a house of this kind from settling the constitution on a partisan basis. But the Liberal ministers, he charged, feared a dissolution, knowing that "deluded hopes, broken promises, oceans of blood unnecessarily shed, a weakened prestige of power abroad, a distracted empire, a discontented Ireland"–all these would be brought against them. It was Midlothian replayed by another hand. Not daring to face the voters, the Liberals had "set up all sorts of shams and counterfeits. They descend into the streets. They call for processions. They imagine that 30,000 Radicals [organized by the caucus] going to amuse themselves in London on a given day expresses the public opinion of the country...They appeal to the streets; they attempt to legislate by picnic."[66]

That the Liberals were seeking "to legislate by picnic" was a palpable hit, often repeated and typically seen as a pejorative reference to the caucus. If they wished to appeal to the country against the lords, Salisbury would remind them that whereas a party might speak by processions and demonstrations, the nation spoke only at the polling booths. Any liberal attempt to substitute "the counterfeit voice...manufactured by the caucus" for a general election would not lead to a true ascertainment of popular feelings and would be indignantly repudiated by the people when they did vote. Nor would the Conservatives "be guided by the public opinion of the streets."[67] Here was an argument with

---

66. The speech is reported in *The Times* July 23. He also made much of the lords protecting the people's liberty against "a dictatorial minister" and "the manufactured opinion of the caucus." A lead article pointed out that the lords had no right to determine when an appeal should be made to the country.

67. *The Times*, July 23. The term legislating by picnic, or a form of it, is also in Ostrogorski, *Democracy and...political parties*, 284 and Jephson, *The platform*, 531–2. See also *The Times*, Aug. 5 for the assertion: "The two parties continue to show, after their several fashions, their appreciation of the method of legislation by picnic."

which not only Conservatives but also conservative Liberals could agree.[68]

At Pomona Gardens, Manchester, Salisbury brought the term "mandate" to the forefront of politics at a meeting billed "to protest against the dictation of the caucus and to support the demand of the house of lords for a complete reform bill." Disavowing any intention of ordinarily bringing into question the commons' representative character, he found it vital to do so at this particular time. When the revision of the constitution was attempted by a commons so old and so departed from its "original mandate," such a house did not in reality and for such a great purpose represent the people. If that house claimed to dictate to the lords, its connection with those who granted its authority and power must be much closer than this. The lords were asking that the people, not a moribund house of commons, decide great constitutional issues.[69]

But Salisbury made no attempt to assert, as he had on other occasions, that the lords might be termed in their own right a representative house. This was early a practice with him; and he sometimes found, or said he did, that the lords were better judges of public opinion than the commons and even that their house represented the permanent opinion of the country unlike the commons who spoke for a fleeting and transient majority. The practice was foreshadowed in Salisbury's remarks during the debate on the Paper Duties Bill in 1861 and again in the events surrounding the Irish Church Act. Speaking to the Suspensory Bill

---

68. Gordon to Lady Sophia Palmer, Oct. 10, *A political correspondence*, 24. Gordon wrote: "What I most mourn over...is the introduction of what seems to me a constitutional novelty fraught with far more danger than the power of forcing a dissolution, the imagined assumption of which by the lords Mr Gladstone so vehemently combats:–I mean the deliberate reference to mobs and meetings as exponents of the will of the country. Surely the rule has hitherto been that a government which failed to carry an important measure had either to acquiesce in the defeat, or dissolve parliament? I apprehend the worst possible consequences from this–both from the invitation to mob rule, and from the implied and pestilent assumption that those who shout loudest are necessarily right. Moreover the notion that the people' and a majority of the people' are convertible terms, has always seemed one of the most curious fallacies." Gordon did not, however, leave Gladstone over home rule.

69. The speech is in *The Times*, Aug. 11.

he had urged rejection on the ground, novel at the time, that the lords were as able to judge the nation's will as the commons. In support of this point he evoked the lords' successful opposition in the 1830s to measures hostile to the Irish church, which had been favored by the commons. The nation had proved indifferent to the question: "In course of time it turned out that you were right," Salisbury told the lords triumphantly in 1868. Then came the conclusion: "You knew the opinion of the nation better than the house of commons."

It will be recalled that in a provocative speech at Hackney in 1880, Salisbury had made use of this idea to counteract the Midlothian campaigns. Though he had employed somewhat different language, his message was clear enough. The lords' main function was to represent "the durable and continued current of feeling and opinion in this country" and "its duty was to represent the permanent as opposed to the passing feelings of the English nation."[70] Two years later he described at Liverpool both lords and commons as "representative institutions," using the words, he stated, in their "lasting sense." The speech was delivered at a meeting of the Liverpool Working Men's Association to a meeting of about 5,000 and it received full coverage in *The Times* of April 14.[71] In 1884 Carnarvon chimed in with the claim that the lords were genuinely popular. According to *The Times* (August 19), he found that the lords reflected the education, sense, respectability, and good feeling of the country. Indeed, he had maintained "that at this moment the house of lords represented more faithfully all that was worthy of representation in this country than the house of commons itself did." He even termed the lords "the people's house."[72]

---

70. Ibid., Nov. 20, 1880.

71. The Liverpool speech, which was one of a series, was delivered at a meeting of the Liverpool Working Men's Association, with 5,000 people in attendance. It is also in Pulling, *Salisbury*, ii, 116 ff. See also Leach, "The house of lords." *Fortnightly Review*, 360.

72. *The Times*, Aug. 19 See also Churchill at Birmingham, Apr. 16. *Speeches of...Lord Randolph Churchill* (1889), ed. Louis Jennings, i, 136–7. In this same time frame, the *Westminster Review*, 66 (July and Oct. 1884), old series 122, 166, in an article favorable to Gladstone insisting that "in this representative country, when the issue is joined, the representative chamber ought to prevail," pointed out that Wellington's stand was altogether different. The author called Salisbury's attention to the pertinent portion of the duke's speech on the Corn Laws.

In a highly publicized speech at the Corn Exchange in Edinburgh, Gladstone dismissed the Conservative allegation. But to speak to it was to give it prominence, even a certain legitimacy; and he paid the Conservatives the compliment of acknowledging that they had constructed their case with great skill. He began with these words: "What is often said and said by clever men in the house of lords is this–that its purpose is to represent not the fleeting opinions of the people, or the passion of the moment, but the permanent, solid convictions of the people." With regard to the notion that the commons were at best a reflection of the fleeting opinions of the people, he would refer the Conservatives to the case of the Ecclesiastical Titles Act of 1851. Despite the strong popular feeling in its favor the statute had proved unworkable and was subsequently repealed with unanimous consent. What had the lords done on this occasion to reflect the solid convictions of the people? Nothing: they had voted overwhelmingly for the measure. The only stand against it was taken by a large minority in the house of commons.[73] This example became an obsession with Gladstone, who harked back to it in the immediate period before the Second Home Rule Bill for Ireland.[74]

If one is tempted to discuss Conservative assertions about the lords' representative character as sheer poppycock, Gladstone did not take this stand. He was serious about the problem posed for his party, and his willingness to discuss it in Salisbury's terms is just as striking. He declared:

> Why gentlemen, it stands thus–we have had twelve parliaments since the Reform Act...and the opinion–the national opinion–has been exhibited in the following manner. Ten of those parliaments have had a Liberal majority. The eleventh parliament was the one that sat from 1841 to 1847. It was elected as a Tory parliament, but in 1846 it put out the Conservative government

---

73. See Gordon's critique, *A political correspondence*, 23–4. He concludes from the voting record, and the editor agrees, that Gladstone was mistaken in his account of the two houses and that Bill. Gordon terms Gladstone's description absurd. Another example of Gladstone's obsession with the subject can be seen in *The private diaries of the Rt. Hon. Sir Algernon West*, ed. Horace G.Hutchinson (1922), 202.

74. H. H. Asquith reports in his *Fifty years of parliament* (1926), i, 269 his discussion with Gladstone on Dec. 12, 1891 about the lords' insistence "on reference of new policy to the people" that Gladstone instanced the Ecclesiastical Titles Bill–"fought strenuously for four months by a small minority in the commons, and then went through the house of lords 'like a shot.' "

of Sir Robert Peel, and put in and supported till its dissolution the Liberal government of Lord John Russell. That is the eleventh parliament.[75]

The twelfth parliament was Disraeli's (Lord Beaconsfield's), which had been largely talked about in the general election of 1880, on its merits and demerits. That parliament, Gladstone would admit, was a Tory parliament from beginning to end. As one looked back for more than fifty years he found ten parliaments on one side, only one parliament on the other. "Which represented the solid permanent conviction of the nation?" Was it "the ten parliaments that were elected upon ten out of the twelve dissolutions, or the one parliament that chanced to be elected from the disorganized state of the Liberal party in...1874?"[76]

Salisbury followed Gladstone in Scotland. A Conservative minority in Glasgow, crowding the railroad station on his arrival, greeted him enthusiastically and cheered when he ended his speech. By this time the referendal theory had matured,[77] and the

---

75. Gladstone, *Political speeches delivered in August and September 1884* (Edinburgh, n.d.), 8–15. See also John Morley, *The life of William Ewart Gladstone* (1903), iii, 128–9. This section of Gladstone's speech is reprinted in Hanham, *Nineteenth century constitution*, 203, under the rubric "Gladstone on the essentially Liberal character of the nation, 1884." This conclusion is all right so far as it goes, but it conceals the important fact that Gladstone and Salisbury were dealing with the more complicated question of whether the lords or commons were better fitted to interpret public opinion. If the lords represented its permanent opinion, at the least the lords were justified in insisting on their referendal function.

76. Gladstone, *Political speeches*, 15. That he was right to take the argument seriously is suggested by Dicey's comment in the "Introduction" to the eighth edition of his extremely influential *Law of the constitution* (1915), xciii-xciv when he writes: "We know...that party government, which to many among the wisest of modern constitutionalists appears to be the essence of England's far-famed constitution, inevitably gives rise to partisanship, and at last produces a machine that may well lead to political corruption and may, when this end is escaped, lead to the strange but acknowledged result that a not unfairly elected legislature may misrepresent the permanent will of the electors." This interpretation, along with other considerations, explains Dicey's advocacy of the referendum. Under the circumstances, it appears that Salisbury's distinction between temporary and permanent majorities can be fairly described as having prospered. See also Asquith's comment in 1904 in Low, *Governance of England*, 87–8, revealing that Salisbury's distinction had taken hold.

77. *The Manchester Guardian* (Sept. 9, 1893) reports that Lord Salisbury was the man who laid down the theory most fully in a series of speeches in 1884. The writer then refers to Salisbury's speech recommending the rejection of the Franchise Bill on July 8, 1884. He sees the lords in 1893 as demanding a plebiscite and expresses the belief that in this great controversy over the Second Home Rule Bill they will yet see reason to regret having been "guided by a Salisbury instead of, as in 1831 and 1841 [1846?] being warned and moderated by a Wellington."

speech rehearsed familiar themes, which can be usefully summarized. In a situation where the houses confronted an intractable problem, on which they were divided, the people must act as arbiter–the theme that Salisbury had enunciated as long ago as 1861 and repeated at length in his "disintegration" article on class struggle in 1883. It was indefensible, he now said, that the commons were unwilling to let the country speak on the question of how best to proceed with parliamentary reform. A house that failed to act in accordance with the country's will was departing from its functions and mission and ought not to complain–especially when the parliament was so old and verging to its close–if the lords called upon it to submit to the electorate from whom the commons' power was derived. As for a Liberal argument, recently advanced by Gladstone, that the commons were the only responsible house, it lacked validity. In dealing with its constitution that house was "just as irresponsible as the house of peers." The speech closed with the warning, noted earlier in this discussion, that the danger to the constitution emanated not from the lords but from the growth of the caucus. The latter enabled the prime minister to control every power in the state.[78]

From Glasgow Salisbury went north to consult with Richmond and Cairns. Somewhat uneasy, he wrote afterwards to his wife: "I left my two wise counsellors in the north in a very fair frame of mind. They will give me trouble in the future–but I hope to pull through."[79] If he was no longer sure of his followers, the Liberal government, too, had problems. "Say what they will," Salisbury declared, "their horror of a dissolution does not go down."[80]

At this juncture Queen Victoria successfully mediated the quarrel, urging Gladstone and Salisbury to enter a bi-partisan conference. On November 17 the government stated publicly that if the Conservative leaders were to give "adequate assurance" that the Franchise Bill would become law by Christmas, the government would discuss with them a seats bill and pledge themselves to carry the agreed measure speedily into law so that a second

---

78. *The Times*, Oct. 2. The speech was given on Sept. 30. See also note 22 above.

79. Cecil, *Salisbury*, iii, 116.

80. Ibid.

reading took place in the commons at the same time that the Franchise Bill went into committee in the lords. In a further exchange with Salisbury Gladstone explained that he would not ask for the "adequate assurance" until the conference's work was complete. Notwithstanding the Liberal offer, it is argued elsewhere that Salisbury's decision to enter the conference stemmed from the royal mediation. Working closely with Richmond and Cairns, now allied with Carnarvon, the queen touched off a rebellion on the opposition front bench that made it impossible to continue the struggle.[81] According to Lady Gwendolen, her father was less than enthusiastic about the political outcome since he preferred a dissolution and a general election, but she also believed that the government's terms were too good to refuse. Whether this was Salisbury's opinion is another matter, but it is clear that he had no alternative except to enter the conference when his following broke up around him.[82]

Despite the Conservative attempt to match Liberal demonstrations in size and enthusiasm, Gladstone had by far the greater popular support.[83] Yet the Conservatives had chalked up a beginning in an area usually thought of as Gladstone's; and, what is more important, the lords had stayed with Salisbury almost to the end in a test of strength with the commons. This was a remarkable feat for them. The lords' fortunes had been on the wane ever since the Great Reform Act; and in 1846 and again in 1869, landmark dates in the post–1832 era, they had adopted a policy of concession counselled in the first instance by Wellington, in the second by Salisbury himself. The 1884 outcome constituted a distinct reversal of the accumulating record. Reform and redistribution would go together, the principle for which the lords had contended for almost five months; and though Salisbury had to give way on a dissolution, still he could take much satisfaction from the lords' performance. Nor was the satisfaction only his. Richmond, Cairns, Carnarvon, and their fellow Conservative peers had stayed the course, true to the end to the goal of a complete scheme of reform.

---

81. See note 52 above.

82. Cecil, *Salisbury*, iii, 121.

83. *Macmillan's Magazine*, 50 (Oct. 1884), 470 states that the Liberals won the battle of demonstrations, and the *Annual Register* of 1884 agrees. See also Jephson, ii, 550. The Liberals claimed to have held 1,512 meetings against 195 on the side of the lords.

The point to be stressed, however, is that the new ideas had been thoroughly tested and proved their worth.[84] This became more evident than ever when the home rule question burst on the political scene. There is, for example, the line taken by Lord Hartington, later duke of Devonshire, a conservative Liberal of very considerable consequence who became a Liberal Unionist in 1886. Addressing the First Home Rule Bill in the commons, he would admit that probably there was no such principle as that of a mandate but contended, nevertheless, that there were certain bounds that parliament was morally obliged to observe in its relations with its constituents. These were violated when the commons, in the immediate aftermath of a general election in which home rule had not figured, initiated legislation "of which the constituencies were not informed, and of which the constituencies might have been informed, and of which if they had been informed, there is at all events, the very gravest doubt as to what their decision might be."[85]

George Curzon, who heard the speech, reported that at the end there was a great shout of approval. "The house felt that it had heard the voice of a statesman & of a possible prime minister," he wrote. Curzon, a man of independent judgment, noticed Hartington's emphasis on the "moral incompetence of parliament, with no mandate from the constituencies to untie the bonds of union." As for Gladstone, he was the "wielder of an influence unequalled in character" who as the crowning act of his political life proposed "the disruption of the United Kingdom & the disintegration of the parliament of the empire."[86]

---

84. McKechnie considers that the lords had successfully at this time demonstrated that they had no intention of resigning their legal rights in legislation. *The reform of the house of lords* (Glasgow, 1909), 48–9. And Richard Henry Gretton, in *A modern history of the English people* (1913–29), i, 148 concludes that Gladstone had steered the Third Reform Bill through in his own fashion but that "true Radicals in later years put down to Gladstone's action on this occasion the confidence with which the house of lords rejected Liberal bills." See also "A democrat's defence of the house of lords," *Nineteenth Century*, 16 (Sept. 1884), 465. This author thought that nowhere had Lord Salisbury shown greater sagacity than in his cry, "Appeal to the people." The article was written by Waltman Berry.

85. The pertinent portion of the speech is in Hanham, *The nineteenth century constitution*, 147. There is an extensive discussion of Hartington's reasons for using the mandate in Kelvin, *The development...of the electoral mandate*, 76 ff.

86. Curzon's account is in an unpublished article entitled "The great debate" (1886). MSS Eur. F. 112/604 in the Curzon papers, India Office.

That is, the referendal theory, used by Conservative peers in 1884 to insist successfully on their approach to parliamentary reform was as soon as this in the service of the very different cause of preserving the Union and the empire, its protagonist no less than a former leading member of Gladstone's government in a memorable speech delivered in the commons. This accession of strength, signalling a broadening base of support for that theory, was singular testimony to Salisbury's remarkable skill and tenacity in pursuing the goal he had set for himself as a young and comparatively unknown MP in a Palmerstonian parliament at a time when Gladstone had already attained national stature. It means that the alliance between public opinion and the lords was falling into place well before Gladstone's electoral victory in 1892 restored him to power with a strong determination to carry into law the Second Home Rule Bill. The renewed threat to the unity of the United Kingdom and the empire provided the critical nudge that closed the ring.

By the early 1890s, then, in the waning days of Gladstone's political career, a persistent Salisbury was in a position to capitalize on the progress already made in promoting his unique interpretation of the lords' power and authority in the political system. By any standard that progress was very substantial–how substantial was apparent by 1895.

Five

The Great Scenario

I

Lord Salisbury's electoral success in late Victorian politics is the more impressive because his aristocratic lineage and aloof, detached personality were so ill-suited to an age of increasing democracy. One contemporary critic noted that he made no effort to "acquaint himself with the personalities and feelings of the rank and file of his own party"; another, that he understood neither the value of the house of commons nor the feelings of constituencies.[1] Yet the seasoned parliamentary reporter, Sir Henry Lucy, describing him as "a man born out of due season," more at home as a royal adviser in the Elizabethan age than his own, writes of a Salisbury who adapted to changing circumstances with increasing skill and success. Here was "crowning proof of his consummate ability."[2] Events seemed to justify this high praise. By 1895, his *annus mirabilis*, Salisbury inspired trust and respect at home and abroad, representing, it has been said, all that was most admirable in Victorian England.[3]

Ushering in a decade of Conservative hegemony, the general election in that year swept away acrimonious issues like home rule for Ireland and the lords' question for the rest of Salisbury's career. The victory–the product of an alliance between Conservatives and Liberal Unionists–is as properly termed a Unionist as a Conservative victory; but either way this question springs to

---

1. Chilston, *The political life and times...first Viscount Chilston*, 35, 172–3. See also Southgate, *The Conservative leadership*, 6.

2. *Memories of eight parliaments* (1908), 125. Cp. Donald Southgate, *The Conservatives: a history of their origins to 1865*, ed. Butler, 224–5.

3. J.A.S. Grenville, *Lord Salisbury and foreign policy: the close of the nineteenth century* (1970), 5.

mind. Did Salisbury profit so much from the breakup of the Liberal party after Gladstone's adoption of home rule in 1886 that a modicum of political skill would yield rich rewards? Or was his a distinctive, personal contribution to the outcome? Although the home rule issue, admittedly, dealt him a winning hand,[4] this does not preclude the need for high political skills to draw maximum party advantage from Gladstone's Irish policy. The period examined here in this context is the Liberal interlude (1892–5) between two Conservative governments, in which Gladstone's Second Home Rule Bill was at center stage. The lords rejected it on September 8, 1893, by the lopsided vote of 419 to 41, the largest vote in their history.

In the following discussion there is no account of the Bill's provisions nor its implications for the United Kingdom and the empire. That road is much travelled. Instead, the emphasis is on the extended proceedings in the commons before the Bill went to the lords. It was in the commons for more than six months; in the lords for less than a week with rejection coming after four nights of debate. A time differential of this dimension excites suspicion that the commons were in fact the scene of the Bill's destruction, the lords confined to ratifying a *fait accompli.* This is not the usual view. Historians, impressed by the size of the lords' vote and sensitive to Salisbury's presence in that house, have treated it as the main arena. On this point Peter Marsh, the standard authority on Salisbury's political career, is representative. Noting the time differential only in passing, he describes an aggressive Salisbury intent on communicating to the country the message that on home rule the lords were more representative than the commons. That is, Salisbury "wanted" the Bill defeated in the lords; and Marsh, in support of this view, invokes Salisbury's remark before Gladstone took office that "in the year that is coming the center of interest and the center of action will be found within these walls."[5]

---

4. Peter Marsh in his *Discipline of popular government* stresses Salisbury's political adroitness, but to Paul Smith he needed only to play a winning hand. *English Historical Review*, xcv, no. 377 (Oct. 1980), 870–3. Lord Blake agrees with Smith, *Salisbury: the man and his policies*, 7–8.

5. Marsh, *Discipline*, 225–6. L. P. Curtis, *Coercion and conciliation in Ireland 1880–1892* (Princeton, New Jersey, 1963), 412.

By taking Salisbury's rhetoric at face value, Marsh overlooks the important fact that the Conservative leader in 1893 was not in a position to control events, indeed that he had to turn to the lords because he had no alternative. This was the situation. Determined at all costs to avoid home rule, which he opposed as destructive to the unity of the British Isles and the empire, Salisbury knew full well that the Unionists could not stop the passage of the Second Home Rule Bill in the commons. Put simply, Gladstone was in charge there because his majority, though only forty and dependent on the Irish vote, was sufficient. The Liberal leader also had at his disposal closure and the guillotine, the latter a severe form of closure. In his second administration (1886–92) Salisbury had used it freely to pass the Irish Crimes Bill (1887) and establish the Parnell Commission, and the new procedures would lead him to comment in 1894 that the commons' majority was "more and more becoming a blind machine."[6] In these circumstances Salisbury, known for his realism in politics, faced Hobson's choice: he either accepted home rule or provided for the Bill's rejection in the lords. It follows, therefore, that there was very little that was voluntary in the decision to rely on the lords; and it is urged here that he was in fact reluctant to do so.

This reluctance to use the lords rose out of his concern for the future of that house. Salisbury had devoted a generation of effort to its resurrection, and it is inconceivable that he blithely undertook a conflict with the highly motivated Gladstone that could undo the progress so evident by 1884. The period of greatest danger would come after the rejection. Should a struggle en-

---

6. Salisbury considered Ireland in its own way as important as India, and as early as 1872 he had warned in an article in the *Quarterly Review* that from the Conservative viewpoint Ireland had to be kept "like India, at all hazards: by persuasion, if possible; if not, by force." Algernon Cecil, *Queen Victoria and her prime ministers* (1953), 313. For the constitutional situation within which Salisbury worked, see his letter to Sidney Low, Dec. 2, 1894, in Low, *The governance of England* (5th impression, 1914), 114–5. Low in an introductory note refers to a paper that he had earlier published, which had led to Salisbury's letter. It, too, should be seen. "If the house of commons were abolished," *Nineteenth Century*, 36 (July-Dec. 1894), 847–55. Excerpts from Low's paper are printed in *Cardinal documents in British history*, ed. Robert Livingston Schuyler and Corinne Comstock Weston (Princeton, New Jersey, 1961), 126–8. See also "The house of lords as a constitutional force," *New Review*, no. 58–March 1894, 257–64. Low seems to have written under Salisbury's influence. There is also pertinent material in Birch, *Representative and responsible government*, 72–8.

sue, there could be only one outcome. A second chamber based on hereditary right in late Victorian England was no match for the people's William. With these considerations in mind Salisbury solved his dilemma by adopting this course: he would commit the lords to battle because he must, but only after bringing the nation to their side. The manner in which the Conservative leader achieved this goal is discussed here under the rubric "the great scenario."

This interpretation fits the known facts. It will be seen that the Unionists took the necessary steps in the commons to win national support before the Bill went to the lords, and that they did so explains both the time differential noted above and Gladstone's patent inability after the event to punish the lords for their temerity though he clearly wanted to do so. His failure to rally his cabinet for an anti-lords crusade certainly attests to the unpopularity of home rule but also to the political skill with which Salisbury insulated the lords against a hostile fallout in the wake of rejection. This phase of the crisis over the Second Home Rule Bill is missing from historical accounts. Yet Salisbury's precautions taken before the event to damp down anti-lords sentiment were at the core of his rejection policy, and that he took this particular course goes far to explain the extent of his party's electoral victory in 1895. By any standard that policy yielded high dividends for him and his party.

The timing in 1893 was different from that in 1861 when the Paper Duties Bill ignited a quarrel between Gladstone and the lords and brought Salisbury into the fray. In the earlier episode he had made his position public after the lords defeated the Bill and without a preliminary preparation of public opinion. His success in 1893 with the new procedure is the more striking because Gladstone had at his back a freshly elected house of commons. This factor so favorable to Gladstone would have to be minimized before Salisbury could launch his campaign to scuttle the Second Home Rule Bill.

II

Gladstone's fourth ministry began in August 1892 and he introduced his Bill in the following February. In the interval Salisbury wrestled with questions rising out of his definition of the lords' referendal function. How could the Conservatives justify the Bill's rejection in the lords after Gladstone won the general election of July 1892? Could the lords safely defy a newly elected house of commons, led by a celebrated exponent of home rule; and had not Salisbury, and Lord Stanley, too, insisted that the lords would give way once the electoral verdict was in, regardless of how distasteful it might be? On a memorable occasion, Salisbury had told the lords: "I quite admit, everyone must admit–that when the opinion of your countrymen has declared itself, and you see that their convictions–their firm, deliberate, sustained convictions–are in favour of any course, I do not for a moment deny that it is your duty to yield."[7] To Sir William Anson, a noted constitutional authority of the period, the tenet became a settled convention of the constitution on which the lords would act, contrary to their action in 1832.[8]

Without Salisbury's ingenuity, or, perhaps better, his willingness to use any politically expedient argument in a crisis, it would have been very difficult to employ the lords' veto with credibility in 1893. For the electorate of 1892, surely acquainted with 1886, would have been aware that a Second Home Rule Bill would follow a Liberal victory at the polls. Anticipating the problem,[9] Salisbury set out to unshackle the lords' veto in his influential "constitutional revision," published in the *National Review* (November 1892). That the veto was his foremost consideration can be seen in his letter to the editor explaining that the article

---

7. Speech of June 26, 1868, *Parl. debs.* (lords). 3rd series cxciii, 88–9. For a more complete discussion of the Irish Church question and Salisbury's espousal of the referendal theory, see Weston, "Salisbury and the lords," 107-17; 127-9.

8. *The law and custom of the constitution* (Oxford, 4th edition, 1909), i, 286. Also, Herbert Paul, *A history of modern England* (New York, 1906), v, 300. Leonard Courtney, *The working constitution of the United Kingdom* (1901), 100–1. William Sharp McKechnie, *The reform of the house of lords* (Glasgow, 1909), 19–20.

9. *Salisbury*, ed. Blake and Cecil, 245. William T. Stead, *Peers or people?* (1907), 3. This work, published originally in 1882, was reprinted with additional materials in 1894. Stead was a strongly Liberal journalist with ties to Gladstone and John Morley. See also *Manchester Guardian*, Feb. 26, 1893 and Garvin, *The life of Joseph Chamberlain*, ii, 577. This is a memorandum of a meeting of Feb. 28, 1893, attended by Salisbury, the duke of Devonshire, A. J. Balfour and Chamberlain, which certainly suggests that Chamberlain was surprised to hear that Salisbury contemplated rejection of the Second Home Rule Bill in the lords "*even after a General Election resulting in a majority for Mr. G.*"

was written "to make it evident either that the house of lords has all the independent right necessary to a second chamber [i.e., a legislative veto]–or, if it is too weak for that, then to force men to face the fact that a stronger body must be substituted." What he most dreaded was the lords' being so bullied and cajoled that their independent right atrophied, leaving the commons with an unchecked supremacy.[10]

To defend the lords' veto, and hence their referendal function, Salisbury developed the concept of a "motley majority," which would justify the lords in ignoring the results of the general election. At issue was the nature of Gladstone's majority, not its size, as Lady Gwendolen explicitly stated.[11] The Liberals were vulnerable on this point. By definition, a motley majority reflected a confusion of voices in the general election, and Salisbury even accused the Liberals of deliberately concealing their home rule bill.[12] The charge had bite because Salisbury had challenged them to put forward an explicit proposal. Unable to agree on the details, they had made a vague and confused commitment and had then muddied the water by adopting the National Liberal Federation's Newcastle program. This proved to be a major tactical error. A mosaic of sectional and other special interests favored by activists, it encompassed home rule and also church disestablishment in Wales and Scotland, local veto on selling intoxicating liquors, triennial parliaments, ending or mending the house of lords, etc. A hostile observer attributed the list to "the logrolling which faddists like."[13]

---

10. Salisbury to Alfred Austin, Oct. 28, 1892, Lady Gwendolen Cecil, *Life of Salisbury*, v, chap. 1, p. 2. This volume of the *Life* was never published. At Hatfield House, it is cited hereafter as Hatfield House MSS 3M/CC. Salisbury's letter to Austin is best interpreted in light of the former's frequent remarks on what he saw as the Liberal determination to keep the house of lords as a sham while destroying it as a reality. They want "to erect a protection which is no protection, but will mislead and destroy all who trust to it." *Parl. debs.* (lords), 4th series, vol. xxx, col. 32. See also Cecil, *Life of Salisbury*, ii, 5, Hatfield House MSS 3M/CC, chap. 1, p. i.

11. Ibid.

12. "Constitutional revision," 289, 295–6. See Marsh, *Discipline*, 222–3 for how easily the partisan nature of this terminology may be overlooked. Indeed, historians at times accept Salisbury's language unquestioningly. See, for example, *The destruction of Lord Rosebery; from the diary of Sir Edward Hamilton, 1894–1895*, ed. with an introductory essay by David Brooks (1986), 107. Brooks uses the referendal theory without labelling it, as an example of how Conservatives borrowed democratic or libertarian ideas from the Liberals. This was, of course, the converse of what had occurred.

13. Weston, "Salisbury and the lords," 125. "Constitutional revision," 295–6. Cp. D. A. Hamer, *Liberal politics in the age of Gladstone and Rosebery; a study in leadership and policy* (Oxford, 1972).

Salisbury had the Newcastle program in mind in asserting that the Welsh vote was notoriously shaped by hostility towards the established Welsh church and that Scottish crofters were full of agrarian schemes but gave little attention to Ireland. Further, "mining constituencies voted for the Eight Hours Bill, the Leicester people voted against vaccination; the dockyard constituencies were fired with indignation against some obscure admiralty wrong." To urge that "amid this multiplicity of questions" the voters had decided for home rule was "to use language without meaning."[14]

Even if it were granted for discussion's sake that the general election had turned on home rule, the fact remained that England and Scotland had voted against it. Unhappily their majority had been transformed into a minority by Wales and Ireland. Salisbury was now evolving the novel concept of the "predominant partner," which was phrased at times in terms of England alone. According to Lady Gwendolen Cecil, her father considered that Gladstone in embracing home rule had pledged his party to the concept of "an independent individuality in the three nations which formed the United Kingdom." Yet the most powerful of them had decisively repudiated the "proposed revolution." Repeal of the Act of Union, to which Great Britain as much as Ireland was partner, was to be carried out despite a hostile majority of 70 in English constituencies and more than 20 in England and Scotland combined. This provocative use of a temporary majority must evoke the constitution's defensive powers. In the first draft of her manuscript she wrote that the use of such a majority to carry the Second Home Rule Bill would challenge the lords to come forward as the champion of the nation's rights.[15]

These dismissive comments on the house of commons, redounding to the lords' benefit, recall Salisbury's practice in the early 1880s of denigrating the lower house. Chagrined that highly organized parties after 1867 had transformed the house into a very different institution, he had contributed to its eroding prestige by targeting the National Liberal Federation as the source of

---

14. "Constitutional revision," 295–6.

15. Lady Gwendolen Cecil, *Life of Salisbury*, Hatfield House MSS 3M/CC, chap. 1, 1–2. Weston, "Salisbury and the lords," 124–6. "Constitutional revision," 297–8.

the commons' alleged servility whenever the Liberals held office. It will be recalled that in Salisbury's rhetoric the Federation was a caucus, directed by wirepullers who bound Liberal MPs with detailed instructions. Closure made the commons the virtual prisoner of caucus and prime minister alike;[16] and at the center of this dismal picture was a dictatorial Gladstone, so powerful that he, not the lords, posed the greater danger to national liberties.

This provocative language, replete with negative images of the commons,[17] enabled Salisbury to reinforce the political message in his *National Review* article. Capitalizing on his past practice of consistently downgrading the house of commons, he now stage-managed a great scenario at Westminster aimed at making concrete an otherwise abstruse political argument and rendering it intelligible to a wide audience. In the midst of the greatest emergency of his long political career, Salisbury worked in unison with his lieutenants Balfour, Chamberlain, and Devonshire–in particular, the two Liberal Unionists[18]–to develop the necessary scenario. If matters worked out as planned, the lords would reject the Second Home Rule Bill with impunity, assisted by national distaste for home rule, certainly, but also by the popular perception that the manner in which the Bill passed the house of commons had violated constitutional norms.

Salisbury's decision to proceed in this way could have been stimulated by a timely letter from Jesse Collings, Chamberlain's right-hand man, stressing the need to place before the constituencies, especially the humbler classes of voters, "by endless repetitions of plain facts and truths...the real nature of the political situation."[19] Salisbury's scenario reflected this formula, but his

---

16. Weston, "Salisbury and the lords," 122–3. Taylor, *Salisbury*, 77–8.

17. Ibid., 78. *Speeches of Salisbury*, ed. Lucy, 123–5, 138, 140–1, 142–4. The Liberal response is in Lady Askwith, *Lord James of Hereford* (1930), 135.

18. Marsh writes of the rare meetings of the Conservative and Liberal Unionist leaders but notes one on May 25, 1892 before the general election of that year. *Discipline*, 221. See also note 9 above where mention is made of a meeting of Feb. 28, 1893. It came eleven days after the Second Home Rule Bill's first reading, and Chamberlain reports that the meeting was to discuss procedure on the Bill. At this time Salisbury made it plain that the lords would reject the Bill when it reached his house; and it would appear, though Chamberlain's memorandum does not say so explicitly, that the party leaders also decided on the tactics to be used in the house of commons on the second reading, which began on Apr. 7 and lasted twelve days before the Bill went into committee. For other comment on contact between the Liberal Unionist and Conservative leaders, see Robert Taylor, *Lord Salisbury*, 149 and *Salisbury*, ed. Blake and Cecil, 240.

19. Collings to Salisbury, Aug. 18, 1892, Salisbury papers, unbound correspondence.

personal touch was evident in the provision for a large-scale obstruction in the commons forcing Gladstone to choose between resorting to the guillotine and abandoning his Bill. During his second administration Salisbury, confronted by a combined Liberal and Irish obstructionism, had used the guillotine vigorously to control the commons.[20] In 1893 Gladstone was to be compelled in a comparable situation to adopt the same procedure.

The Unionist leader in charge of the obstructionist campaign was Joseph Chamberlain. A dynamic leader with high motivation and outstanding parliamentary skills, he was, in Lucy's words, "in constant attendance, relentless, implacable, resolved at any cost to baulk Mr. Gladstone's desire and destroy a Bill, which, as he knows, his old chief cherishes as the apple of his eye."[21] If all went as planned, Chamberlain would convey graphically to the country the unforgettable image of a domineering prime minister at Westminster bent on driving a highly controversial major bill, without proper consideration, through a captive house of commons, his strict control over its proceedings manifested for all to see by his repeated use of the guillotine. The outcome must benefit the lords, especially since the legislation in question affected so deeply both the constitution and the empire. The nation, contrasting the pliant commons with the lords, where there was neither closure nor guillotine, would know where to place its trust. It would go to an untrammeled chamber, equipped with a referendal function that assured the nation a decisive voice in so vital a matter.

The Unionists were positioned to reap full benefit from the scenario since they constituted almost half of the commons and even a half dozen obstructionists could tie up the house. Speaker Peel gave them free rein in the early months of the parliament when he ruled that the Liberal majority of forty was too small for any more than the occasional use of closure. Unionist leaders like Lord Wolmer, Salisbury's son-in-law and earlier Liberal Unionist Whip, seized the opportunity to offer frequent amendments; and Gladstone's self-defeating response was to di-

20. Southgate, *The Conservative leadership*, 129.

21. *A diary of the home rule parliament, 1892–1895* (1896), 143. S.H. Jeyes, *Mr. Chamberlain: his life and public career* (1903), 348.

vide the house and use the Liberal majority in the voting lobby to strike down opposition amendments.[22] John Morley, Gladstone's biographer and confidant, after referring to the obstruction as "freely practiced and without remorse," writes that Gladstone's following, frustrated by the dilatory conduct of business, besieged Liberal ministers–"calling out for a drastic closure, as simple tribes might clamour to a rainmaker."[23] Little wonder! Depicting Chamberlain as "the life and soul of obstruction," Lucy wrote of the second reading: "I have known the house of commons pretty intimately for twenty years, and cannot call to mind any epoch of obstruction exceeding in deliberation and pertinacity that which clogged the wheels of parliament during the past eight weeks."[24]

That Unionist strategy was on the lines depicted here appears from the very valuable account in Garvin's official life of Chamberlain. Garvin edited *The Observer* from 1908–42. A contemporary of Chamberlain and his devoted follower, Garvin presumably wrote from private information as well as the parliamentary debates when he described Chamberlain as intending "to the utmost to play out time" with definite goals in mind. Thus he would defeat the ministerial plan of carrying home rule as part of "the Newcastle program and its 'logrolling federation' " and implant the Unionist cause more deeply in the country's mind. Indeed, he would so "delay and thwart the government that closure [the guillotine] in the commons might furnish a crushing argument for the expected action of the house of lords." This obstruction, Garvin writes, "was deliberate and looked beyond the immediate inch-by-inch contention to the purposes of a final strategy."[25]

The major effort came after the Bill went into committee on May 8, where it remained for four months as Chamberlain

---

22. Lucy, *Home rule parliament*, 80, 154–5. Wolmer's activity can be seen in *Parl. debs.*, 4th series, xii, 1569, 1578–80, 1641, 1645–6, 1648–9. Ibid., xiv, 705–11, 729, 731, 978, 1025, 1027. In Lucy's view Gladstone's tendency to speak often and to indulge in long speeches served the Unionists well though this was not his intent. *Home rule parliament*, 97–8, 161–2, 146–7, 222.

23. *The life of William Ewart Gladstone* (New York, 3 vols. in 2, 1911), ii, 499, 503. In Morley's opinion a mistake was made at this juncture.

24. Lucy, *Home rule parliament*, 93, 143.

25. James L. Garvin, *Life of Chamberlain*, ii, 565, 568.

dissected it piece by piece. Of thirty-seven clauses, only four had passed by the end of June, and at this juncture the frustrated Liberals entered the trap set for them. Protesting that there was no alternative to forcing the Bill through committee before the end of July, the majority voted on June 30 a resolution providing that the guillotine would fall every Thursday. Every week a block of clauses would be carried, whether or not these had been discussed.[26]

Chamberlain and Salisbury had obtained their immediate objective. Penetrating to the heart of the matter, Garvin writes: "To put the ministers in this dilemma was just what Chamberlain had purposed, knowing that it would do them more harm in the country than it could do them good in parliament." He describes the impact in these words: "With each weekly decapitation of Unionist argument, exasperation increased, until the mother of parliaments was disgraced before the world." Assailing the "gag" placed on parliamentary deliberations, Chamberlain referred to the government's Tammany methods. Then came the charge of a bargain with the Irish, which underlay the procedure, silencing the predominant partner while ignoring and overrunning the deepest convictions of the bulk of Great Britain.[27]

At this juncture Salisbury entered the picture with a highly publicized speech to the Junior Constitutional Club on July 7. He reinforced the message from Westminster to the country when he described Gladstone as demonstrating "how the ancient privilege and power of the house of commons" could be "converted into the subtle instrument of the caprices of a single man." He had done this with "a reckless application of the party screw" and without regard for consequences. But Gladstone's activity had boomeranged when he inadvertently demonstrated that either an effective second chamber or the referendum was essential "to provide against dangers of this kind and to furnish a mode by which the people of this country can have their voice when enterprises of this kind upon their liberty are attempted."[28]

---

26. *Parl. debs.*, 4th series, xii (June 29), 373. Ibid. (June 30), 590.

27. *Life of Chamberlain*, ii, 566–7.

28. This speech was reported in *The Times*, July 8, 1893. See also Salisbury, "Lord Rosebery's plan," *National Review*, 24 (Sept.-Feb. 1894–5), 459. *Quarterly Review*, 177, 268–9.

After the Bill emerged from committee it proved necessary to resort to the guillotine to carry forward the usually routine report stage. At once an alert Chamberlain gave notice of an amendment protesting, in Garvin's words, "against the degradation of the house of commons to a registration agency, and demanding the dissolution of parliament...in order that the nation...might pronounce on matters concealed or at least unknown at the last general election."[29] Chamberlain moved the amendment on August 21; once more Garvin is helpful: "In rather less than an hour he supplied the Unionist campaign in the constituencies with a store of arms."[30]

This store of arms came straight from Salisbury's article on constitutional revision. Witness the sentiments that Garvin attributes to Chamberlain, who is reported as stating:

> There was no true majority in the country for any single item in the medley of the government's prospectus. The government itself was the creation of a system of "political log-rolling" carried beyond example. The ministerial sections only voted together for anything because each of them wanted something else. The Welsh members voted for home rule because they wanted disestablishment; the teetotallers voted for disestablishment because they wanted local veto; and the Labor party voted for everything because they wanted an eight-hours day. The government "trample on the liberties of the house and they gag opponents they are unable to answer...To destroy an empire...he [Gladstone] must also stifle discussion and humiliate the house of commons...And so I say that your majority is not a homogeneous majority and...it...will be swept entirely away when once more an appeal is made."

And Chamberlain forecast that three-fourths of the Bill would go to the lords exactly as it left Gladstone's hands, "without consideration either by friend or by foe."[31]

This powerful speech, delivered by a great parliamentary speaker, probably killed the Bill in the country. This was Chamberlain's conclusion when he wrote confidently on September 2, as the Bill was leaving the commons, that the more serious

---

29. Garvin, *Life of Chamberlain*, ii, 575.

30. Ibid.

31. Ibid., 575–6. *Parl. debs.*, 4th series, xvi (Aug. 21,1893), 666.

Gladstonians knew they were beaten. All of his accounts from the country were favorable; and he believed that if there were a general election during the autumn, they would have a good majority.[32]

National publications with the notable exception of the *Manchester Guardian* severely censured the manner in which the Bill passed the commons. On July 31 the highly influential *Times* rendered Salisbury a signal service by printing the text of the Second Home Rule Bill in the form that it had assumed by that time. The clauses that had been discussed were italicized, and so were numerous amendments. Clauses also stood out that had received no discussion at all; and only a quarter of the Bill's clauses had been discussed, some of them to a very limited degree. Garvin's account, which includes a description of the text in *The Times* of July 31, certainly points to the conclusion that the Unionists had from the first worked to project this pejorative image of the commons' handiwork to the country at large.

Materials in the Chamberlain collection of the University of Birmingham Library support this view of their strategy. These include a fifty-page Home Rule Notebook, in which Chamberlain recorded the Bill's journey through the committee stage as the clauses came before the house. Among other things it reveals that the Unionists made singularly effective use of the amending process to produce the results presented so graphically in *The Times*. Chamberlain also referred to the resolution of June 30, which he termed a "gagging resolution"; and he noticed after its adoption certain clauses approved without any discussion. Finally, it should be observed that the germane pages (13–4) of *The Times* of July 31 had been folded within the Home Rule Notebook,[33] presumably as a trophy of the political wars.

On August 22 an indefatigable *Times* did the political arithmetic for its readers. The pertinent sentence reads: "A majority of 38 yesterday decreed that three-fourths of the Home Rule Bill shall leave the house of commons without examination or discussion of any kind." A similar note sounded in *Blackwood's*

---

32. Garvin, *Life of Chamberlain*, ii, 577.

33. Ibid., 575. Chamberlain collection, JC 8/6/2. Lucy points out that the most important clauses were discussed. *Home rule parliament*, 142–3, 225.

Edinburgh Magazine when the anonymous author of "The Peers and the People" pronounced the preceding parliamentary session unprecedented. "Never before has a government carried through the house of commons a measure involving imperial disintegration," he wrote. And never before had a government "by brute and arbitrary force driven through the house a bill effecting a series of constitutional changes, refusing all discussion on twenty-six out of thirty-seven clauses."[34]

The curtain came down on the great scenario when the lords, after a debate of less than a week, refused the Bill a second reading. Salisbury had at his side the great body of the house, all except a handful of Gladstonian peers and office holders.[35] Conspicuous among his supporters was another great peer, Devonshire, leader of the Liberal Unionist peers and one of the most respected figures in political life. In 1886 as Lord Hartington, with a seat in the commons, he had moved the rejection of Gladstone's First Home Rule Bill; now in 1893 he would do the same for the Second Home Rule Bill. In his speech, as in Chamberlain's, Salisbury's seminal article on constitutional revision provided the point of departure. Not only did Devonshire deny that Gladstone had won a mandate in 1892 for his home rule bill but he also discerned, so he stated, a positive hostility in the country towards the Liberal leader's policy.

The product of the brain and will of one man, who had imposed it on his followers, the policy had never been approved by the country. To be sure, it was an issue in the general election of 1886, but the Liberals had lost; and it had been kept in the background as late as 1892 to such an extent that it was impossible to determine the question on which the present government had been returned. Under the circumstances there was only one

34. *Blackwood's Edinburgh Magazine* (Oct. 1893), 154, 597. See also G. Lowes Dickinson, *The development of parliament during the nineteenth century* (1895), 166. He writes: "More and more every year the constituencies, or rather the caucuses, do actually dominate the house [of commons], and, as a direct consequence, the debates in parliament are coming more and more to be regarded as mere dialectical exercises. The party that may happen to be in power is beginning to act upon that hypothesis; opposition is labelled obstruction, and put down by the gag; and the only effect of a debate is to excite passion to that fever-point at which the decision of the majority is felt by their opponents not as a national award but as an arbitrary and tyrannical exercise of brute force."

35. Marsh, *Discipline*, 226–7.

satisfactory way to learn the country's will: the Bill itself must go to the electorate. So grave a policy must have the country's approval in advance of parliament's for the principle of self-government for Ireland and also for the form that it would take and the provisions by which it would be carried out. This procedure was the more necessary because the conditions under which the commons had considered the measure made it impossible for the lords to learn whether the Bill reflected the commons' judgment. The commons' journal revealed that three-quarters of the Bill's contents were never discussed.[36]

It was a remarkable performance, and a puzzled *Manchester Guardian* (September 7, 1893) found it particularly odd in a whig. Devonshire had broached a theory leaving no place for the people's elected representatives and none for the government proceeding from them. But in light of Salisbury's teachings over the years and at this juncture in his career, it was really not odd at all.

For the time being this episode strengthened the house of lords. There was a marked tendency at the time, and there has been since then, to describe the lords as more faithfully reflecting the country's will in 1893 than the commons. An entry in a contemporary journal kept by Lady Monkswell reflected the lords' new-found popularity. She was not in London at the time of the rejection, but a friend who was there had referred to an unprecedented wave of public feeling. For the first time in history the lords had represented the people's feeling and the commons had not. On leaving their house the peers were greeted by cheering crowds singing "Rule Britannia" and setting off fireworks. The Gladstonians had threatened that if the lords dared to throw out the Bill, they would sign their own death warrant; but there had been only one meeting to censure them, this one in Shoreditch. Throughout England there was "the most complete indifference."[37]

Another way of gauging the national impact of Salisbury's scenario is to look for signs that his message reached its audience

---

36. *Parl. debs.* (lords), 4th series, xvii, 26–32. Holland, *Devonshire*, ii, 251–8.

37. *A Victorian diarist: extracts from the journals of Mary, Lady Monkswell, 1873–1895*, ed. E.C.F. Collier (1944), 238–9.

in the intended form. Germane comment on this matter is present in W.E.H. Lecky's *Democracy and liberty* (1896). A polemical tract, begun by the Liberal Unionist historian in the winter of 1890–1, it was virtually complete by that of 1894–5. When the Second Home Rule Bill was before the commons, and Chamberlain's efforts were at their peak, Lecky attended a meeting of some 1,100 Unionists at Albert Hall; and two days later, at a Hatfield House reception for its delegates, he listened to stirring speeches from Salisbury, Devonshire, Balfour, and Chamberlain. He may well have seen Chamberlain carried shoulder high by cheering Ulstermen around the front court.[38]

In the timely *Democracy and liberty*, Lecky expressed regret at the commons' changed tone during his lifetime. Much of what had gone wrong was due to the Irish Nationalists who had set out to "degrade, dislocate, and paralyze the parliamentary machine till their objects were attained." But the responsibility was not just theirs: their example was contagious, and others had connived with them. Moreover, the new corrective parliamentary rules had been abused, and Lecky turned to the events at Westminster in 1893. Debates had been closed arbitrarily in order to "prevent discussion on matters of momentous importance." Thus

> many clauses of a home rule bill which went to the very root of the British constitution; which, in the opinion of the great majority of competent British statesmen, would have proved the inevitable prelude to the dismemberment and downfall of the empire; which was supported by a party depending on the votes of men who were ostentatiously indifferent to the well-being of the empire, and was strenuously opposed by a great majority of the representatives of England, and by a considerable majority of the representatives of Great Britain, were forced through the house of commons by the application of the closure, and without any possibility of the smallest discussion.

Only the lords' veto had prevented "*a measure of the first importance, carried by such means and by a bare majority* from becoming law."[39]

---

38. *A memoir of the Right Hon. William Edward Hartpole Lecky, by his wife* (New York, 1909), 269, 288, 303. Lady Gwendolen Cecil, Hatfield House MSS 3M/CC, chap. 1, p. 4.

39. *Democracy and liberty* (Indianapolis, Liberty Classics, 1896), i, 123–4 and more generally chaps. 2 and 4. See also the restatement of the referendal theory to reflect the early 1890s in Anson, *The law and custom of the constitution*, i, 287, 289.

This passage from Lecky's *Democracy and liberty*, supplemented by the account of the Hatfield House meeting in his *Memoir*, reveals that Salisbury's message was reaching the public on the desired lines and scale. Together they support the idea that the manner in which the Conservative leader delivered his anti-home rule argument was almost as important as its substance. Perhaps as much so. For having a message is one thing; communicating it successfully to the country at large is something else again.

Gladstone stayed on for a time after the rejection but, unable to persuade his cabinet to test the lords' position in a general election, he gave way in March 1894 to Lord Rosebery. Although the latter at first blundered by agreeing publicly with Salisbury on the need for the predominant partner's consent to home rule before it could be legislated, he soon decided that the lords were a great obstacle to the Liberal program; and in October he launched a campaign to curb the lords with a major speech at Bradford. It converted the general election of 1895 into a referendum on the lords' referendal function when he defined the main issue that the electors would have to consider. If they believed that the lords understood their wishes better than their representatives, they should dispense with representation and "abide contentedly by the unbiased, the patriarchal, and the mellow wisdom of the house of lords."[40] That Salisbury had won a national consensus in support of his lords' policy was attested when the Conservatives, allied with the Liberal Unionists, now won their greatest electoral victory since 1832. Little wonder that contemporaries concluded that conservatism, with Salisbury at his party's helm, had become the dominant credo. Thus the Liberal Sir Edward Hamilton, earlier one of Gladstone's private secretaries and Rosebery's lifelong friend, wrote in his diary that "among the contributory causes to the Unionist triumph" was "the fashion of Conservatism."[41]

---

40. This speech was printed in *The Times* on Oct. 29, 1894. It was also given currency in Stead, *Peers or people?* 4, 5. Rosebery reported to Queen Victoria that the speech had fallen flat and made no progress in the country. Peter Stansky, *Ambitions and strategy: the struggle for the leadership of the Liberal Party in the 1890s* (Oxford, 1964), 140–1. Moreover, by-elections at this juncture began to run against the Liberals. *Destruction of Lord Rosebery*, ed. Brooks, 52–3.

41. Ibid., 270, 272.

This judgment was confirmed by Rosebery's remarks. Looking back after Salisbury's death to the Conservative leader's despair at his party's surrender to parliamentary reform in 1867, Rosebery described Salisbury as lamenting that the monarchical principle was dead, the aristocratical foredoomed, and the democratic principle triumphant. Yet these prophecies were falsified in his lifetime. Rosebery reported that before Salisbury died "the monarchical principle was infinitely stronger than it was in 1867, the aristocratical principle was so much stronger that it seemed almost to have assumed a permanent predominance, and the democratic principle, which he thought would govern the country from 1867 onwards, has had a rather sickly time of it."[42]

Then there is the evidence of the historian David Brooks, an authority on Rosebery's government. He explains the failure of the Liberal campaign against the lords in the terms discussed here but without reference as such to the referendal theory. But that it was rampant can be seen readily from his comments on the electoral campaigns waged by Balfour and Chamberlain in 1895.[43] Brooks also introduces his own observations. "So far from building up a head of steam against the upper chamber," he writes, "the government had witnessed a sharp decline in its own electoral popularity."[44] Why had they failed? The answer could not have been more to the point: "*The premise on which ministers' arguments had been based, that the lower chamber was the legitimate organ of the nation's will, no longer appeared to have much validity, at least as far as the existing house of commons was concerned.*"[45] The commons' unpopularity was partly due to the new machinery developed to speed up their proceedings. The fear was that the guillotine would permit a tiny majority to legislate radical programs such as the Norwich program of the Trades Union Congress, with its stress on nationalizing the land and major industries.[46] Paradoxically, Salisbury, a political leader often de-

---

42. *The unveiling of the memorial bust of the late Marquess of Salisbury on Monday, Nov. 14, 1904.* Published by authority, 12–3.

43. *Destruction of Lord Rosebery*, ed. Brooks, 85, 97.

44. Ibid., 54.

45. Ibid.

46. Ibid., 44, 54, 57, 200–1, 214. The Norwich program is in *The Times*, Sept. 7, 1894. Taylor, *Salisbury*, 81. Low expressed the same concern in his "House of lords as a constitutional force," *New Review*, 262–3. Southgate, *The Conservative leadership*, 109–10.

picted as rigidly conservative in his principles, was fast becoming a mecca for moderate opinion–in his own way, like so many others, the heir to the Palmerstonian tradition.[47]

The appraisal of the Salisbury household is of special interest. Fortunately, there are available comments on the general election from Lady Gwendolen Cecil, her father's secretary and close companion. More than anyone else she was intimately acquainted with Salisbury's thought processes; and she found in the 1895 election "a fact of very actual importance":

> It made concrete the fundamental contention of house of lords champions. If the second chamber had not possessed the power of compelling an appeal to the electorate, a vast constitutional change would in fact have been passed into law, to which the large majority of that electorate–amounting in Great Britain to more than two-thirds of its constituencies–were now shown to have been consciously and definitely opposed. From that conclusion there was and could be no escape. *The place which a second chamber, fully equipped for the purpose, can claim as a constitutional safeguard for democratic rights, was established as a matter of history by the record of the parliament of '92–95 and of the election in which it came to an end.*[48]

Add to this assessment that of a shrewd and disinterested observer of the parliamentary scene. On the eve of the general election Lucy recorded that Salisbury had "triumphed all along the line" against the commons.[49]

Well he might write this way. For the general election was an unqualified triumph for Salisbury and the lords, and an unmitigated disaster for Rosebery and the commons. Gladstone's majority of 40 was wiped out, and Salisbury emerged with a majority of 152 in the new parliament. While other explanations–agricultural depression on the countryside, a decade of expanding imperialism, growing concern about socialistic legislation, more possible if the lords' referendal function were weakened, the mismatch between Salisbury at the height of his powers and an aged Gladstone, followed by the inexperienced Rosebery, etc.–can be advanced to shed light on the electoral result, surely there is a

---

47. Lady Gwendolen Cecil, Hatfield House MSS 3M/CC, chap. 2, p. 11. Taylor, *Life of Salisbury*, 81.

48. Hatfield House MSS 3M/CC, chap. 2, p. 11. *Salisbury*, ed. Blake and Cecil, 60.

49. *Memories of eight parliaments*, 120.

place in this litany for the political skills with which Salisbury and his associates convinced contemporaries that national and imperial problems could be entrusted more safely to the Conservatives (Unionists) than to the Liberals; to the lords than to the commons.

The political leader who shaped his party's policy in these years was a knowledgeable politician who had learned how to manipulate images and symbols so as to shape public perception of the government at Westminster. Starkly realistic in appraising the political change brought by parliamentary reform,[50] deeply distrustful of Gladstonian leadership and a Liberal commons, and politically pragmatic, he utilized the referendal theory to give his party and the lords a populist cast that struck a sympathetic chord in Victorian England. In the end he discovered a formula for a great electoral success when he combined his party's attack on the provisions of the Second Home Rule Bill with a pejorative image of the Gladstonian house of commons that approved the measure.

Salisbury's attitude during the passage of the Second Reform Act is instructive in this connection. Convinced that Derby and Disraeli had betrayed their party by sponsoring household suffrage in the boroughs, he bitterly impugned their integrity in the *Quarterly Review.* The impact of that measure, he wrote, would "depend very much on the judgment which the nation ultimately forms of the conduct of those who have brought it about."[51] Salisbury's nephew expanded on this theme when he wrote of the Conservative leader's recognition that "changes must be effected in such a way as to preserve their agents from the reproach of want of principle such as the opponents of Gladstone's Reform Bill of 1866 must of necessity incur by the passage of their

---

50. Salisbury's realism, compared with that of modern scholars writing on this period, can be seen in Birch, *Representative and responsible government,* 72–8. His name could have been properly included in Birch's list of late nineteenth-century observers–Sir Henry Maine, Ostrogorski, Low, and A. L. Lowell–who had a true sense of how the government was changing. In this connection see John Roach, "Liberalism and the Victorian intelligentsia," *Cambridge Historical Journal,* 13, 1 (Cambridge, 1957), 58–81. Salisbury published a short pamphlet in 1893 that dealt with the case against home rule from an imperial and international standpoint. Lady Gwendolen Cecil, Hatfield House, MSS 3M/CC, chap. 1, p. 4.

51. *Lord Salisbury on politics,* ed. Smith, 256, 259, 260.

own far further-reaching Act of 1867. It was, indeed, not so much the measure in itself that shocked him [Salisbury] as the means by which it was carried."[52]

In 1867 Salisbury had lacked the necessary self-confidence to mount a successful resistance to Derby and Disraeli. But in the early 1890s this was not the case. An experienced political leader in his own right and an ex-prime minister fresh from a long tenure of power, he set out to organize a country-wide consensus against the Second Home Rule Bill, not only on the basis of its provisions, which he abominated, but also on the ground that in a great constitutional-imperial crisis the Liberal house of commons could not be trusted to respect the nation's will or protect its welfare. How well he succeeded is attested by the outcome of the general election of 1895.

III

Yet the crisis over the Second Home Rule Bill and the lords' role in it had exacted a toll, and there are signs of a concern on the part of the Unionist leadership that the burden of exercising a referendal function was too heavy for the lords. This concern was reflected in the new willingness to consider the referendum a viable option. An instrument of direct democracy, it served the same purpose as the lords' referendal function without engaging the lords' credit in the outcome. Thus Salisbury in writing on constitutional revision hinted that the referendum was in itself desirable though he did not use the word. But, significantly, it was present in the original version of the article, which referred specifically to the Swiss referendum. The latter was the more radical because it provided for an appeal to the people after the houses

---

52. Algernon Cecil, *Queen Victoria and her prime ministers*, 299. See also Grenville, *Lord Salisbury and foreign policy*, 22 for an analogous outlook in conducting foreign policy. The journalist Sidney Brooks, a friend of Garvin, writes of Salisbury that "he came early to his beliefs, and can hardly be said to have parted with any of them"–an observation borne out by the parallel between Salisbury's attitude in 1867 and that at the time of the Second Home Rule Bill. *North American Review*, 175 (1902), 157. There is also pertinent material in "Lord Salisbury," *Monthly Review*, 13 (Oct.-Dec. 1903), 2–6, signed "X." Robert Cecil, Salisbury's son, is thought to have written the article. On this point see the *DNB* article on Salisbury.

of the legislature agreed on a given measure. That Salisbury was favorable to the referendum was apparent when he wrote of the existing system as defective because it contained no procedure by which the nation could directly express its attitude towards organic change. Safeguards found elsewhere as in the United States, Belgium, and Holland were absent; and they had the further advantage of having the means needed to ask the electorate a clear question and obtain a clear answer. A vote was taken on a constitutional change, and an unambiguous answer was returned.[53]

To Salisbury, these defects in the English constitutional system seemed a potential source of disaster after the advent of home rule. The Ulster problem, which aroused his strongest emotions, provided him with a case in point. A political leader who placed a high value on loyalty and gave it unstintingly to his followers–who condemned out of hand Charles I's desertion of Strafford in the Stuart century, Peel's betrayal of his party in 1846, Disraeli's adoption of parliamentary reform in 1867–Salisbury saw in home rule a rejection of an Ulster that the English themselves had created. In the discussion that followed Salisbury seemed to be lamenting the absence of a referendum, which would enable the country to speak on Ulster's future.

As he said, "no more fundamental change could be adopted than this surrender of a race who...assumed their present position of danger at our bidding, and whom we are commanding to exchange their present allegiance...for a new, untried, sinister jurisdiction which they abhore and despise." Before it could be made, the nation would have to be consulted. To define what this involved, Salisbury recommended elaborate and careful provisions for isolating an issue before it went to the electorate. And he would compare the provisions in other constitutions with "the confused din of miscellaneous utterances" that the English were asked to accept as "the people's voice on the most momentous question of constitutional revision" that could be proposed to them.[54]

Moreover, unless there was a very substantial majority for

---

53. "Constitutional revision," 292–4.

54. Ibid., 295.

a constitutional change as fundamental as home rule, no permanence was possible. To tell Ulstermen that home rule would be forced upon them by a decision turning on a handful of votes was to proclaim that "the caprice of today may well be cancelled by the repentance of tomorrow." Perpetual conflict must further embitter this portion of Ireland and deepen division there. In the countries that Salisbury had mentioned, assent to constitutional change required either a two-thirds vote as in the United States or three-quarters as in Greece. Not only was there no such security in England, the majorities on which great decisions turned were at times ludicrous. For instance, in the last general election the shift of 703 votes where the Unionists had been victorious would have returned them to office. "Does the most sanguine Radical expect that Ulstermen would ever accept the vote of 703 electors scattered over England and Ireland as a sufficient warrant for surrendering them forever to the good pleasure of Archbishop Walsh and his party?" Salisbury wondered.[55]

In lieu of a more appropriate procedure Salisbury would rely on the lords to reject the Home Rule Bill. Here was the only power in the constitution capable of securing that the nation's will would be ascertained and obeyed with anything like the accuracy of constitutional provisions elsewhere. Unfortunately, the lords could discharge this duty only incompletely because they could not isolate the issue to be presented to the electorate with the exactitude that characterized the American and Belgian systems. Nor could that house insist upon a specified proportion in the majority of votes to be obtained. Yet the lords could see to it that a special election was held to return a house of commons empowered to deal with home rule. And it could insist that there be no fundamental change without England's and Scotland's assent. Granted that the house of lords was an illogical institution, so too was the present method of learning whether the nation wanted change. "At worst the house of lords is the anomalous corrective of an anomalous system of constitutional revision," he wrote. The notion that some day its constitution might be improved could not excuse the peers at this time from doing their duty if an emergency arose. "For the part which they fill in the

---

55. Ibid., 296.

process of constitutional revision is one which cannot be supplied," Salisbury explained. They alone possessed "the power of securing that in a great project of fundamental change–a change in the framework of the empire–the nation shall be honestly consulted, and that its voice shall be faithfully obeyed."[56]

The import of this language is unmistakable. After reading the article, Dicey sent one of his own to Salisbury that supported his views on constitutional revision. Dicey considered that sooner or later, though sooner than people anticipated, a provision like the referendum would be introduced into the constitution. It was one means at least of protecting the nation against sudden changes by a party that happened to have a parliamentary majority. It was the only change he knew that was both democratic and conservative in its effects.[57] In reply Salisbury concurred with the idea that some form of the referendum was coming. It was the only way to terminate the divergence of views between the houses, but he doubted that it would come as soon as Dicey believed. There would be a great deal of troubled water to pass through first.[58]

There are other signs that the Unionists were thinking in terms of the referendum. For example, the subject came under discussion on February 28, 1893 at a meeting of the leaders to develop their strategy when the Second Home Rule Bill reached the lords. At that time Salisbury, in the presence of Devonshire, Balfour, and Chamberlain, described himself as favoring the referendum.[59] He moved still further in this direction in his speech to the Junior Constitutional Club, on July 7, 1893, which is mentioned above. That this speech was a sequel to the article on constitutional revision, appeared when he declared:

> I am a strong believer in the necessity of a second chamber, and yet I doubt whether the whole of the stress of resisting the great constitutional attack ought to be thrown upon such a chamber. I think we ought to have some power of appealing to a far weightier tribunal–namely, to the opinion of the nation

---

56. Ibid., 298–300.

57. Dicey sent an article on the referendum to Salisbury, by way of Arthur Balfour, on Nov. 11, 1892. Hatfield House MSS; A. J. Balfour 1892, #459a.

58. Salisbury to Dicey, Nov. 26, 1892. Weston, "Salisbury and the lords," 125, note 75.

59. Garvin, *Life of Chamberlain*, ii, 577. Cp. Marsh, *Discipline*, 226.

itself. That power exists in almost every other constitutional government in the world. It exists in Switzerland, in France, in America, in Sweden, Norway, Holland, Belgium and in Greece. Wherever the foundations of the country itself are to be dealt with and attack is intended upon them in one form of machinery or another, the nation is directly called into council upon this issue and this issue only, and asked whether it will have it so. I confess I think that the nations which are in that condition are in a safer position than ourselves, and I earnestly hope that the attention of the lovers of the constitution in this country may be drawn to the question whether under the changed circumstances–whether, considering that the house of commons now works without the faintest regard to the considerate and honourable traditions by which it was formerly influenced–we do not now require some more definite, technical, absolute safeguard that the constitution by which the nation lives shall not be changed without the nation's will.[60]

In a lead article on the following day *The Times* commented that there was much force in Salisbury's contention that something like the referendum, as it worked in Switzerland, was needed "to save the country from being hurried into vast constitutional changes without due consideration." But in the absence of the referendum, its author agreed with Salisbury that it was the lords' duty to see to it that the question was submitted to the constituencies.

Salisbury's speech at the Junior Constitutional Club had a surprisingly long life. It was quoted during the debates on the Parliament Bill to demonstrate his support for the referendum, which the Unionists of Edwardian England sponsored as their alternative to the Bill. The speaker, Lord Saltoun, a diehard who voted against the Parliament Bill, considered that the subject had not been dropped since Salisbury brought it forward eighteen years earlier.[61]

The same theme had resonated in the debates on the Second Home Rule Bill, emanating in this instance from Devonshire. A leader of conspicuous importance in the alliance between the Conservatives and the Liberal Unionists, he had insisted that the

60. *The Times*, July 8, 1893.

61. *Parl. debs.* (lords), 5th series, ix, 45, 1076.

Bill itself go to the electorate. This should be done, he urged, because its form and provisions were "the very essence of the question." This had been recognized by the measure's promoters when they told the country that Irish independence was inadmissible, that the Irish parliament of 1792 [Grattan's parliament] was impracticable, that home rule would be conceded only on conditions such as maintenance of parliamentary supremacy, enough authority for parliament to safeguard all imperial interests, provision of an equitable financial arrangement between the two countries, and the like. Moreover, no details of the Bill were available during the general election. How then was it possible, he asked, "to contend that the country has given its decision on the measure, the form of which is now shown to be only less essential than the principle itself?"[62] Nor was it sufficient to be told that the general election had provided a mandate for the Bill and hence authority for working out the organic details. If there were a mandate, it was at best conditional, the conditions unknown to the country. Before this measure became law, the lords had the right to demand that the country's judgment be given on a completed work. The measure under consideration had never even been fully examined in the Commons; their journal revealed that three-quarters of it had not been discussed. In summary, the Bill should be "submitted to the country for its approval, aye or no."[63]

Although Devonshire stopped short of demanding a referendum by name, Liberal peers challenged him outright on the point. He was referring to the referendum, they charged; and they spoke of it as a very democratic instrument for which there was no precedent in the history of their house when faced with far-reaching measures. Lord Playfair asked: "Is he going to ask you to adopt that most democratic of measures, *a referendum ad hoc?*" In his view it was unnecessary–there had been a clearly expressed mandate for home rule in the general election.[64] The Marquis of

62. Ibid. (lords), 4th series, xvii, 30–1.

63. Ibid., cols. 31–2. See also Andrew Bonar Law's comment that preliminary to writing his well-known Blenheim speech (July 29, 1912) he read the speeches in 1886 and 1893 of Randolph Churchill, Salisbury, Balfour, and the dukes of Devonshire and Argyll. Bonar Law to Lord Lansdowne, Dec. 10, 1913. Bonar Law Papers, 33/6/111, fos. 4–5.

64. *Parl. debs.* (lords), 4th series, xvii, 238, 239. *Manchester Guardian,* Sept. 6, 1893.

Ripon, on the other hand, thought the doctrine of a mandate totally new to the constitution. He had never known any measure to be so much discussed as this one. As for the referendum, this was a "new-fangled idea...very rife now." There was no past precedent convincing him that the lords had this sort of function. He would ask what had been the past practice "I should like to ask," Ripon went on, "of the great measures which have been passed within the last fifty years, in which of them has the actual bill been laid before the country, and in regard to which of them you have claimed this right of referendum?" He could not find that the bill had been before the country on former great occasions when the lords had accepted controversial measures. He instanced the Corn Bill of 1846, the Reform Bill of 1867, and the Irish Church Bill of 1869. Of the Irish Church Bill, Ripon declared: "You did not talk about the referendum then. Your lordships did not say that the Bill itself had never been before the country but you passed it, and one of its authors was the noble duke."[65]

This means that the Unionist emphasis on the referendum, so conspicuous during the constitutional crisis over the Parliament Bill, had long roots. By 1911, and indeed much earlier, Selborne was its standard bearer. His political ideas had ripened under the influence of his father-in-law, Lord Salisbury; and as the Liberal Unionist Whip Lord Wolmer, he was active, as has been seen, in the politics of 1893. Moreover, he was a great admirer of Chamberlain, with whom he had close professional ties. Selborne's strong interest in the referendum requires lengthy consideration, but for the moment it should be noted that the 1890s were the breeding ground for his and his followers' political ideas though these were not at center stage in politics until the Liberals brought forward their Parliament Bill late in 1910.

The early 1890s were equally seminal for Curzon though in a decidedly different way. He had been friends with Selborne since their Oxford days, and their entrance into politics coincided with Gladstone's First Home Rule Bill in 1886. In 1895 both inherited titles that compelled them to leave the commons for the lords; but even before this period ended, the seeds of discord

---

65. *Parl. debs.* (lords), 4th series, xvii, 296–7.

between them were noticeable, and their career paths had begun to diverge. In 1893 Selborne had worked with Chamberlain to destroy the Second Home Rule Bill, and his hostility towards home rule was fully displayed when he played a conspicuous role in Salisbury's great scenario. In his opinion, home rule for Ireland would be disastrous for the empire. It would serve as the prelude to Ireland's independence; and he believed that if Ireland left the empire, India would follow.

What then of Curzon? Here, too, there is no doubt about where he stood on home rule. To begin with, he had no part in the great scenario, apparently from personal choice. Surprising as this may seem, Curzon had no interest in home rule, not a whit. According to one of his biographers, Kenneth Rose, Curzon on August 26, 1893 told his close friend, David Spring Rice, that he did not "care a damn about the Bill." Curzon added, in a display of irritation, that the whole house had "discussed it with portentous seriousness from the start, just as if it was coming into operation tomorrow." Rose also reports that Curzon's record as a backbencher at Westminster was meager. He "spoke infrequently even on imperial affairs, shunned social questions and, except to record the votes demanded by the party whips, took almost no interest in the controversies of Irish Home Rule that continued to burden the legislature for year after year." As was earlier noted, the article in the *Dictionary of national biography* on Curzon depicts him as a lukewarm Unionist, and its author, Harold Nicolson, offers the same assessment of Curzon's attitude towards home rule as Rose. In sum, Curzon would not have stated, as Balfour allegedly did in 1910, that "his whole history forbade his being a party to any form of home rule though younger men less involved in the controversies of '86 and '93 might be free to contemplate what he could not accept."[66]

The explanation for Curzon's very different response to the issue of home rule for Ireland seems to be rooted in a very strong interest in the empire as a whole. Accustomed to thinking

---

66. *Superior person: a portrait of Curzon and his circle in late Victorian England* (1969), 139, 421. See also ibid., pp. 371–2. Balfour's remark is quoted in Weston, "The Liberal Leadership and the Lords' Veto," *Historical Journal*, 11, 3 (1968), 536. For Selborne's attitude as described above, see MS Selborne 191, fos. 39–40; MS Selborne 192, fos. 65–9.

in terms of such distant lands as China, India, Siam, Persia, and Afghanistan, which fascinated him, he may have considered the Irish question a provincial matter, too close to home to excite the interest of a political leader who reasoned in global terms. Despite his well-known physical difficulties, Curzon was continually travelling in the years from 1882 to 1895. The situation in 1892 is of special interest. On August 11 Gladstone took office, determined on a final effort to give Ireland home rule, and on the thirteenth Curzon was en route to New York on his second trip around the world. In March 1893 he was once more in England and on September 1 the Second Home Rule Bill passed the house of commons. Just five days earlier Curzon had made the dismissive remark regarding that Bill, which Rose reports. When Curzon was in England, he had little time to spare for the Irish question. His time was taken up with writing weighty tomes on such demanding subjects as Russia in Central Asia, the Persian question, and the problems of the Far East.

Finally, it should be remarked that it was Curzon's practice to carry out any task before him with exemplary thoroughness and in minute detail, leaving almost no time for parliamentary business. He said as much in a letter written to Mary Victoria Leiter, a wealthy Chicago heiress who became his wife. Complaining of the strain of answering letters without sufficient secretarial help, he wrote:

> Next week I have got to go away making long speeches in the country. And all this while I have four or five articles on hand for magazines, lecture for the Royal Geographical Society, business of boards, and the lord knows what.

The letter was written on March 26, 1893, shortly after Gladstone introduced the Second Home Rule Bill in the commons.[67]

The contrast between Selborne's and Curzon's outlooks on two major questions of the day was complete when Curzon published an article in 1894 that denounced the referendum. An independent-minded man, who had already made public his own views about reforming the lords, Curzon took up an anti-referen-

---

67. Marquis of Zetland (earl of Ronaldshay), *The life of Lord Curzon: being the authorized biography of George Nathaniel Curzon; marquess of Curzon of Kedleston, K.G.* (3 vols., 1928), i, 71, 190, 194. The author is cited subsequently as Ronaldshay.

dum posture although both Salisbury and Balfour had announced publicly their willingness to adopt the referendum if there were no other way to stop home rule. But the two leaders, despite their aloof, detached, and generally unapproachable personalities, were moved by a passionate dislike of home rule and the prospect of an independent Ireland. This means that a direct relationship existed between a marked hostility towards home rule and a willingness to adopt the referendum if there were no other viable means of stopping home rule. It follows that Curzon, who had no interest in home rule, had no difficulty in rejecting the referendum. In the early twentieth century the points on which Selborne and Curzon were divided gave rise to serious friction between them and their respective followers; and by 1911 it was a nice question whether or not party unity would survive. But before developing further the subject of the incipient Selborne-Curzon rivalry, and the reasons for it, it is necessary to complete this discussion of Salisbury's policy after the lords in 1893 rejected the Second Home Rule Bill.

IV

Salisbury's "consummate ability," in Lucy's felicitous phrase, was also evidenced in his cautious policy before the general election of 1895. Above all, he aimed at consolidating the gains already made, and in this enterprise he could count on Chamberlain's active support. Nowhere was Salisbury's caution more fully demonstrated than in his response to Sir William Harcourt's Death Duties Bill in the Liberal Budget of 1894, as both great parties prepared for the anticipated general election. The Bill was highly provocative to the inheritors of large landed estates and hence to many peers, prominent among them Salisbury himself. It posed a double threat. The first rose out of the steeply graduated duties, the other out of the provision to assess the duties, for the first time, on the full capital value of the land. According to Lady Gwendolen, the principles adopted "constituted in their effect on individuals the heaviest blows that had been struck by parliament since the repeal of the corn laws against the interest most largely represented in the house of lords."[68]

If the Liberals anticipated a violent reaction from the Unionist leadership, they were disappointed. Salisbury's references to the Death Duties Bill were surprisingly meager for a political leader whose antipathy to direct taxation was long- standing. It will be remembered that he viewed it as a form of legalized spoliation reflecting the historic class struggle. Direct taxation, if used at all, should be confined to emergencies. His reticence at this time affords striking evidence of his high regard for the lords' referendal function, which he had done so much to nourish. Compelled to choose between its retention and public opposition to a measure of the first importance in advancing direct taxation, he had no difficulty in establishing his priorities. Lady Gwendolen describes her father as practicing great self-restraint on behalf of a larger cause when confronted with Harcourt's Death Duties though other Unionists were less forbearing. Independently of Salisbury Devonshire waged an opposition campaign out of doors; and Conservative MPs were hostile. But Salisbury was silent, as was Chamberlain.

Nor did Salisbury speak out when the Bill reached the lords, even when the government's majority sank to fourteen on the second reading. Lady Gwendolen's commentary, which she repeatedly rewrote, is well worth quoting for its insight into her father's reasoning, its very length revealing the significance attached in the family household to his inactivity at this time:

> There were strong protests in the debate from many of the peers; a final warning of rural disaster from...Devonshire, a fiercely eloquent phillipic from the duke of Argyll; but the leader of the opposition never opened his lips and the Bill was passed without a division being called. He intervened briefly on July 30th at the conclusion of the third reading, to enter a formal demurrer to statements which had been made in the country as to the legal incompetency of the lords to amend a money bill. He could not allow the creation by default of a precedent derogatory to their rights and, while not disputing, he said, the evidence of accepted practice, he felt it important for

68. Hatfield House MSS 3M/CC, chap. 1, p. 12.

> members of the house "to adhere rigidly to their legal powers, whatever they might be." The fact that this protest was deliberately deferred until the last moment of the Bill's passage corroborates the indication of his previous silence. He was resolved that the lords should not fight on this issue and he was aware of the danger lest, after their recent triumphs in defiance, their present individual sense of financial injustice might rouse them to uncontrollable action.[69]

And then she undertook to explain the problem confronting her father.

He had to decide how best to proceed without arousing his followers. Little could be said safely since the vigorous language natural to him might ignite passions better left undisturbed. In Lady Gwendolen's opinion, there was no "oratorical reward for which it would have been worthwhile to imperil *the alliance which he was now hopefully establishing between the second chamber's authority and the popular will."* And she concluded: "The exigencies of his house of lords policy called for this silent stifling of revolt against the '94 budget."[70]

That the referendal theory was always present in his thoughts about the lords also appears from Salisbury's speech on finance, to which Lady Gwendolen alluded. It contained his favorite themes regarding the lords' power and that house's position in relationship to the commons. Unwilling to surrender the claims of the house of lords to amend money bills, he nonetheless recognized that such a power could only be exercised on rare occasions. This was because it impinged on the question of executive authority. Since the amendment of finance bills or their rejection by the house of lords would make for the greatest inconveniences in dealing with public finance, he did not dispute the necessity of the accepted practice by which that house as a rule left the finance of the year alone. Yet it was also very important, in view of the changes in the commons, that the peers adhere rigidly to their legal powers.

In Salisbury's opinion, the houses enjoyed the same legal power, that of one no less than the other's; and he noted that a

---

69. Lady Gwendolen Cecil, Hatfield House MSS. 3M/CC, chap. 1, p. 15.

70. Ibid., 16, 17.

majority of even a single vote permitted the commons to exercise their legal rights. Yet these rights were distinct from that house's moral authority. Under certain circumstances its moral authority was irresistible. This occurred when that house in theory and practice represented "a distinct expression of the will of the people of these three countries." There were, however, other occasions when the commons' authority was diminished and conceivably might disappear. He then came to the Death Duties Bill. "I repeat," he declared "that the legal authority is good if it is exercised by a majority of a single vote." But the commons' moral authority depended on the popular strength that it represented and that lay behind it. Since he found that Harcourt's Bill lacked popular sanction, he presumably would have rejected it had there not been the necessity of consolidating the gains accruing from the lords' rejection of the Second Home Rule Bill. That is, Salisbury had no qualms about the lords' vetoing or amending a finance bill under ordinary circumstances, all this despite the episode of the Paper Duties Bill.[71]

If Salisbury refused to contest Harcourt's Bill, he was more militant in the fall of 1894 when faced with Rosebery's ill-starred, anti-lords campaign. At Bradford and Glasgow the latter, after stating that he was a two-chamber man, seemed to accept from his colleagues the idea of limiting the lords' power of delay to a single year as John Bright had proposed in 1884. Asquith, the home secretary, went further than this when he favored single-chamber government.[72]

With Gladstone gone from the political scene and perhaps with the perception that it was less necessary to exercise caution in the new situation, Salisbury undertook to deal with Rosebery and Asquith in another article. Entitled "Lord Rosebery's plan," it was also published in the *National Review* (Sept.-Feb. 1894–5). Its most interesting feature is a corollary now advanced to Salisbury's usual description of the lords' referendal function. The lords had the duty not only to make sure that legislation reflected the nation's permanent opinion but also to checkmate the logrolling measures of a party too subservient to special interests.

---

71. *Parl. debs.* (lords), 4th series, xxvii, 1222–5 (July 30, 1894).

72. *The destruction of Lord Rosebery*, ed. Brooks, 45–51.

The Liberals were a changed party from Palmerston's day; they had become not only anti-empire, but also anti-property, and Salisbury now referred to their espousal of ideas associated with Henry George and Keir Hardie.[73]

In these circumstances it is unsurprising to find Salisbury, in response to Rosebery's campaign to reform the lords, taking the following tone in 1894:

> The longer the struggle lasts [on this question] the more carefully men will study the ways of the house of commons, the sovereign to whose tender mercies they are to be consigned. They will realize that, there, party government is rapidly coming to mean government by an iron party machine, blindly fulfilling the bargains which its conductors have made in order to procure the votes of fanatical or self-interested groups. The more familiar they become with its procedure and its springs of action at the present time, the less disposed will they be to surrender to its uncontrolled discretion either the rights of classes who are in a minority, or the unity of the empire.[74]

That is, wirepullers and logrollers had created the Newcastle program with which Gladstone was so closely associated; and if the lords were to be rendered impotent, a house of commons, subservient to such interests, would be free to enact into law such programs regardless of their impact on the rights of minorities and on the empire.[75]

On this note, so familiar to contemporaries, Salisbury's long campaign to maintain the lords' authority while aspersing that of the commons came to an end; and the electoral results of 1895, which seemed to confirm his views of the two houses, may well have induced a hubris in his party that explains its response to the Liberal landslide of 1906. In its wake, Balfour, Salisbury's successor in the party leadership, explained that regardless of the electoral result the Unionists had the duty of controlling the destinies of England's great empire. As LeMay perceptively observes, more than rhetoric was involved. The Unionists would use against the Liberal government their majority in the lords in

---

73. "Lord Rosebery's Plan," *National Review*, 24, 450–2, 457, 459.

74. Ibid.

75. Ibid.

accordance with Salisbury's mandate doctrine.[76] The Conservative leader was gone from the scene, to be sure, but he had left his party a fateful ideological heritage that would lead in due course to the Parliament Act of 1911. It has also been seen that in this period the roots of the Selborne-Curzon rivalry were firmly planted.

76. LeMay, *Victorian constitution*, 190. The same signal emanated from the lords' ill-judged rejection of the Finance Bill of 1909. Weston, "Salisbury and the lords," 107, note 12.

Six

Selborne and the Imperial Factor

I

By providing that the lords could delay ordinary legislation for no more than two years and a finance bill only a month, the Parliament Act of 1911 brought to an end the referendal theory. Lord Lansdowne spelled out the Act's ideological message in these words: "The will of the people, *as interpreted by the house of commons of the day*, is to prevail, in spite of two rejections by the lords within the life of a single parliament."[1] The Parliament Act was followed by the passing of the Third Home Rule Bill (1912–14) and, by forcing parliamentary opposition out of doors, the extremist Unionist tactics referred to as the Tory rebellion. The outcome could hardly have surprised the Liberals. They must have anticipated, in Charles Townshend's words, "that the twin blows of the Parliament Act and the Home Rule Bill would strain to its limits the system of politics founded on gradualism and compromise."[2]

The Unionist alternative to the Parliament Bill was the referendum. To Roy Jenkins, writing about its passage from the Liberal standpoint, this commitment was a straw-clutching maneuver to stave off political disaster, and he virtually ignores Salisbury's impact on the generation of Unionists who came to maturity in the early 1890s and took the lead in shaping party policy in the early twentieth century. Jenkins only notes the Conservative stand

---

Selborne often kept copies of his letters to other people. To avoid repetition, these letters are not cited as copies in these notes.

1. Cromer papers, Public Record Office, FO 633/34/3079. Landsdowne to Cromer, Jan. 5, 1911, fo. 2.
2. *Political violence in Ireland: government and resistance since 1848* (Oxford, 1983), 245–6. George Dangerfield, *The strange death of Liberal England* (1935), part ii, chap. 2.

against the Irish Church Bill and its relationship to Salisbury's letter to Carnarvon in 1872.[3]

Yet the referendal theory, which has so much in common with the referendum, was taken very seriously in Salisbury's day. There is, for example, Gladstone's complaint in 1886 that the Conservative leader, by identifying himself with "a new creed of tory democracy" was encouraging radicalism.[4] The more usual practice in that period was to associate such a creed with Randolph Churchill. So often was this done in late Victorian England that according to a modern scholar Churchill and tory democracy became "a cliché topic in late Victorian historiography."[5]

The words are those of R. E. Quinault, whose recent analysis of Churchill's tory democracy not only calls attention to his innate and conventional conservatism but also his interest in Salisbury's success with the working classes during his provincial tours. Salisbury's theme, as was earlier pointed out, was the relationship between the lords' referendal function and the preservation of English liberties. In his "Elijah's mantle" (1883), Churchill equated Salisbury's populism with Disraeli's. The latter had begun the work of creating a great democracy, and Salisbury was completing and perpetuating his legacy. Even before Disraeli's death, Churchill had lighted on Salisbury as the next leader of the party, and he gave Salisbury unstinting support in his struggle with Northcote for the sole leadership. Moreover, Churchill was more than willing that the party leader be in the lords. That house was "the nucleus of the party," and they would stand or fall together. Whatever exalted the lords would strengthen the party and would not endanger the constitution.[6]

---

3. *Mr. Balfour's poodle: an account of the struggle between the house of lords and the government of Mr. Asquith* (1954, repr. 1968), 31, 200. Ronaldshay, *The life of Lord Curzon*, iii, 55 refers to a deathbed repentance in this connection.

4. Gladstone to Queen Victoria, Mar. 8, 1886, *Letters of Queen Victoria*, ed. Buckle, 3rd series, i, 76. In 1895 Gladstone said of Salisbury that he was "imbued with less constitutional principles than any other public man." *The destruction of Lord Rosebery from the diary of Sir Edward Hamilton 1894–1895*, ed. David Brooks (1986), 258.

5. R. E. Quinault, "Lord Randolph Churchill and Tory democracy, 1880–1885," *Historical Journal*, 22, i (1979), 141.

6. Ibid., 143–4, 148, 150, 153, passim. Churchill, "Elijah's mantle," Apr. 19, 1883, *Fortnightly Review*, 197, new series–May 1, 1883, 619.

Similar sentiments were expressed in an anonymous article in the highly influential *Quarterly Review* in 1902. Its author wrote of Salisbury's rendering great service to his party by adapting conservatism to the new conditions produced by the reforms of the preceding epoch. Disraeli had "laid down the broad lines of this adaptation on the historic occasion when he boasted that he had 'educated his party' "; but it was Lord Salisbury who had "worked out the scheme in detail."[7] Add to these populist ideas Conservative sponsorship of the broad-based Primrose League, and the conclusion follows that more than opportunism moved the Unionists to adopt the referendum.

Nor should it be overlooked that there were Unionist leaders favorable to the referendum on its merits. Taking the same realistic view of the political system as Salisbury, they parted company with the Liberals when they defined the constitutional problem not in terms of lords versus commons but of the lords versus the cabinet-dominated commons, whose power was the greater because of the doctrine of parliamentary sovereignty. The Parliament Act, they prophesied, would produce an omnipotent single-chamber government, which would elevate the prime minister's power. Thus P. Lyttelton Gell, one of Lord Milner's associates, wrote in its wake of "the change which has thrown our former parliamentary methods on the scrapheap." Since 1905 the cabinet had become a dictator, parliamentary conflict a sham. Liberal MPs, aware of this, treated parliament as a *lit de justice*, "in which the mandates of the dictator [i.e., the cabinet] are registered after certain hollow and unrespected forms have been complied with." The only real battlefield was the constituencies.[8] This perspective rendered the referendum attractive in its own right, and its adoption seemed the more urgent because of the British empire. By this means, it was said, stability would return to Westminster and the far-flung empire that it governed.

---

7. Vol. 196 (July-Oct.), 652.

8. Gell to Selborne, Nov. 7, 1911, MS Selborne 77, fos. 2–2v*. Birch, *Representative and responsible government*, 72–8.

II

The driving force behind the referendum in Edwardian politics was Lord Selborne, Salisbury's son-in-law and ideological disciple. An habitué of Hatfield House, where political talk was incessant, he could have heard the referendum canvassed; but in any case he had personal memories of the Unionist struggle to defeat the Second Home Rule Bill. He was an active participant, and his father had supported Devonshire in the lords. In this period Salisbury had hinted broadly on two occasions that the Unionists would turn to it if the referendal theory could not protect the lords' legislative veto. And in 1894 Balfour also stated publicly that he could envisage circumstances in which the referendum should be used.[9]

But if Salisbury and Balfour turned reluctantly to the referendum as their last resort in stopping home rule, Selborne from the first had little difficulty with the idea of adopting it. It would have long been familiar to him as a Liberal Unionist. Ever since 1886 the Liberal Unionists had entertained the idea. This was true, for example, of Dicey, who devoted a generation of effort in a fruitless attempt to secure its adoption. The eminent constitutional scholar had canvassed the idea as early as 1884 when he proposed using the referendum to break the deadlock between the houses over the Third Reform Bill. The introduction of the home rule issue in 1886 turned his thoughts in this direction once more, and four years later he published his important article "Ought the referendum to be introduced into England?" in the *Contemporary Review*. This was followed by his *Leap in the dark* (1893), in which he recommended applying the referendum to the Second Home Rule Bill. It appeared in a second edition in 1911 on the eve of the Third Home Rule Bill. In these years he was ably seconded by John St. Loe Strachey, editor of the *Liberal Unionist* (1887–92) and the influential *Spectator*. More than anyone else outside Westminster Dicey and Strachey gave the referendum currency, doing so in a variety of ways. One of the most effective was a symposium in the *National Review* in April 1894,

---

9. Blanche E. C. Dugdale, *Arthur James Balfour, first earl of Balfour*, 2 vols. (1936), i, 81. The *Spectator*, Feb. 10, 1894. Cp. view in *The Times*, June 26, 1907.

which originated with Strachey and included such other participants as Dicey and Curzon. Another sign of the growing interest in the referendum came when Chamberlain sponsored the referendum in 1903 as the means of winning support for tariff reform. It remains only to add that in a bibliography compiled by Selborne there are references to Dicey's *Contemporary Review* article and the *National Review* symposium.[10]

Much is known about Selborne although there is no biography. Son of Gladstone's lord chancellor, he was in the commons for ten years before going to the lords in 1895. Thereafter he held a series of posts from which he emerged with an enviable reputation as an administrator. The most notable was an appointment as high commissioner for South Africa. Not thought of as a Unionist leader of the first rank, still he was a familiar figure in high political circles; and even before his tour of duty was over in South Africa, he was influencing party policy from afar. The process went on apace after his return to England, where his impressive success as an imperial proconsul and nation builder brought him an attentive audience. The esteem in which he was held by the time that he retired from politics in 1922 was attested by Jack Sandars, Balfour's private secretary, who wrote of Selborne's having given "eminent service in public life and in the private councils of his party." Nor was there need to invite the world's attention "either to his virtues or abilities, for in every field of political and official labour they have been alike admirable and conspicuous." Although Sandars had more reservations than this statement reveals, Selborne was nonetheless a man of parts.

---

10. Pertinent to Liberal Unionism and the referendum are the following: *Memorials of Albert Venn Dicey*, ed. Robert S. Rait (1925), 122–4; Cosgrove, *The rule of law*, 105–9; and Vernon Bogdanor, *The people and the party system: the referendum and electoral reform in British politics* (Cambridge, 1981), 10–5; 16–7. For further insight regarding Dicey, see his important "Ought the referendum to be introduced into England?" *Contemporary Review*, 57 (Jan. to June, 1890), 489–511. For Strachey, the pertinent sources are *The adventure of living: a subjective autobiography* (New York and London, 1922), and Amy Strachey, *St. Loe Strachey, his life and his paper* (1930). The latter tells about Strachey's connection with Balfour of Burleigh's "Reference to the People Bill," introduced in the lords on Mar. 2, 1911. *St. Loe Strachey*, 229–30. For Selborne's reception of the Bill, see *Parl. debs.* (lords), 5th series, vii, 277–82. The *National Review* Symposium is in the *National Review*, 23 (Mar. to Aug. 1894). Selborne's bibliography, titled "Literature & text books on the subject of the referendum" is in Selborne MS 76, fos. 294–6. See also note 47 below.

He began political life as a Gladstonian Liberal, but a change set in after marriage to Lady Maud Cecil, Salisbury's older daughter. A militant champion of women's rights, she brought to the marriage a high intelligence, capacity for plain speech, the practice of discussing politics, and the assets accruing from her family background. Given his great affection for her and admiration for her intelligence, so freely expressed in his memoirs, it may be supposed that her influence helps explain his receptivity to her father's teachings. The Cecil connection fostered his political rise, and so did his father's legal and political eminence.

It was due, too, to Selborne's personal traits. According to the Reverend J. D. Brewis, author of the sketch in the *Dictionary of national biography*, he displayed at Oxford and in later life "very good ability without literary brilliance or strictly scholarly qualities, keen insight into practical issues, and a great capacity for concentration."[11] He also notes Selborne's political acumen. Contemporaries praised his administrative ability, and the editor of his domestic papers singles out his fair-mindedness. Selborne was independent in thought and self-confident in dealing with important political leaders and extraordinarily tenacious in pursuit of his goals. In his person he was less than scintillating; but Lord Balcarres, the Chief Unionist Whip and a man of very different gifts, though he found Selborne dull, adjudged him nevertheless a great man.[12]

Abandoning the Liberal party after Gladstone's conversion to home rule, he had every opportunity after 1886 to hone his political skills. As Chief Liberal Unionist Whip with responsibility for party organization in the country and duties in the commons, he worked amicably with his Conservative counter-

---

11. *Studies of yesterday* (1928), 86–7. See the discussion of Selborne and the honors system, suggesting a difference between his attitude when he was Chief Liberal Unionist Whip in 1892 and that taken towards David Lloyd George on this matter in the early 1920s. T. A. Jenkins, "The funding of the Liberal Unionist party and the honours system," *English Historical Review*, cv, no. 417 (Oct. 1990), 920–38.

12. *The Crawford papers: the journals of David Lindsay, twenty-seventh earl of Crawford and tenth Earl of Balcarres, 1871–1940*, ed. John Vincent (Manchester, 1984), 179. See also 63, 79–80. *The crisis of British Unionism: the domestic political papers of the second Earl of Selborne, 1885–1922*, ed. George Boyce (1987), xix. There is comment on Selborne's essential political moderation in an essay written by Corinne C. Weston, "Lord Selborne, Bonar Law, and the 'Tory revolt,' " published early in 1995 in a volume of essays on the house of lords edited by R. W. Davis.

part, Aretas Akers-Douglas, and cooperated with Captain Middleton, both highly skilled in the mechanics of politics. He also associated with other Liberal Unionists such as Devonshire and Chamberlain and Conservative leaders in the commons. On May 25, 1892, when the decision was being made to dissolve parliament prior to the general election, he was present at a discussion of the leaders of both Unionist parties, with his fellow whips; and after the election he resigned his post to fight "Mr. Gladstone's Second Home Rule Bill & his bill to disestablish the Church in Wales."[13] Then came his activity at Chamberlain's side during the famous obstruction of 1893. Dissecting the Second Home Rule Bill, Selborne inserted words, removed others, advanced and withdrew sub-sections, sought clarification of clauses, and gave lengthy speeches, in short doing everything possible to compel the Liberals to adopt the guillotine.[14]

In this period, too, he acquired the powerful interest in empire that inspired and sustained his lifelong pursuit of the referendum. On at least one occasion he asserted that, compelled to choose between party and empire, he would come down unhesitatingly on the side of empire.[15] These sentiments were displayed conspicuously in the home rule crisis and were fostered as well by his long and fruitful association with Joseph Chamberlain. The latter's influence on Selborne bears comparison with Salisbury's. In 1895 he was termed, along with Austen Chamberlain, one of Joseph Chamberlain's immediate followers, and in that year he went to the colonial office as Joseph Chamberlain's under-secretary. Chamberlain treated Selborne as a colleague and kept no secrets from him; and Selborne responded with affection, whole-hearted admiration, and respect. Searching in his mind for a "second Chatham" during the First World War, he concluded of Chamberlain that more than anyone else he had the leadership qualities needed to end the national travail. So close was their relationship that Ronald Robinson and John Gallagher in their *Africa and the Victorians* (1961) invariably couple

---

13. MS Selborne 191, fos. 23–6. Akers-Douglas, *Chilston*, 231.

14. See note 22 in Chap. 5.

15. Selborne to Alice [Lady Salisbury], Sept. 25, 1908. MS Selborne 115, fo. 44. Selborne wrote that he cared a great deal for his party but "an enormous deal more for the B.E." The former was the means, the latter the end.

their names in referring to the colonial office; and Selborne was the spokesman for colonial policy in the lords. When Salisbury's last administration began, Selborne served as intermediary between the prime minister and Chamberlain; and the practice continued thereafter. Chamberlain also relied on Selborne to make the colonial office's case privately to Salisbury, doubtless a wise practice in light of his tendency to trust only relatives and men with whom he was familiar.[16]

An ardent imperialist in the Chamberlain mold, Selborne associated with such kindred spirits as Milner, Cecil Rhodes, and Dr. Jameson, leader of the notorious raid on the Transvaal that provoked the Boer War. In the anti-imperialistic aftermath, Selborne remained steadfastly loyal to Milner, as did George Wyndham, parliamentary under-secretary at the war office and later chief secretary for Ireland. The bond established between them at this time probably explains their political alliance in 1911. Selborne's imperial consciousness quickened with the great imperial conference of 1897 celebrating Queen Victoria's diamond jubilee, and in its wake he piloted the Commonwealth of Australia Act (1900) through the lords. By 1908 Jem Salisbury, fourth marquis* of Salisbury and Selborne's closest friend and confidant, was saluting him as "one of the leaders of the imperial party."[17]

The mainstay of Selborne's reputation was the South African experience. In an area seen as a graveyard for ambitious politicians, he scored a resounding success as the architect of a new dominion, the Union of South Africa. At the time he noted the use to which Natal put the referendum in deciding on union, and it became a favorite example with him.[18] The English public, thoroughly disenchanted with war, welcomed arrangements for the Boers to take charge of home affairs within an imperial frame-

---

16. *The destruction of Lord Rosebery*, 265. MS Selborne 191, fos. 76, 86. Robinson and Gallagher, 432. Eric Stokes, "Milnerism," *Historical Journal*, 5, 1 (1962), 57. See the letter quoted there from P. Lyttelton Gell to Milner on Sept. 21, 1899. There is also pertinent material in Selborne to Robert Palmer, Aug. 1, 1915, MS Selborne 109, fo. 60.

17. Ibid., 54–5, 57, 58. MS Selborne 191, fo. 86. Robinson and Gallagher, *Africa and the Victorians*, 445, 460. Salisbury to Selborne, July 29, 1908, MS Selborne 5, fo. 216.

18. *Parl. debs.* (lords), 5th series, vii, 279, 282.

work; and this diplomatic triumph facilitated Selborne's re-entry into politics after his return in June 1910. Honors flowed. Edward VII bestowed the Garter on him, he carried the new dominion's standard at George V's coronation, and Cambridge and Oxford awarded him honorary degrees.

While in South Africa he was kept informed about Westminster politics by Jem Salisbury. As earlier noted, Selborne was a member of the Hatfield House circle, and he later recalled with pleasure that Lord and Lady Salisbury had treated him as a son. He loved them dearly, he declared. There are letters at Hatfield House in which during his father's lifetime Selborne addressed Salisbury as "Dear Papa," and he wrote warmly of Hugh and Robert Cecil, his brothers-in-law. As for Balfour, Selborne was ambivalent, writing of him at times in negative terms but usually praising his attractive personal qualities. Very probably relations between them were strained in Salisbury's last government after Balfour opposed unsuccessfully Selborne's appointment to the admiralty with access to the cabinet.[19] But the ultimate test in the long run was Balfour's capacity to give his followers a clear lead in a crisis; and here he too often failed, most miserably of all in 1911.

Selborne differed from the Cecils in one critical area. Unlike them he was no free trader. He sided with Chamberlain in 1903 when his crusade for tariff reform was launched and thereafter was wholly devoted to policies favoring imperial unity. Like Chamberlain he would develop "the empire into a completely self-sustaining economic unit."[20] This policy required tariff protection for industries, i.e., tariff reform, which could protect the empire as a trading unit against the outside world, but also highly controversial food taxes by which Canada and other parts of the empire would be given preference in English markets. Selborne belonged to the extreme group of protectionists known

---

19. MS Selborne 191, fos. 11–2. Grenville, *Lord Salisbury and foreign policy*, 323. Balfour had his own candidate.

20. Alan Sykes, *Tariff reform in British politics* (Oxford, 1979), 34. Selborne was also very active in promoting the empire's political unity. J. E. Kendle, *The round table movement and imperial union* (Toronto, 1975), passim.

as "whole hoggers," who sponsored both tariff reform and food taxes.[21]

The Cecils, on the other hand, remained faithful to Lord Salisbury's teachings. Though he had supported protection at Oxford, he subsequently accepted it in certain circumstances but not in the form of food taxes. These were politically out of the question; the people would never accept them. Lady Gwendolen writes: "For his party to become associated with any such proposals he spoke of to the end as a calamity–unquestionable and disastrous."[22] To be a free trader in many cases meant to accept the referendum; and Selborne worked with Jem Salisbury and Robert Cecil for its adoption. Sharing in key respects the main ideas of both the Cecils and the Birmingham crowd, Selborne tried to mediate between them. That his efforts had considerable success appeared when in the great crisis of 1911 Austen Chamberlain, his father's political heir, was leagued with Selborne and the Cecils. It was Selborne who bridged the gap.

This political relationship is the more remarkable in light of Selborne's penchant for the referendum. To what avail an extensive campaign for tariff reform, one might ask, if in the end the issue had to be submitted to the electorate for a second opinion? Yet the goals seemed compatible to Selborne. He would keep tariff reform steadily in view but revise the timetable to give the constitutional problem priority. Well before the lords' rejection of David Lloyd George's Finance Bill, which set in motion the events leading to the Parliament Bill, and before the Unionists decided to subordinate tariff reform to the constitutional problem, Selborne concluded in South Africa that the empire's and the party's future demanded a lords policy dependent on the referendum–a judgment from which he never receded. Indeed he

---

21. *The crisis of British Unionism*, ed. Boyce, x, 35–9, 49. Selborne's position can be seen in letters to Jem Salisbury. See, for example, Selborne to Jem Salisbury, May 23, 1907, MS Selborne 5, fos. 163–7; Aug. 15, 1907, MS Selborne 5, fos. 179–82. Selborne to Joseph Chamberlain, Dec. 20, 1909, MS Selborne 9, fos. 177–9. See also Amery, *Joseph Chamberlain*, vi, 590–5, 607, 673, 971, 984. Wyndham had the same sympathies as Selborne. Ibid., 932. See also Selborne to Balfour, Dec. 24, 1910, MS Selborne 1, fo. 139 and Ronan Fanning, "'Rats' versus 'Ditchers'; the diehard revolt and the Parliament Bill of 1911," *Parliament and community*, ed. Art Cosgrove and J. I. McGuire (Belfast, 1983), 202.

22. *Biographical studies*, 86–9.

became obsessed with the idea that only the referendum could bring the political stability at home required to sustain the empire. Conditioned to thinking in terms of the referendum in 1893, when Salisbury, Devonshire, and Chamberlain discussed its adoption in the shadow of the Second Home Rule Bill, Selborne veered sharply towards direct democracy in 1907 and thereafter never looked back.

III

The imperial factor was the causal agent. Determined to attach South Africa securely to the empire, Selborne found his mission jeopardized by the great Liberal victory of 1906. Although his appointment originated with Balfour, he stayed on to complete the work of reconciliation and reconstruction under Sir Henry Campbell-Bannerman. In the new political climate he decided that the barrier to a new dominion was not the defeated Boers but the Liberals in the house of commons. Selborne pronounced the Liberal colonial secretary, Lord Elgin, "very unhelpful & unreceptive, unsympathetic & uncommunicative."[23] This was a strong indictment from a man typically described as having much common sense and a conciliatory disposition. On another occasion he declared: "Altogether my relations with him were very difficult, & he is the only politician in my public life who I think behaved to me badly."[24] Selborne believed that Elgin had even sought his resignation.[25]

But Selborne reserved his harshest criticism for the Liberal house of commons. Willing to unite the British and Boer colonies even if it meant a Boer majority in the new parliament, he explained in 1908 that interference from Westminster had made unification necessary. If the Liberal house of commons persisted in treating South Africa on the present lines, he believed that the British there would become disloyal. Unhappily, this interference would persist so long as the "malignant lunatics of the home rule

23. Ensor, *England since 1870*, 390. MS Selborne 191, fo. 116.

24. Ibid., fos. 116–7.

25. Ibid., fo. 119.

Cobdenite party" intruded "their baneful influence and interference into S.A. affairs." But since the Liberals did not dare to lay hands in the same way on a united Canada or Australia, he had concluded that the way to protect South Africa from the "curse of the house of commons" was to unify it.[26] Indeed, the house of commons was a far greater menace to South Africa's connection with the empire than the Boers,[27] and later in the year he told his wife that he would never trust any Liberal government on an imperial matter again so long as he lived.[28]

Deciding, however, that more was needed than a new dominion to curb a Liberal house of commons, Selborne set out as early as 1907 to reëstablish political stability at Westminster. The task was the more pressing because the Liberal majority was so large. Fearful lest the lords under stress blunder seriously, he turned to the referendum as his preferred means of protecting that house. It had numerous advantages. It alone could bring stability at home, preserve the essential features of the house of lords, and protect the empire against Liberal excesses. A logical supplement to the house of lords, when the two houses were deadlocked, the referendum would lessen its burden by bringing the people into the political process between general elections. Here was the wisest and safest solution to the Unionist party's problems, and in language that bespoke Salisbury's enduring influence he described the people as "the ultimate custodians of the constitution, and the final arbiters when their servants, the two houses of parliament, quarrel."[29]

Running through Selborne's letters is an unqualified confidence in the people's political instincts and just intentions if they had time to reflect. These statements applied to men and women alike, whether or not they had the vote.[30] In 1911 he published

---

26. Selborne to Joseph Chamberlain, Feb. 24, 1908, MS Selborne 9, fos. 162–3. See also Selborne to Jem Salisbury, Aug. 22, 1908, MS Selborne 6, fos. 1, 3.

27. MS Selborne 9, fo. 162.

28. MS Selborne 101, fo. 69. The letter is dated Sept. 14, 1908.

29. Selborne, "The Unionist Party and the referendum," reprinted in 1911 from the July number of the *Oxford and Cambridge Review* (July 12, 1911), 7. This is cited hereafter as MS Selborne 182/7. Selborne's ideas are also expressed in *The state and the citizen* (1913) and *Rights of citizenship: a survey of safeguards for the people* (1912), 224–32.

30. Selborne to Jem Salisbury, Aug. 15, 1907, MS Selborne 5, fos. 176–7. Same to same, Apr. 12, 1917, MS Selborne 6, fo. 208.

an article favorable to women's suffrage,[31] and on another occasion he referred to Lloyd George's miscalculation in seeking to bribe electors with budgets that appealed to class hatred. As Selborne put it, "the British democracy is still the least unfit democracy to wield power of which the world has yet furnished example."[32] During the First World War he found no man indispensable; the people's resolve was the necessary spring to victory.[33]

Also notable about Selborne was his ease in mingling with a variety of people. In South Africa he was as accessible to the Boers as the British, and he distinctly relished an experience in the countryside with Boer farmers, which he related at length. Indeed, he professed great respect for the agricultural population everywhere, priding himself, for example, on his relations with Hampshire agricultural laborers. He stressed the value of this class to the nation.[34] On another occasion he criticized Lloyd George and Balfour as too quick to disparage high-ranking soldiers and sailors because they lacked skill in dialectics.[35]

Whatever the attraction of the referendum's democratic features for Selborne, he was keenly aware that its adoption could serve party purposes. He had been a candidate for a history degree at Oxford in 1881; this interest may explain his assembling a small library on the referendum. An examination of its contents provides further insight into the reasons why he took up the referendum. Rarely commenting on passages in his books, he at times marked in the margins or underlined in the text materials of the greatest interest to him. Thus his eye was caught by certain pages in Jane Stoddart's *Against the Referendum* (1909, repr. 1910), in which she warned the Liberals against the referendum. Selborne translated the pertinent passages into positive benefits for his party. Thus she noted that in America, where the referendum was a bit and bridle on the legislature, it had a distinctly

31. Phillips, *The diehards*, 83.

32. Selborne to Robert Palmer, Apr. 16, 1912, MS Selborne 109, fos. 54–6. See also MS Selborne 191, fos. 223–4.

33. MS Selborne 80, fo. 287. See under discussion of Bonar Law as member of the cabinet. See also MS Selborne 191, fo. 159.

34. Ibid., fos. 12–3, 193, 224–8. For South Africa, see ibid., fos. 128–33, 145.

35. Ibid., fo. 100.

conservative effect inimical to progress; and the popular vote that it evoked showed a dislike of large expenditure, centralization, and violent innovation. She was explicit that the referendum would work steadily to the Liberals' disadvantage. Then came her explanation, clear enough to anyone familiar with the Unionist charge, as Selborne certainly was, that the Liberals thrived on "log-rolling." It was obvious, she stated, that there would not be enough enthusiasm for a given reform to carry it in the face of the formidable opposition that would be displayed in a referendum. When the people voted, they had before them a number of reforms; and the voter who cared about one might be indifferent to another.[36] This could have been the clinching point for Selborne.

Not that this analysis inspired his policy. The moment of truth had come earlier, in June 1907, when Campbell-Bannerman unveiled his plan to limit the lords' veto to six months. The principle was too radical for his cabinet, and a member (Lord Crewe), forecast that the Unionists would ride off on the referendum unless the Liberals also provided for quinquennial parliaments.[37] Not much prescience was required for the forecast. The referendum was after all intimately related to the referendal theory, which the C-B veto plan would end; and of this theory Selborne could say with justice that his party had proclaimed it on a thousand platforms.[38] Borrowing from Salisbury, he asserted that the referendum would check the tyranny of a temporary majority in the commons.[39] Thereafter Selborne's commitment was firm; and whatever the vicissitudes, his energy was unflagging, his fervor intense, his devotion complete.

He initially thought only in terms of ending legislative deadlocks. At the cabinet's instance, a rejected or unsuitably amended measure would be sent to the electorate. Usage would

---

36. MS Selborne 182/1, fos. 15, 25–6, etc. See note 67 below for further comment on this book.

37. Weston, "The Liberal leadership and the lords' veto, 1907–1910," *Historical Journal*, 11, 3 (1968), 520. This article is reprinted in *Peers, politics and power: the house of lords, 1603–1911*, ed. Clyve Jones and David Lewis Jones (1986), 489–518.

38. MS Selborne 74, fos. 36–9. See *The crisis of British unionism*, ed. Boyce, x-xii for descriptions of Selborne's views that place him squarely in the Salisbury tradition.

39. Selborne to Jem Salisbury, Aug. 15, 1907, MS Selborne 5, fo. 178. See also "Reform of the house of Lords and referendum," Balfour papers, B.L. Add. MS 49, 708, fo. 192.

be infrequent, and there was no provision for the initiative, which he and his fellow Unionists disliked. To Selborne, it was a red herring, dragged across the trail by enemies to the referendum.[40]

His referendum proposal was vulnerable for several reasons. Despite Selborne's denial that the lords were a rival to the commons,[41] it assumed an equality between the houses unacceptable to the Liberals. At the same time it was too radical for the Unionists because he would apply the referendum not only to constitutional but also to ordinary legislation on the ground that it was impossible to distinguish between them. There was still another formidable objection. To confine the referendum to deadlocks was inherently unfair to the Liberals because these existed only when they held office.

The solution was obvious. A Liberal minority in the commons must have access to the referendum when the Unionists had majorities in the two houses. To take this route would subvert, however, the long accepted doctrine of parliamentary sovereignty, an outcome much too drastic for Selborne. As he said, "to give the power of any body of persons to appeal directly to the electorate against a bill passed by both houses of parliament" constituted "a revolution" in the constitution. An infinitely greater change would be introduced than the proposal to refer a dispute between the houses to the people. Still, even a radical referendum was preferable to no referendum at all. On November 12, 1910, following the Constitutional Conference of that year, he stated to Balfour a willingness to take the referendum both ways–in the case of a deadlock, to be sure, but also when the houses were agreed, if this were necessary to protect "grave matters" from the will of a Liberal house of commons. His preference, however, was the more conservative version.[42]

By itself the referendum would not solve the constitutional problem. Foreseeing a crisis that might produce a royal creation of peers, Selborne would forestall this eventuality by reforming

---

40. MS Selborne 182/7, p. 12.

41. Selborne to Jem Salisbury, Aug. 15, 1907, MS Selborne 5, fo. 176.

42. Selborne to Balfour, Feb. 23, 1910, B.L. Add. MS 49708, fo. 185. The same to the same, Nov. 12, 1910, ibid., fo. 212. Weston, "Liberal leadership," 530. MS Selborne 76, fo. 2. See also Selborne to F. S. Oliver, Mar. 30, 1911, MS Selborne 74, fo. 71.

the house of lords. The intention was to secure a less partisan house, which would obviate the need to thrust the Crown into the political arena. This was Selborne's attitude towards the Crown in politics in 1907; four years later, as will be seen, it had gone full circle. But to return to the subject at hand. If the referendum were adopted, a moderate reform of the lords would become acceptable: a mixture of the hereditary principle and life peerages would suffice. The interest in reform was always subsidiary to keeping the house's power strong, a concern also dominant with Salisbury. In short, until the lords question reached crisis proportions, Selborne's main reliance was on the referendum as the solution to the constitutional problem. It was to do three things: keep the lords essentially unchanged; in conjunction with a moderate reform of that house, fence off the Crown from the political arena; and restore the Unionists to office. The only way to prevent a Liberal victory in the next general election, he warned in 1907, was to adopt the referendum: "by it alone" could the house of lords be preserved "whether reformed or unreformed, as a reality and a strength to the constitution and not as a sham."[43]

As earlier noted, Selborne in forwarding the referendum worked closely with Jem Salisbury, the man in public life whom he most admired.[44] High churchmen with a reputation for exceptional probity, they seem in many ways Victorians left over from the previous century. For example, at a time when it was unfashionable to do so they criticized the manner in which their party awarded honors; and their distaste for Lloyd George's practices led them in 1922 to oppose successfully the continuation of his wartime coalition. In contemporary opinion, Selborne and Salisbury were straightforward and sincere, unbending in principle, and consistent in purpose–qualities, it might be noted, that were often attributed to Lord Salisbury. Temperamentally different from Balfour, whom they considered a flawed leader because he allegedly lacked serious purpose in constitutional matters, they

---

43. Memorandum to Lansdowne, Feb. 28, 1910. MS Selborne 74, fos. 3–4. Selborne to Balfour, Nov. 25, 1909, MS Selborne 1, fo. 115. See also MS Selborne 76, fos. 274–87. Whether this is Selborne's memorandum is unclear, but it contains his usual arguments.

44. MS Selborne 191, fo. 54.

came to see in him a source of debasement in public life, from their viewpoint the most damaging of charges. In 1911 they spearheaded the diehard revolt against his authority, an action that eventuated in his resignation from the party leadership. Thereafter an undeviating loyalty to the lords and the referendal theory led them to relive the trauma of these years; and they spent the rest of their political lives vainly seeking to replace the Parliament Act with the referendum or its equivalent. This was their goal long after other Unionists had fallen away.[45]

Salisbury, too, was deeply interested in empire, and he was as determined as Selborne to maintain the Act of Union. Like Lord Salisbury earlier, he and Selborne believed that if Ireland were to go its separate way, India would follow–a viewpoint common to Unionists. Although the imperial factor explains Jem Salisbury's willingness to advocate the referendum, he was less eager than Selborne; but once committed he favored a more radical usage. The explanation of the seeming paradox lies in his free-trade ideology. Hostile to food taxes, which his party sponsored, he was as prepared to use the referendum to forestall drastic changes in Unionist policy as to use it against the Liberals. He would employ it even when the two houses were agreed, territory that Selborne refused to enter until late in 1910. Given the latter's high opinion of Salisbury's advice, it is possible that in this respect he shaped Selborne's views. Hugh and Robert Cecil also supported both the referendum and free trade. Doubtless Austen Chamberlain had this influential group in mind when he reported that "a section of the Unionist party was strongly in favour of the referendum on its merits."[46]

The dominant figure was Selborne, the most effective and active proponent of the referendum in high Unionist circles. With

---

45. Rose, *The later Cecils*, 59, 73, 79–81, 87–90. Maurice Cowling, *The impact of labour* (Cambridge, 1971), 70, 71, 72, 75, 90, 147, 257. Max Egremont, *The cousins: the friendship and activities of Wilfred Scawen Blunt and George Wyndham* (1977), 275. This has Wyndham's opinion of Balfour, which may have reflected Selborne's. Sandars, *Studies of yesterday*, 85–106. MS Selborne 191, fos. 38, 54, 163–4. Ibid., 192, fos. 70–1. *Crawford papers*, ed. Vincent, 425, 427, 552. Fanning, "'Rats' versus 'ditchers,' " 205. Peter Fraser, "The Unionist debacle of 1911 and Balfour's retirement," *Journal of Modern History*, 35 (1936), 364–5. See also David Cannadine, *The decline and fall of the British aristocracy* (New Haven, 1990), chap. 7.

46. *Politics from inside: an epistolary chronicle, 1906–1914* (1936), 194. Cowling, *The impact of labour*, 71, 75–6. Jem Salisbury to Selborne, Jan. 11, 1910, MS Selborne 6, fo. 37.

the help of the Cecils, he placed it on the party agenda, where it remained until 1914. This is a valid description of Selborne though Balfour of Burleigh, a Unionist peer with whom contemporaries linked Selborne's name in this respect, introduced in the lords on March 2, 1911, a Referendum Bill that reached a second reading before it was withdrawn. Unhappily for the future of his plan Balfour of Burleigh was a free trader, as was the real author of the Referendum Bill, John St. Loe Strachey, Unionist editor of the *Spectator*. Along with Dicey, also a free trader, Strachey had publicized the referendum steadily since the early 1890s.[47]

Unlike Strachey and Dicey who are routinely mentioned in scholarly accounts of the referendum, Selborne was a tariff reformer with the highest of credentials in the Chamberlain wing of the Unionist party. That Selborne was safe on tariff reform and food taxes facilitated the referendum's acceptance though it could not ensure it. For Joseph Chamberlain's tariff reform campaign and the general election of 1906 had so decimated the free-trade elements in the party that no one not a tariff reformer could have hoped in these years to place the referendum at the very center of party policy. It took Selborne to do that. In 1903–4 he had worked with Chamberlain in capturing the Liberal Unionist Association, which as Chief Liberal Unionist Whip he had helped found. He and Lansdowne, also a Liberal Unionist, became its vice-presidents. About this time Selborne wrote: "The more I study the question the more I am convinced that, if this country is to maintain herself in the years to come in the same rank with the U.S., Russia, & Germany, the [economic] unit must be enlarged from the UK to the empire."[48]

As earlier noted, Selborne's priorities differed from Chamberlain's despite long experience as his subordinate and lieutenant. Not only did he place a higher value on political and constitutional arrangements, but Selborne also made the point that tariff reform would be more permanent if sanctioned by a

---

47. Sir John Marriott, *Second chambers* (Oxford, 1927), 225. Strachey to Balfour of Burleigh, Mar. 2, 1911, Strachey Papers, Record Office, House of Lords, S/2/5/35. See also Strachey, *The referendum* (1924), 40, 42, 59–75, 95. Robert Cecil and Lord Balfour of Burleigh cooperated in promoting the referendum. Jem Salisbury to Selborne, Apr. 29, 1910, MS Selborne 6, fos. 56–56v.

48. Cited in Philipps, *The diehards*, 107.

referendum. And he sought other solutions to the difference between them, at one stage suggesting a special convention to settle the fiscal issue.[49] Still it was not easy even for a whole-hogger to win support for the referendum, given the fear of his fellow tariff reformers that it would be used to wipe out their gains. Not until events on the eve of the general election of December, 1910, seemed to demonstrate that food taxes were in the way of the Unionists' return to power, did resistance soften. They now proved willing to use the referendum to offset the unpopularity of those taxes; and by this time, too, the lords' question was at center stage. The major holdout was Austen Chamberlain, and his opposition seems to have been based on economic and fiscal considerations but not constitutional.[50]

As early as December 20, 1909, Selborne addressed the whole-hogger dilemma in a letter to Joseph Chamberlain. Recognizing that his party's return to office in the forthcoming general election would mean dealing with tariff reform, he pointed out that it was equally necessary "to apply a remedy to the constitutional deadlock, which has really arisen." The relations between lords and commons could not remain permanently as they were. If a remedy were not found, "the home rule–pro-Boer–little England–socialist party" would one day return to power and in time establish a single-chamber tyranny. He spelled out the consequences, as he envisaged them. A house of commons with a majority of the present size or larger could reverse the Unionist policy of tariff reform, denounce the preference presently extended to the colonies, and, most surely, disrupt the empire. There was, in his biting words, "no depth of malignant lunacy, to which such a majority, if constitutionally uncontrolled, would not sink."[51]

While Chamberlain's reply was reassuring, political reality made it less so. In 1906 he was stricken with the paralysis that ended his political career; and his son Austen, who was notoriously hostile to the referendum, was now ascendant among the

---

49. Selborne to Salisbury, Aug. 15, 1907, MS Selborne 5, fos. 180–82.

50. Jack Sandars to Balfour, Dec. 24, 1910, B.L. Add. MS 49767, fo. 52. See Neal Blewett, *The peers, the parties and the people, the general election of 1910* (1972), chap. 9 for the whole-hogger movement to accept the referendum.

51. *The crisis of British Unionism*, ed. Boyce, 44–5.

tariff reformers. Thus the anomaly of the two Unionist leaders most trusted by Joseph Chamberlain locked for many months in 1911 in an internecine struggle within the shadow cabinet. For Selborne, whatever his respect and admiration for Joseph Chamberlain, was bent on securing the referendum. In his letter of December 20, 1909, he had stated simply: "I plump for the referendum." And in another passage he stated: "My feelings on the subject are very strong and my judgment deeprooted." In a letter on the same day to Jem Salisbury he announced his unwillingness to join a new Unionist government unless Balfour promised to support the referendum and other changes in the lords. Whatever help was possible outside the government he would give, but he would not abandon the referendum. "I should strain every nerve," he wrote, "to force my party into accepting and adopting my policy in this matter."[52]

Selborne with good reason assumed Balfour's familiarity with his plan. He was in London in the late summer and early fall of 1909 when the lords had before them Lloyd George's Finance Bill. While the debates were still underway he returned to South Africa; but very much aware of the emergent crisis he composed on shipboard some "Notes on Referendum" and arranged for their transmission to Balfour. Lady Selborne was to forward them via Robert Cecil. Not until five months later did Selborne realize, on February 23, 1910, that the letter had miscarried. He at once sent another copy to Balfour, accompanied this time with a critique of passages hostile to the referendum in W.S. McKechnie's *Reform of the house of lords* (1909). He then telegraphed a statement of his plan to Lansdowne and followed it up with a memorandum. Less than a month later Lansdowne composed his own memorandum, based on Selborne's materials, and sent it to the shadow cabinet. He also sent Sandars a letter describing himself as never having favored the referendum on its merits but as now thinking the idea would be popular. "A reformed house of lords and the referendum would not be a bad cry with which to meet the demand for single-chamber government," he now believed.[53] Whatever his mental reservations,

52. Ibid. See also Selborne MS 6, fos. 31–2.

53. Selborne to Balfour, Feb. 23, 1910, MS Selborne 1, fo. 117. The "Notes on referendum" are fos. 120–1 and are dated Sept. 6, 1909. There is a second copy, fos. 122–3. The notes on McKechnie, written a year earlier, are in fos. 124–9. See also B.L. Add. MS

Lansdowne accepted the referendum principle and gradually became one of its more radical advocates.

By April 16, 1910, Selborne's referendum was before the shadow cabinet, but eight days later it received a severe setback when its members voted against sending it to a select committee of the lords. Nor was this all the bad news. Chamberlain had found a powerful ally in Curzon. The latter's political ideas about the lords, which differed sharply from Selborne's, had also crystallized in the late nineteenth century; and they would be put forward forcibly. His objections to the referendum will require consideration, but for the moment it is desirable to turn to Chamberlain's account of what transpired on April 24.

His account was detailed. Jem Salisbury wanted them to take up the referendum, but opposition had come from several quarters including Austen himself and Curzon. Austen had urged that the more frequent the appeal to the voter, the worse the Unionists would do. The voters, bored by it all, would stay away from the polls, and on this score the Unionists would suffer more than the Liberals. Moderate men, on whom the Unionists relied, would tire first, whereas the hardened partisan was a dependable voter. Moreover the Unionists had no organization for the purposes of a referendum, unlike the Liberals who had the chapels. Chamberlain reported that he and Andrew Bonar Law were agreed that the referendum would not help electorally in the present situation; and they, with Curzon, that they had better not rush into such changes without careful thought and knowing the implications. On the other side were Selborne and the Cecils, who were hot for the referendum; and Lansdowne was leaning this way. Chamberlain's account concluded with two observations that in his opinion carried the day. One of them, supported by Curzon, dismissed as fruitless the proposal to refer the referendum to a select committee of the lords. Nothing or very little could come of it; no satisfactory agreement was possible.[54]

Selborne could not have overlooked the fact that Chamberlain and Curzon, in particular, had administered a fateful set-

---

49708, fos. 183–200; MS Selborne 74, fos. 1–4. Lansdowne to Selborne, Mar. 23, 1910, MS Selborne 74, fos. 7–10.

54. Chamberlain, *Politics from inside*, 263–4. Robert Cecil tried unsuccessfully to win over Curzon. Cecil was a promoter of the referendum, working with Balfour of Burleigh. See, too, Robert Cecil to Lady Selborne, Apr. 29, 1910, MS Selborne 74, fo. 26.

back to the referendum. The opportunity now passed to make his plan public simultaneously with the Liberals' Parliament Bill, and circumstances would not again be so auspicious. The Constitutional Conference that had begun on June 7 ended without a bipartisan compromise on November 10; and though the referendum figured in its deliberations, the proceedings were not made public. This means that a whole year passed after Selborne took up his campaign before it penetrated public consciousness. Embodied in the Lansdowne resolutions introduced in the lords on November 21, 1910, before the December general election, it had come too late to acquaint the electorate with a proposal that was both novel and far-reaching.[55]

Curzon was a more formidable foe of the referendum than Austen Chamberlain, whose opposition is often cited. As earlier noted, Curzons's hostility, which is explicable in light of his indifference to home rule, was amply demonstrated in the early 1890s when the Second Home Rule Bill was at center stage; and it had not abated with time. Moreover, plagued with ill health, he had a prickly, combative personality and a high degree of imperiousness and self-righteousness. Unsurprisingly in the circumstances, his rejection of the referendum, combined with these personal qualities, now gave rise to a long drawn-out struggle within the shadow cabinet that culminated in its breakup on July 21, 1911. On that day accumulated emotions and tensions exploded like an underground fire, suddenly bursting forth with great ferocity and roaring out of control. As Balfour commented in a memorable sentence: "In the face of all men the party fabric was, for the moment, violently rent from top to bottom."[56]

55. According to Selborne, the whole position would have altered if the referendum had been out right after the January election, which he thought might have been accomplished. Selborne to Balfour, Dec. 24, 1910, MS Selborne 1, fo. 139. But Selborne was hardly urgent when he sent the referendum materials to Balfour. He hoped that they might talk these over in June but in the meantime did not expect an answer. MS Selborne 1, fo. 117. The referendum had been canvassed in politics ever since the mid-1880s but did not enter the Unionist agenda until Selborne took it up. For a useful summary of the earlier discussion, see Stoddart, *Against the referendum*, especially the introductory note and part III, chaps. i-v. As was earlier noted Lord Salisbury advocated the referendum in the early 1890s. That he did so was recalled by Lord Saltoun in the parliamentary debates. *Parl. debs.* (lords), 5th series, vol. ix, columns 45–6. He spoke on July 3, 1911.

56. *Politics from inside*, 350–1.

The time has come, then, to consider more fully Curzon's reasons for rejecting the referendum and to explore further the personal qualities of the leading protagonists, which shed so much light on the discord in the shadow cabinet.

IV

Like Selborne, Curzon was a distinguished imperial proconsul accustomed to command and a political leader of prodigious industry. Salisbury appointed him viceroy of India in 1898, at the early age of thirty-nine; and until 1905 he controlled the fate of the teeming millions in the subcontinent. He is said to have returned to England "an angry and embittered man." Contemporaries had mixed feelings towards him, some never forgiving him when he won a great victory on behalf of the Parliament Bill in 1911. Reviled by its opponents, he was denigrated by Leo Maxse, the vitriolic editor of the *National Review*, as the "pushful proconsul."[57] Yet his political career, taken as a whole, shone with success. After serving in Asquith's wartime government, he was foreign secretary in the Lloyd George coalition of 1916 and then in Bonar Law's government.

When the latter resigned in 1922, Curzon expected to become prime minister, only to have the glittering prize elude him. A sense of fairness led Salisbury to support him, but by this time neither he nor Selborne considered Curzon a friend. He and Selborne had been for many years on cordial terms; but their friendship, according to Selborne, ended abruptly in 1910. Concerned and puzzled, Selborne made unsuccessful enquiries of Curzon's authorized biographer, the earl of Ronaldshay. But withdrawal in this way was characteristic of Curzon; he steadily reduced the number of his friends until at his death he had almost none.[58]

If Curzon broke with Selborne, it was the other way round with Jem Salisbury. With him, Curzon's role in passing the Parliament Act was decisive. According to Lady Gwendolen Cecil,

---

57. *National Review*, vol. 58, p. 511.

58. MS Selborne 191, fos. 50–1. The year seems to be 1910 though it is difficult to read.

"Jem's struggle for a charitable judgment of George Curzon's proceedings is more than his nervous system is equal to, and I'm quite longing to find an adequate defense for that worthy."[59] The break was long in the making. On Curzon's return from India he had every right, based on precedent, to anticipate finding cabinet members at Charing Cross Station when he entered London. But before leaving India he had quarrelled with the Balfour cabinet, and not a single member was there. Selborne was in South Africa, but Salisbury's absence requires further explanation. During his viceroyalty Curzon had emerged as a bitter critic of Lord Salisbury's policies. At the time of his return Jem Salisbury wrote a letter to Selborne expressing doubt that they could work with him if he returned to public life, so different was his view from Lord Salisbury's.[60] Moreover, in his last years in India Curzon was involved in an unsuccessful struggle with Lord Kitchener. During its course Salisbury's wife was intermediary between Kitchener and the cabinet; and the Cecils sided with him.[61]

Unlike Selborne and Salisbury, Curzon was primarily interested in reforming the composition of the house of lords. Seeing in the referendal theory the necessary safeguard for its legislative veto, he saw that house's composition in a different light. After entering the commons in 1886, he grew uneasy about Salisbury's lopsided majority in the house of lords; and his worst fears were realized when Labouchere introduced resolutions to abolish it. Curzon's response took the form of two articles in the *National Review* for 1888 urging the addition of new elements to that house. He would bring in men of culture with the highest education and attainments; men of service, such as ex-MPs, judges, ambassadors, civil servants; even colonials recruited from distant but loyal lands.[62]

---

59. Quoted in Rose, *The later Cecils*, 81. The original letter is at Hatfield House. She added: "but it's difficult. Only the old truth that there's nothing so bitter as faction fighting–& the closer the factions to one another the more unscrupulous the weapons they will use." Hatfield House GWE, Lady Gwendolen Cecil to Lady Selborne, Aug. 14, 1911.

60. MS Selborne 5, fo. 149. The letter is dated Mar. 2, 1907. Grenville, *Lord Salisbury and foreign policy*, 296–7.

61. Rose, *The later Cecils*, 83–4.

62. "A purified British senate," *National Review*, (Mar. 1888); "Reconstruction of the house of lords," ibid. (Apr. 1888). See also "The Referendum," ibid. (Mar. 1894), "Peers' disabilities," *Nineteenth Century* (April 1894). See also Ronaldshay, *The life of Lord Curzon: George Nathaniel*, i, 134–40.

In that year Curzon worked with Lord Rosebery on the problem of reforming the house of lords, and when the question became acute once more in Edwardian England, Curzon was appointed to a committee, chaired by Rosebery, to consider its reform. The agreed report of the Rosebery Committee in 1908 recommended limiting the hereditary qualification, but the major breakthrough came in March 1910 when Rosebery won acceptance for the principle that the possession of a peerage should no longer of itself give the right to sit and vote in the lords. Curzon was Rosebery's most enthusiastic supporter in the parliamentary debates.[63] Both were associated with the principle that the reformed house should have an elective element, and a provision to this effect appeared in the Lansdowne Reform Bill of 1911, which Curzon was reputed to have "had a large share in shaping."[64]

The already wide gulf between Curzon and Selborne on the lords question expanded still further when Curzon in 1911 threw all his energy into defeating the diehard revolt, which was associated in the public mind with the referendum. His action signalled if not a downright opposition to the referendum at least a decided reluctance to go the last mile on its behalf. As earlier noted, Selborne and Salisbury were diehard leaders of conspicuous importance; and both favored the referendum. Nor did they have any sympathy for Rosebery's or his disciples' views. Salisbury thought "very poorly of the Rosebery Report,"[65] and he and Selborne adamantly opposed an elective principle in relationship to the lords. At a later date Selborne, remarking on his detestation of parts of Lansdowne's Reform Bill, condemned a provision for the indirect election of a group of peers by MPs acting as an electoral college. Indeed, he considered bringing in a reform bill a tactical error.[66]

In 1894 Curzon had stated publicly his opposition to the referendum in remarks well known in the 1910–1 period. A participant in a *National Review* symposium, he rejected categorically even the relatively moderate proposal of using it to break dead-

---

63. Jenkins, *Mr. Balfour's poodle*, 137–41.

64. Jem Salisbury to Selborne, Mar. 19, 1910, MS Selborne 6, fos. 44–5. Sir Almeric Fitzroy, *Memoirs*, 2 vols. (1925), ii, 444.

65. Jem Salisbury to Selborne, Jan. 11, 1910, MS Selborne 6, fo. 34.

66. Ibid. See also Selborne to Lord Halsbury, Aug. 31, 1911, B.L. Add. MS 56374, fo. 182.

locks between the houses. The referendum would strengthen an already powerful house, armed with the referendal theory, and revolutionize its constitution without solving the home rule question and defeating a policy of disintegration.[67] Nor did the referendum possess the democratic character assigned by adherents. He warned of the potential injury to parliamentary government. For one thing, powerful and unscrupulous governments could emerge. Outrageous proposals in the commons would lead to the full employment of the guillotine to carry a measure and hence the destruction of free speech there. Indeed Curzon forecast a new star chamber registering the decrees of a parliamentary tyrant, checked only by the haphazard aye or no of a plebiscite. The referendum, intended to buttress the lords, would destroy the commons. Damaging electoral techniques would be the consequence, resulting either in instructed parliamentary members or bamboozled constituents. When measures were in dispute, there would be a flood of electioneering literature and what Curzon referred to as miniature general elections.

Then there was the point that the referendum as contemplated was unfair to Liberals. The arrangement would not work since the houses rarely disagreed when the Unionists were in office. Nor was the proposal attractive to those already complaining "that the house of lords enjoys an extraordinary initiative"; and its pandering to the electorate's self-interest was distasteful. Finally, in an outburst revealing Curzon's conservatism, the electorate would be convinced of its infallibility as it learned to ignore parliamentary debates. As he said, "Let us...save our democracy from the danger to which all previous democracies have succumbed, viz., the license of untempered power."[68]

---

67. *National Review*, 23 (Apr. 1894), 73. Other contributors were A. V. Dicey, Lord Grey, Strachey. Curzon's comments were revived in 1910 when these became the subject of discussion in Sir Robertson Nicoll's *British Weekly*, a highly influential non-conformist publication sympathetic to Lloyd George, and in Jane Stoddard's *Against the referendum.* This influential book was composed of articles on the referendum that had run serially in the *British Weekly*. She was for thirty years Nicoll's assistant. Her book received much attention. Strachey admired it in the *Spectator*, the British Constitutional Association discussed it, and it was mentioned in the lords in the debates on Balfour of Burleigh's Bill in Mar. 1911. Curzon noticed the revived interest in his position of 1894 in *Parl. debs.* (lords), 5th series, ix, 189.

68. *National Review*, 28, pp. 74–6.

It was much easier to assume in the late nineteenth century that the lords could carry out indefinitely their referendal function than after 1906, when Selborne took up the referendum; and this assumption partly explains Curzon's stand against the referendum in 1894. So too does the disparity between his political experience in the early 1890s and Selborne's, which was previously noted. He was also more conservative by nature than Selborne. In Lloyd George's view, expressed at a later date, Curzon was "not very accessible to new ideas."[69] Whatever the primary explanation, Curzon was inveterately hostile to the referendum thereafter except on the rare occasions when party loyalty compelled him to defend it publicly, as in 1911, or party exigencies were operative, as in 1914, when it appeared that the Unionists might take office without a thought-out lords policy. At such times Curzon would allow the referendum to be rushed into the breach; otherwise, no. Thus he worked steadily in 1910 and 1911, within the shadow cabinet, to confine the referendum to a tentative and uncertain status even though it was the central item in Unionist policy. Writing in 1916 Selborne described Curzon as being as opposed to the referendum as to women's suffrage. At that time Curzon had been for four years president of the National League for Opposing Women's Suffrage.[70]

If Selborne had been less infatuated with the referendum or Curzon more conciliatory in disposition, party unity would have suffered less from their very different approaches to the lords question. But given their personal characteristics and outlooks, to say nothing of their experiences as imperial proconsuls, these strong-willed, self-confident political leaders were bound to wreak havoc once face to face on the referendum issue in a shadow cabinet weakened and demoralized by successive electoral defeats. Selborne was more flexible and better-natured. His

---

69. Stoddart, *Against the referendum*, 96. *The political diaries of C. P. Scott 1911–1928*, ed. Trevor Wilson (New York, 1970), 325.

70. Selborne to Jem Salisbury, Sept. 20, 1916, MS Selborne 6, fos. 198–9. Discussing the Parliament Act, Selborne stated: "The referendum is the least we can go for." Ibid., fo. 198 See also Fraser, "The Unionist debacle of 1911," 357. Curzon's presidency is mentioned in a prefatory note to the Curzon papers at the India Office. MSS Eur F 112/807. See also MSS Eur F 112/95, fos. 56v, 57, 58, 71.

political pragmatism, displayed to full advantage in South Africa, helped reconcile the defeated Boer leaders to the imperial connection, whereas the tactless Curzon in a troubled period in India publicly insulted the Indian intellectual élite. Nor did his disposition improve when on his return to England he failed for some time to secure a parliamentary seat. The reception he encountered was altogether different from Selborne's, doubtless a fact not lost on him and certainly not conducive to mellowing an already difficult personality. The death of his wife at this time left him a lonely and embittered public figure.

More gifted intellectually than Selborne, Curzon, as earlier noted, had disagreeable characteristics that converted longstanding friendships into political animosities. If contemporaries saluted his wit, charm, and brilliance, still stories abound of his insensitivity, greed, excessive ambition, and arrogance, even brutality towards those around him, whatever their positions on the social and political scale. Balcarres went to the heart of the matter when he described Curzon in these terms: "It is partly a question of manner–somewhat professorial and challenging, partly also because of his assurance which seems to provoke opposition." He "perhaps presses his view too far, for as he is always convinced he is right, he seldom if ever is prepared to concede a point. Whoever differs from him must be wrong and must therefore be vigorously opposed. And he is quite merciless in pressing his views, and untiring as well."[71] Given Curzon's personal attributes and the habit of command habitual with both men, a difference between them on so fundamental a point must sooner or later create friction; and a member of the shadow cabinet, Lord Midleton, recorded that by July 1911 "recrimination previously acute, became violent."[72]

It will be recalled that in April 1910, while Selborne was still in South Africa, Curzon, leagued with Austen Chamberlain, dealt the referendum a severe blow in the shadow cabinet. A month later he went further, expressing his opposition publicly.[73]

---

71. *Crawford papers*, 400. Balcarres referred to Curzon repeatedly as "All-Highest." Ibid., 465, 481, 482–3. See also 422, 425, 462, passim.

72. Earl of Midleton, *Records and reactions, 1856–1939* (1939), 270, 273, 274.

73. Strachey to Balfour of Burleigh, May 12, 1910. Strachey papers. Strachey: "I was so sorry to see Curzon giving a leader against the referendum."

Before the year was out they may have once more frustrated Selborne, now back in England. On November 20, following the breakdown of the Constitutional Conference, where the referendum was prominently featured, an important meeting of the Unionist leaders at Hackwood, Curzon's country estate, made final decisions about the Lansdowne resolutions that were read in the lords on the following day. Two provisions are of prime interest: a pledge to reform the lords and, then, to apply the referendum to the settlement of any "matter of great gravity." Not only was the referendum to be used to break deadlocks between the houses, it would also afford "if need be a check upon legislation even when both houses are agreed"–so Lansdowne stated on November 21. The promise to give the Liberals fairer treatment when they were a minority in the commons was a genuinely radical step, but its impact was lessened by the failure to include finance in the arrangement. No such concession was offered because of the compromise reached at Hackwood. At that time Balfour apparently intervened to secure for the advocates of the referendum the provision pledging the party to apply it to "grave matters." Critics found the concession too broad, opening the door for the future development of the referendum; and neither Chamberlain nor Curzon would have found it acceptable. In return, Chamberlain received assurance that the referendum would not be applied to finance.[74] There may have been a struggle on this point. An anonymous memorandum in the Selborne papers, written shortly before the December election of 1910, warns that silence about finance would make the party vulnerable in the coming general election by suggesting that the referendum was only for Liberal measures.[75]

The Hackwood compromise crumbled within twenty-four hours. This is apparent from the proceedings in the lords when Lansdowne was explaining his resolutions. Salisbury, writing to

---

74. Chamberlain, *Politics from inside*, 342–3. Sir Charles Petrie, *Life and letters of the Rt. Hon. Sir Austen Chamberlain*, two vols. (1939–40), I, 269. Chamberlain wrote to Richard Jebb, Dec. 7, 1910, "Balfour's Albert Hall declaration was a bitter pill for me to swallow...because it reversed a decision which we had deliberately taken and embodied in the Lansdowne resolutions–that budgets, whether tariff reform or not, were not fit subjects for the referendum." See also Alice Wilson Fox, *The earl of Halsbury lord high chancellor, 1823–1921* (1929), 274.

75. MS Selborne 76, fos. 3–6.

Balfour, described what occurred. "Then in accordance with what had been settled at Hackwood he [Lansdowne] stated...clearly but diplomatically, that financial bills even if they were called in question as going beyond pure finance would be subject to a joint sitting [of the two houses] but not to a referendum." Crewe, speaking after Lansdowne, "did not miss the point and interpreted it to mean that tariff reform could not be sent to a referendum." But the debate took a different turn when Lord St. Aldwyn pointed out that Lansdowne's attitude towards "minorities" modified the resolutions, bringing tariff reform within the scope of a referendum. Though Salisbury stated that in his opinion the Hackwood decision was wrong, he steered clear of the subject, contenting himself with dwelling on Lansdowne's view of minorities while passing "the other matter by." Since then it had been aired in the newspapers; and Lord Cromer, a free trader, had written to *The Times* supporting St. Aldwyn.[76]

Taunted by the Liberals with unfairness and insincerity, Balfour responded with the well-known Albert Hall declaration (November 29, 1910), pledging the Unionists to submit the principles of tariff reform to a referendum. If it gave Chamberlain his notorious case of referendum sickness,[77] it also placed the official party imprimatur on the radical version of the referendum. Tariff reform would become law only when the Unionists held office, and at such times they controlled both houses. Their agreement to subject tariff reform to the referendum meant an acceptance as a political fact of life that the votes of both houses would be by-passed. In short, St. Aldwyn's assessment was on the mark. As late as 1909 this version was unacceptable to Selborne because it portended a popular rather than parliamentary sovereignty, but by 1910 he had come full circle. So, too, had the Constitutional Conference, it might be noted, with which he and Curzon, too, were in contact. Salisbury, a free trader, never had the problem. Both men were at Hackwood, and either one or both could have authored the anonymous memorandum.[78]

---

76. Salisbury to Balfour, Nov. 29, 1910, B.L. Add. MS 49758, fos. 247–8. For Lansdowne's remarks, see *Parl. debs.* (lords), 5th series, vi, 844. He stated that he was only speaking for himself, but he could hardly have been doing that. See Blewett, *The peers, the parties, and the people*, 181–8.

77. Chamberlain, *Politics from inside*, 332.

78. Selborne to Balfour, Dec. 24, 1910, MS Selborne 1, fo. 140. Selborne to F. S. Oliver, Mar. 30, 1911, MS Selborne 74, fos. 71–4. Among the Unionists not in attendance at

Despite a seeming harmony at Hackwood, the Unionists were in disarray on the eve of the general election. Ill-prepared for the Liberal challenge to the Hackwood compromise, they rushed, in public view and at the instance of their political enemies, for the nearest exit; and to cap it all, the Albert Hall declaration was too late to affect the electoral outcome. Whether an earlier decision to bring tariff reform within the ambit of the referendum would have changed the result may be wondered, and presumably the question crossed Selborne's methodical mind. In any case, he must have known that a more realistic policy could have emerged at Hackwood had the problem been confined to dealing with Chamberlain. But Curzon, too, had to be satisfied; and he was just as determined as Chamberlain to keep the referendum within narrow limits, though for different reasons.

Chamberlain's unhappiness with the Albert Hall declaration is notorious, and it is well-known that he stood alone on the fiscal issue when his fellow tariff reformers deserted him.[79] The disunity now rampant among the Unionist leaders was due, then, to the constitutional question and, in particular, to the division on the referendum within the shadow cabinet.[80] This became obvious when they considered how best to implement the Lansdowne amendments. On January 10, 1911, a committee of the shadow cabinet–consisting of Lansdowne as chairman; Sir Robert Finlay, a distinguished constitutional lawyer and later lord chancellor, who favored the referendum; Selborne; and Austen Chamberlain–was instructed to prepare three bills: a "reform bill" reconstituting the house of lords; a bill dealing with relations between the houses; and a referendum bill detailing the machinery of the referendum.

The committee's report, in circulation by February 3,

---

the Constitutional Conference of 1910 but kept informed of the deliberations were Curzon and Selborne. Alfred Gollin, *The Observer and J. L. Garvin, 1908–1914* (1960), 231. This is a useful reminder that the rivalry between Curzon and Selborne is a central theme in discussing the Unionist party before the Parliament Act.

79. Chamberlain to Jebb, Dec. 7, 1910, *Life and letters*, i, p. 268.

80. By this time the controversy over tariff reform and free trade, so prominent in the years from 1903 to 1909, had been superseded by the constitutional crisis that arose with the rejection of Lloyd George's Finance Bill. Alan Sykes writes: "During 1909 and 1910 most Unionist free traders sacrificed their free trade principles to join in this defence [of the constitution] alongside the more powerful tariff reformers." "The Radical Right and the crisis of Conservatism before the First World War," *Historical Journal*, 26, 3(1983), 675–6.

would put aside for the time being the first two bills as too difficult to draft, given the complexities of the situation and differing views about procedure. The shadow cabinet should center its attention instead on drafting amendments to the Parliament Bill. Meanwhile the committee would proceed with a referendum bill on the grounds that it was relatively simple to prepare and its production was vital. The bill would deal with the machinery of the referendum, not the occasions and circumstances in which it would be deployed. The report read: "Unless we are able to produce a bill of some kind, we shall be told that the idea of the referendum is impracticable, and that we have never dared to get to close quarters with it." Such a statement must do the party "infinite harm," and the production of a referendum bill was "the only answer to it."[81] The failure to produce a referendum bill in these months tells, therefore, a great deal about the state of mind of Unionist leaders on the eve of the Parliament Act.

The situation was inauspicious. Meeting on February 25 to consider the committee's report, the shadow cabinet, so Lansdowne reported to Balfour, had a "considerable divergence of opinion." To be sure, members agreed with the committee on the impossibility of introducing at this time a bill dealing with the two houses' relations. This was to set aside the draft of a bill focusing on the referendum but not one dealing with its machinery. Discord now set in as Curzon firmly opposed the majority. Refusing bluntly to accept the committee's recommendation to set aside the reform bill as well, he would proceed with it. The party and the press desired it, and failure to produce such a bill would bring into question the sincerity of the promise to reform the lords. Lansdowne thought Curzon had the support of George Wyndham, Lord Derby, and Henry Chaplin. But at least in Wyndham's case, this did not denote hostility towards the referendum; on this issue he sided with Selborne.[82]

A few days after the shadow cabinet an uneasy Selborne sought out Curzon to learn whether he proposed to jettison the

---

81. MS Selborne 76, fos. 7–15.

82. Lansdowne to Balfour, Feb. 15, 1911, B.L. Add. MS 49730, fos. 188–9. See also Jack Sandars to Balfour, Feb. 15, 1911, B.L. Add. MS 49767, fos. 114–114v. Wyndham's views on the referendum are in a letter, Mar. 24, 1911, B.L. Add. MS 49806, fos. 100–1.

referendum. He missed seeing Curzon but subsequently received from him a letter of February 19 denying any such intention. His views about how to proceed, Curzon wrote reassuringly, were contingent on their continuing to adhere to the plan in the Lansdowne resolutions; but he held firm to his position in the shadow cabinet. He would consider, however, proceeding at the same time with a bill regulating the relations of the houses and would meet on the matter with Selborne or Balfour.[83] In the end a reform bill was introduced (though not as early as Curzon wished), but not a bill dealing with the two houses' relations or the referendum.

The outcome was foreshadowed in Lansdowne's comments to Balfour on March 19. The reform bill produced "a cleavage between the front & the back benches," he explained, but with regard to the referendum their colleagues were "deeply divided among themselves." He wondered, was Balfour aware "of the views held on one side by Austen & Curzon, & on the other by Finlay & Selborne?" When he coupled these names, he did not mean to suggest that "either the first two or the second think exactly alike." Balfour should talk with Finlay, who had worked especially hard on the matter; but in any case it was imperative to decide the line to be advised before the next shadow cabinet.[84] The parting of the ways came a week later. Austen Chamberlain reported the decision taken on March 26: "At last I found myself in a majority again, and, strongly supporting Curzon's objections, succeeded in defeating the project of introducing a referendum bill of our own as well as a lords reform bill."[85]

The decision was pivotal. To bring in such a bill would

---

83. Curzon to Selborne, Feb. 19, 1911, MS Selborne 10, fos. 159–61.

84. Lansdowne to Balfour, Mar. 19, 1911, B.L. Add. MS 49730, fos. 198–9. Lansdowne to Jack Sandars, ibid., fos. 203–4. In this letter to Sandars Lansdowne expressed the hope that Balfour would also meet with Selborne, Curzon, Chamberlain, and a few others for about a half hour apiece.

85. Chamberlain, *Politics from inside*, 333. There had apparently been a less successful meeting from his standpoint on Mar. 23. This appears from Chamberlain's own comment and also from a letter of Selborne to Sandars, Mar. 24, 1911, B.L. Add. MS 49708, fo. 219. The decision of the shadow cabinet on Mar. 26 explains why the Unionists did not support Balfour of Burleigh's Bill on the second reading. See Lansdowne to Balfour, Mar. 19, 1911, B.L. Add. MS 49730, fo. 197. If they could not agree to bring forward a referendum bill of their own, they were hardly in a position to support someone else's.

have been to affirm publicly a constant support for the referendum, moving it out of the realm of speculation and into the limelight.[86] Thereafter it met with a continuing scrutiny, which seems to have been hostile. On May 26, Lansdowne wrote to Sandars about a forthcoming meeting to be attended by Selborne, Salisbury, Curzon, and Midleton, the last-named working with Curzon on the Reform Bill. Lansdowne wanted Balfour to bring Austen Chamberlain.[87] At the meeting Selborne warded off an attempt to limit the application of the referendum to home rule; but his confidence remained unimpaired, or so it appears, since he advanced though without success an argument for broadening its scope to include ordinary as well as constitutional legislation.[88]

The Reform Bill was introduced on May 8, and a week later Lansdowne proceeded to a second reading. So frigid was the reception that a motion for rejection might well have carried. According to a contemporary account, "feeling was much fomented by the ostentatious way in which on one or two occasions Curzon prompted his leader: his personality does not command enthusiasm, and he is credited, rightly or wrongly, with having had a large share in shaping Lord Lansdowne's scheme. At any rate, this morning he received a number of peers at his house and expounded the measure to them."[89]

The Reform Bill now slipped from sight, and the referendum moved to the forefront of consideration. It was embodied in the second of several amendments introduced in Lansdowne's name in the lords on June 26 with the aim of retaining an appeal to the people. This amendment, thereafter referred to as the Lansdowne amendment, reads:

> Any bill
> (a) which affects the existence of the crown or the Protestant succession thereto; or (b) which establishes a national parliament or assembly or a national council in Ireland, Scotland, Wales, or England with legislative powers therein; or

---

86. See for example Finlay's memorandum of Feb. 20, 1911.

87. B.L. Add. MS 49861, fo. 153.

88. Ibid. 49730, fo. 238. Ac 9/1/23 May 30, 1911.

89. Jenkins, *Mr. Balfour's poodle*, 201–4. Fitzroy, *Memoirs*, ii, 444. *Crawford papers*, 184.

(c) which has been referred to the joint committee [to be set up], and which in their opinion raises an issue of great gravity upon which the judgment of the country has not been sufficiently ascertained shall not be presented to his majesty nor receive the royal assent under the provisions of this section unless and until it has been submitted to and approved by the electors in manner to be hereafter provided by act of parliament.

(2) Any question whether a bill comes within the meaning of paragraphs (a) (b) of sub-section (1) of this section shall be decided by the joint committee.

This was more than a deadlock plan. According to Lansdowne, the Unionists, so long as the lords were unreformed, would allow references to the joint committee by a substantial majority in the commons or by the speaker on behalf of a minority. That is, a bill of the kind described above, would go to referendum if so decided by the joint committee, fairly constituted between the two parties, even if both houses accepted the measure. Lansdowne also promised, if his amendment met with encouragement, to bring in a referendum bill in a few days.[90]

But time had run out. The commons promptly rejected the lords' amendments *en bloc*, and Balfour learned that the king had agreed to create enough peers to ensure the passage of an unamended Parliament Bill. A letter from the Liberal prime minister, H. H. Asquith, to Balfour on July 20 confirmed the information. On the following day the shadow cabinet met to decide policy. At this juncture the quarrel between the lords and the Liberal government entered a final phase. The time for compromise, if it had ever existed, had come and gone; and in the angry months that ensued the Unionist leadership virtually collapsed.

---

90. *Parl. debs.* (lords), 5th series, ix, 100–14. Lansdowne spoke on July 4, 1911.

Seven

The Closing Door

I

The last phase of the referendal theory began with the shadow cabinet's breakup on July 21, 1911, and ended in 1922 with the decision by the Unionists, now called Conservatives, to treat the Parliament Act as permanent. The theory had a revival when the fifth marquis of Salisbury (Jem Salisbury's son) invoked it in dealing with the nationalizing agenda of the Attlee government (1945–51). But the episode, though a useful reminder of its long association with the house of Cecil, was no more than a postscript to the politics of 1911.

The Selborne-Curzon rivalry was once more conspicuous when the shadow cabinet considered party policy in light of George V's pledge to create peers to carry the Parliament Bill. According to Lady Gwendolen, any difference over tactics, however public and stormy, would have been overcome had it not been for the strong undercurrent of discontent with Balfour's leadership. As it was, "the whole thing" was so unstable that "anything would topple it."[1]

"Anything" in this instance was Balfour's and Lansdowne's advice to the lords to surrender without a struggle; and although it prevailed, the price was high. The vote of ten to eight revealed that whatever unity remained had now disintegrated. Lord

---

1. Lady Gwendolen Cecil to Lady Selborne, July 21, 1911, Hatfield House MSS GWE. The year given in these notes, unless otherwise stated, is 1911. *The Crawford papers: the journals of David Lindsay twenty-seventh Earl of Crawford and tenth Earl of Balcarres, 1871–1940, during the years 1892–1940*, ed. John Vincent (Manchester, 1984), 175.

Balcarres, the chief Unionist whip, left this record of the voting pattern:

a) for acquiescence without forcing creation of peers:

A.J.B.	Londonderry	Broderick
Lansdowne	Walter Long	Alfred Lyttelton
Curzon	Bob Douglas	
Chaplin	Steel-Maitland	

b) for driving government to create peers:

Selborne	F. E. Smith	Carson
G. Wyndham	Austen Chamberlain	and (I suppose)
Salisbury	Lord Halsbury	myself

The majority for the surrender policy were known as the hedgers; the minority for driving the government to create peers as the diehards or ditchers. Curzon led the hedgers while Selborne was the most determined of the diehards.[2]

That afternoon Lansdowne outlined at Lansdowne House the alternatives before the lords. Favoring resistance was the discouraging effect of surrender on the rank and file, who would think it inconceivable that their leaders would sanction so revolutionary a measure without a peerage creation. Yet resistance had penalties. A large creation would destroy the lords' independence, obviate any benefits accruing from the Parliament Bill, and make that house an object of ridicule in the civilized world. Since the Bill would pass whatever the lords' policy, Lansdowne would accept it without taking responsibility for its contents and at the first opportunity restore the constitutional balance.[3]

Although Curzon took the lead in rallying support for Lansdowne after the meeting, his role during its course is problematic. According to Lansdowne's memorandum on the meeting, it appears that it was St. Aldwyn who set the tone when he warned the lords that forcing a large peer creation might alienate the country. Curzon was said to have spoken similarly.[4] Lansdowne also referred to Selborne's speech, characterizing it as one

2. Ibid., 196.

3. Newton, Thomas Wodehouse Legh, Baron, *Lord Lansdowne: a biography* (1929), 422.

4. Ibid. See also Ensor, *England, 1870–1914,* 429.

"of great force and earnestness";[5] but more can be said than this since the speech is in the Selborne papers. The message was stark: there should be no surrender. The Unionist party and the lords would survive as living forces even if 500 peers were created. Not so, if the lords simply surrendered. Doing so would discredit their leadership, damage the party, and place that house in an odious light. With radical legislation still threatening, the lords would be viewed as abandoning their trust; and whatever the outward appearance, their house would not be the same. Sooner or later it would be swept away. Denying any feelings about "the glory of death in the last ditch," Selborne would resist to the end and throw the whole responsibility for breaking up the constitution on the radical party, as he termed the Liberals.[6] His views were echoed by such prominent diehards as Lord Halsbury, Jem Salisbury, Willoughby de Broke, and the dukes of Bedford and Norfolk.[7]

It is usual to cite the fiery Lord Halsbury, aged 87, who was thrice lord chancellor under Salisbury, as the diehard leader; but the attribution is questionable. A contemporary stated categorically that Halsbury was too old to lead a party, and Wilfrid Blunt, Wyndham's cousin, referred to Halsbury as the "nominal leader" chosen "because of his great age." Otherwise, "there would have been jealousies."[8] If not Halsbury, who did lead the diehards? Probably Selborne. His speech at the Lansdowne House meeting points to this conclusion; and so does his prominent position in the diehard campaign, which he directed as Halsbury's chief of staff and head of a small committee. Also part of the picture is his authorship with Jem Salisbury of the well-known diehard manifesto, which circulated among supporters of

---

5. Newton, *Lord Lansdowne*, 422.

6. MS Selborne 76, fos. 155–7. These words are written on the speech: "meant for Friday 21-7-11."

7. Newton, *Lord Lansdowne*, 422. Bedford is discussed at length in David Spring, "Land and Politics in Edwardian England," printed in *Agricultural history*, published quarterly for the Agricultural History Society by the University of California Press, 17–42. This article provides a valuable economic and social frame of reference for the Conservative ideology discussed in this study. So, too, of course, does the elaborate discussion in Cannadine's *Rise and fall of the British aristocracy*.

8. Max Egremont, *The cousins: the friendship, opinions and activities of Wilfrid Scawen Blunt and George Wyndham* (1979), 276. See also Lord Henage to Lord Cromer, Aug. 5., Cromer papers, PRO FO 633/34/3079, fo. 69.

the Lansdowne amendment. It was the irreducible minimum that the diehards would accept; and the amendment's rejection in the lords on August 10 opened the way for the Parliament Bill's passage.[9]

Also conspicuous in the diehard leadership were the hitherto obscure Lord Willoughby de Broke and the diehard whips, Lords Lovat and Mayo. Willoughby's organizational skills won high praise from contemporaries, Lovat had a national reputation as the leader of Lovat's Scouts during the Boer War, and Mayo was a prominent Irish landlord. All three, along with Halsbury, Selborne, and Salisbury, signed the diehard manifesto; and Willoughby raised successfully an important point about its contents. Yet it was Selborne who decided the number and identity of the signatories,[10] a point to be noted since an authority on this period, following Leo Maxse's *National Review*, assigns Willoughby a status equal to Selborne's; and the *National Review* went further. Moreover, their reputations as political leaders and administrators were not comparable, and the tone of Willoughby's letters to Selborne is that of a subordinate. On one occasion he reported that Selborne's whip was being sent to receptive peers. According to Halsbury's biographer, Selborne was chief of staff for the diehards; Willoughby, his adjutant."[11] Then there was the contemporary practice of referring to the diehard leaders collectively as Selborne and company, Selborne and friends, etc., the terminology being applied to Selborne, Salisbury,

---

9. For Selborne as the diehard strategist, see A. Wilson Fox, *The earl of Halsbury Lord High Chancellor, 1823–1921* (1929), 234, 242, 251–2, 258–9; and Ronan Fanning, "'Rats' versus 'Ditchers': the diehard revolt and the Parliament Bill of 1911," *Parliament and community*, ed. Art Cosgrove and J.I. McGuire (Belfast, 1983), 202. Selborne wound up the debate for the diehards on the night of Aug. 10. *Parl. debs.* (lords), 5th series, ix, 1072–4. Selborne's name is identified by contemporaries with the revolt in the leading role as often as Halsbury's. See, for example, St. Aldwyn's speech in the lords on Aug. 9, ibid., 929, where mention is made of Selborne and Salisbury as the organizers of opposition to the policy on the Parliament Bill enunciated by Lord Lansdowne and Balfour. See also Hatfield House MSS 4M/70/107. This is a copy of the diehard manifesto. On the back of it, in Jem Salisbury's writing, appears the notation: "July 1911 (Diehard Memorandum Drafted by Ld Selborne in consultation with me)" and see Halsbury Papers, B.L. Add. MS 56374, fos. 98–98v.

10. MS Selborne 74, fos. 102–3v; 121–3.

11. Fox, *The earl of Halsbury*, p. 233–4. Willoughby to Selborne, July 27, MS Selborne 74, fo. 149v. Gregory Philipps, "Lord Willoughby de Broke and the politics of Radical Toryism, 1909–1914," *Journal of British Studies*, 20, 1 (1980), 209. *National Review*, 58 (Sept. 1911-Feb. 1912), 7–9.

Willoughby and such Unionist MPs as F. E. Smith, Leo Amery, Chamberlain, Hugh Cecil, and Wyndham.[12]

Evidence of a different kind comes from the memoirs of Almeric Fitzroy, clerk to the privy council and the confidant of statesmen. On July 20–the day before the shadow cabinet's breakup–Fitzroy described a singularly interesting conversation with the hedger Lord Bath. The latter considered that Lansdowne from the first should have refused to amend the Parliament Bill and postponed action until the Unionists were returned to office. Unfortunately, he had "yielded to pressure from the advocates of more violent courses." At this point Bath became more specific. Fitzroy continued:

> Selborne, as I was prepared to hear, he described as the man who, in season and out of season, was urging resistance with ability of a certain order, but obstinate in his adherence to a limited point of view. Bath thought him blind in the handling of the present difficulty: but his persistence made him formidable.[13]

When Fitzroy the following night engaged Speaker Lowther's wife on the subject, she "with the fullest knowledge confirmed what Bath had said the night before about the malefic influence exercised by Selborne on the deliberations of the Unionist leaders."[14]

But how to explain Selborne's influence on party policy so soon after his return from South Africa? Once more Fitzroy is helpful. "The weight of sheer pertinacy which sees one aspect of a situation with extraordinary clearness and determination," he pointed out, had "always to be reckoned with in estimating the probable decision of a number of men at a critical juncture." The reputation won in South Africa had enhanced "the ponderable qualities of Selborne's judgment at a moment when altogether different intellectual attributes should be cast into the scale."[15]

The condition of the Unionist party when Selborne re-

---

12. See the comment on St. Aldwyn's speech of Aug. 9 in note 9 above. For use of the term "Selborne & Co.," see Lord Monteagle to Lord Cromer, July 31. Cromer papers, PRO FO 633/34/3079, fos. 41–2. *Crawford papers*, 208–17.

13. *Memoirs*, ii, 454.

14. Ibid., 455.

15. Ibid.

turned to England also explains his rapid rise to a position of great influence. Its members, demoralized by repeated electoral defeats, displayed, he related, "a want of faith, a vacillation, an opportunism." The rot was due to Peel and Wellington, who had taught the party to abandon its cherished beliefs and conform to its adversaries' notions. Selborne had only contempt for what he termed "sheer opportunism in fact."[16] Given the party's state, a strong-minded leader with a penchant for decisive action, who had thought through his goals, might well shape party policy, his effectiveness the greater if he was motivated by principle and the conviction that his course was right. This was Selborne. In harking back to Peel and Wellington as the source of his party's ills, he could have been referring to their rejection of agricultural protection but also to their hostility towards the referendal theory. With these qualities and outlook, Selborne would have seen a surrender policy in 1911 as one of sheer opportunism, to be resisted to the very end.

The same value judgments appear in the comment of his sister-in-law, Lady Gwendolen. Like her father and the Cecils generally, she found an important place in politics for principle:

> My real reason for hoping that the h. of lords will fight it out to the end [she wrote] is that on large and fundamental issues it is always right to do so...I expect always reasons of expediency when the crisis comes, for surrendering instead of resisting–but I don't think you will find a case in history where it has succeeded, though it has often been tried.[17]

Here is a key element in the diehard revolt that ought not to be overlooked.

To be principled in politics does not ensure wisdom in political action, and the diehard policy is usually thought of as disruptive and misguided. Yet the Unionists as a party were more realistic than the Liberals in interpreting the constitutional changes since 1867; and so, too, were the diehards. Drawn from the party's progressive wing, they were interested in social and economic reform, experienced in politics, and above all con-

---

16. Selborne to Andrew Bonar Law, Dec. 19, 1912, *The crisis of British Unionism*, ed. Boyce, 93–4.

17. Lady Gwendolen to Lady Selborne, Jan. 6, Hatfield House, GWE. See also note 52, in chap. 5.

vinced that their actions rested on the bedrock of principle. Jem Salisbury, as committed a diehard as Selborne, declared on one occasion: "Sincerity indeed is everything in politics and not only sincerity of the heart but sincerity which will shine before men."[18] Nor should the constitutional objectives of these leaders be dismissed out of hand. Selborne and Salisbury believed wholeheartedly in the lords' referendal function and its role in maintaining an element of balance in the constitution. These objectives and their personal qualities put in doubt the unqualified condemnation of the diehards often present in historical accounts though this has begun to change.[19]

Curzon has had a much better press. He is usually seen as the very personification of wisdom and moderation among Unionist leaders at this time, though Balcarres's portrayal suggests that here, too, revisionism is in order. In a delineation of the political scene on July 31 Balcarres wrote of the Selborne-Curzon rivalry as "*a personal embittered fight* between two determined and somewhat jealous statesmen." Both were proconsuls of convinced toryism, Selborne "senior qua cabinet minister and knight of the garter, Curzon more pre-eminent as an ex-viceroy and popular figure." As for their personal traits, Selborne was "persistent, obstinate, and full of common sense"; Curzon, "brilliant, witty, paradoxical, and not wholly devoid of cunning." Each was "out for blood" and "determined to win," but Selborne would be "content to secure his object by the creation of peers." Curzon on the other hand would "seldom forget and never forgive the smallest triumph of his adversary, even though it be limited to the ennoblement of one single solitary Radical snob."[20]

This description of Curzon accords with the account in Sandars' diary. When the latter met him on the street a few days earlier, Curzon had exclaimed excitedly that "he had got 260

---

18. Salisbury to Selborne, Sept. 12, MS Selborne 6, fos. 116v.–7.

19. See for example the influential George Dangerfield, *The strange death of Liberal England 1910–1914* (1935, repr. Capricorn Books, New York, 1961), chap. 3. Fanning "'Rats' versus 'Ditchers,' " 193–210. In recent years revisionism has set in. Gregory Philipps, *The diehards: aristocratic society and politics in Edwardian England* (1979). Michael Brock, "The strange death of Liberal England," *Albion: a quarterly journal concerned with British studies*, 17.4 (winter, 1985), 409–23.

20. *Crawford papers*, 206. See also Balcarres' appraisal of Curzon in 1906 and 1921. Ibid., 93, 414.

peers to follow Lord Lansdowne, that the dinner the previous evening [honoring Halsbury with Selborne in the chair] had been a failure, and that there would not be 50 peers to follow Lord Halsbury." Sandars attributed this state of mind to Curzon: "His exultation was great, and his language only appropriate to the defeat of a political opponent."[21] Not, he might have added, to the defeat of fellow members of the shadow cabinet. So far had matters come since the referendum penetrated to the center of Unionist politics.

Although little is known about Curzon's speech at Lansdowne House, he was certainly hostile in the summer of 1911 towards the creation of even a single peer. His dislike of diehard policy, which owed much to this attitude, was fully displayed in his later castigation of its leaders' resistance to the Parliament Bill as "unstatesmanlike, ill-considered, unpatriotic & unwise." Professing never to have seen two sides to the matter, he considered that events in the next two years demonstrated "how foolish & misguided the policy of the diehards would have been." He had responded, he stated, by organizing the hedgers shortly after the Lansdowne House meeting, the direction falling to a committee composed of the duke of Devonshire, Lord Midleton (known as Curzon's henchman), Lord Dunmore, Lord Hindlip, and Curzon himself. Its members met daily at his residence for a fortnight with Lansdowne in attendance. According to Curzon, the policy of the hedgers was to abstain in the final division, and he denied that they had in any way trafficked with the Unionist peers who went into the government lobby. Guided by conscience, the latter had voted in unexpectedly large numbers to prevent the lords from being swamped and the constitution converted into an object of ridicule.[22]

Despite his vehemence in denouncing diehard policy, Curzon, as is well-known, was himself a diehard early in the parliamentary crisis. At least twice after the December general election in 1910 he expressed willingness to die in the ditch before yielding to the threat of a large peerage creation. He did this at a

21. Balfour papers, B.L. MS 49767, fo. 221.

22. Ibid., fo. 213. Curzon, "Correspondence on the Parliament Bill and the crisis of 1911," MSS EUR F 112/89, fos. 2–3v.

private luncheon of Unionist candidates and MPs and again at Hatfield House before the duke of Portland, Lord Derby, Hugh Cecil, and Lord William Ormesby-Gore. Nor was this the first or last time that Curzon changed sides, with marked advantage to his political career. Some historians have commented harshly on this aspect of his character. One of them referred to Curzon as the ditcher renegade, and to A.J.P. Taylor he was "one of nature's rats." Taylor quoted approvingly Lord Beaverbrook's caustic characterization of Curzon as "a political jumping jack." Nor did he escape contemporary censure. Ormesby-Gore, a Unionist MP with ties to Smith and Wyndham, memorialized the Hatfield House scene for Willoughby in a 1913 memorandum, its preparation at this late date pointing to a residual diehard resentment at Curzon's apostasy.[23]

As earlier noted, the more usual approach is to depict Curzon as an innately moderate leader who unlike the purblind diehards read the handwriting on the wall in 1911 and moved promptly to take preventative action. The author of the sketch of Curzon in the *D.N.B* was representative in writing: "When he realized...that the Liberal government was in deadly earnest, he had the wisdom to retreat, and it was Curzon's sensible advice which largely decided the debate of August 8–10...and secured for the Liberal government a bare majority in support of its proposals." But whatever Curzon's praiseworthy qualities, the reasons why he took a vigorous anti-diehard policy in 1911 were more complicated than this description allows. To see this, it is necessary to note, first of all, his preoccupation with securing a permanent seat in the lords. Ever since his return from India in 1905, he had sedulously though unsuccessfully sought a hereditary peerage of the United Kingdom, only to have it elude him. Edward VII was willing to gratify his wish, but not Balfour or Campbell-Bannerman.

Curzon's prospects brightened in 1911. At a critical stage in passing the Parliament Bill, the new king, George V, was receptive. But it should be stated that some months before this stage

---

23. *The political papers of the 19th Lord Willoughby de Broke, 1907–1929*, WB/6/13. *National Review*, 58, p. 20. Jenkins, *Mr. Balfour's poodle*, 215. Dangerfield, *The strange death of Liberal England*, 64. Taylor, *English history, 1914–1945* (Oxford, 1965), 204.

was reached the move to give Curzon the kind of peerage that he desired was underway. In March of that year, at a time when Asquith believed that the Parliament Bill would pass without a crisis, Curzon's name was on the coronation honors list that would be made public in the following November. And Curzon was well aware, months ahead of time, that he was to be the recipient of an earldom. In a letter of June 25, Sir Arthur Bigge (Lord Stamfordham)–with Lord Knollys private secretary to George V–wrote in response to a letter from Curzon of having conveyed the Unionist leader's thanks to the King. According to Bigge, George V wanted to assure Curzon that it had given him great pleasure to confer an earldom upon Curzon; and Bigge added his own congratulations.[24]

The presence of this letter in the Curzon collection at the India Office attests the recipient's pleasure at its contents. Nor did Curzon's correspondence with the court now slacken. Another letter from Bigge, equally timely, arrived on July 24, three days after the shadow cabinet's breakup. A letter that day from Curzon to *The Times* had explained his policy to a wide circle of readers, and it was apparent that George V liked the letter and wanted Curzon to pursue the policy expressed in it. The King had read Curzon's "admirable" letter, Bigge wrote, with "the greatest interest and satisfaction"; and he thanked Curzon for placing before the public a review of the situation that was both wise and dispassionate. Further, the King hoped, so Bigge stated, that Curzon's position and influence in the opposition, along with the arguments in his letter to *The Times*, would induce some advocates of forcing a peerage creation to follow Curzon's lead. There is a notation on the letter, presumably written by George V, that reads: "*private* very satisfactory 24 July 1911." Finally, on the night of August 10, when the lords accepted the Parliament Bill without a peerage creation, a third letter from Bigge reached Curzon. This one expressed George V's deep gratitude for Curzon's very valuable service in saving the situation.[25]

---

24. "Curzon," *Dictionary of national biography*, Bigge to Curzon, June 25, Curzon papers, MSS Eur F 112/18, fos. 5–6.

25. Stamfordham to Curzon, July 24, MSS Eur F 112/89, fos. 10–11v. Kenneth Rose describes Curzon's long pursuit of an hereditary peerage. *Superior person*, 366–73. Rose, *The later Cecils* (New York, 1975), 82. According to Selborne, his stand on the Parliament Bill cost him George V's confidence; and he attributed the King's attitude to Knollys' persuasiveness. MS Selborne 191, fos. 184–5.

It may be assumed that Curzon's mind in this crucial period often turned to the pending earldom; and his preoccupation with the subject was clearly manifested in July when he requested the inclusion of a special remainder. Despite resistance from Asquith, who thought the King disinclined to such creations, Curzon prevailed. Two days after his letter appeared in *The Times* he learned that his request had been granted; and in the following November he was created Earl Curzon of Kedleston, Viscount Scarsdale (with reversion to his father and heirs male) and Baron Ravensdale (with reversion to his daughter and heirs male).[26]

That these negotiations affected Curzon's activity in the summer of 1911 can hardly be doubted. No one exceeded him in zeal when it came to battling the diehards in the months between Bigge's letter and the coronation ceremonies or when he sought to maintain Balfour as party leader. The prospect of the peerage creation that the diehard leadership was provoking must have galvanized Curzon still more. If the diehard revolt were not ended, the coveted title would be devalued before it was received. At least one perceptive contemporary sensed the relationship between this facet of Curzon's personality and his anti-diehard stand. This was Selborne's closest associate, George Wyndham, who traced Curzon's dislike of a peerage creation to social snobbery and even concluded that this personal trait gave rise to his campaign as a whole for the surrender policy. The biographer-historian, Max Egremont, wrote briskly: "The ex-viceroy could not bear, Wyndham thought, to see the peerage contaminated by such a glut of unsuitable parvenus, and snobbery, rather than prudence, was the motive behind his moderation."[27]

Guided by Lord Salisbury's ideological teachings, Selborne, as earlier noted, advocated altogether different tactics. He would compel a creation of 500 peers before the lords surrendered. A creation was vital to alert the nation to the silent revolution underway at Westminster where the Liberals were destroying the lords' referendal function. This was the worst possible kind of revolution. Seeing the house of lords with the same outward appearance, the nation would have a false sense of security, lulled into the mistaken belief that its liberties were intact. What

26. The pertinent materials are in the Royal Archives at Windsor Castle.

27. *The cousins*, 278.

Selborne dreaded, and Salisbury earlier, was a "sham" house of lords. At Kelso in 1884 Salisbury had warned against any proposal by which the house of lords was seemingly unchanged even as it was being reduced to inactivity and impotence. Stripped of the referendal function, and hence its legislative veto, it would be a "sham" house of lords, "a mere screen and mask for any enterprise that the [prime] minister might like to undertake." How much better for that house to be abolished than for it to bleed to death![28] To Selborne, admonitions of this kind seemed profoundly wise;[29] and in 1911, when he was confronted with the Parliament Bill, they haunted him.

Unless there was a peerage creation, affixed as a hallmark to the Parliament Bill, the Liberals would establish with impunity "single chamber government in the most dangerous form possible, because the uncontrolled autocracy of the house of commons would be partially concealed by the existence of a sham house of lords." This was the thrust of the diehard manifesto, which, it will be recalled, Selborne and Salisbury authored. The point to be stressed is that this set of ideas was longstanding with Selborne and tenaciously held through the years. As early as 1907 this language was conspicuous in a letter from Selborne to Jem Salisbury; and its contents, when compared with the diehard manifesto, established beyond doubt the intellectual relationship between Lord Salisbury's ideological pronouncements in late Victorian England and the diehard mentality of 1911. Selborne charged the Liberals with employing Campbell-Bannerman's veto plan to get rid of a second chamber while denying that this was in fact their aim. Following out Salisbury's line of argument, Selborne insisted that their new system would make a temporary majority in the commons absolutely despotic and at the same time retain a sham house of lords or second chamber so as to mislead the nation. Like Salisbury before him, Selborne thought it would be "infinitely wiser and infinitely safer...to have no second chamber at all than to have a sham one." And he then added: "You will remember how brilliantly your father put that 20 years

28. *Speeches*, ed. Lucy, 123–4, 142–3. See also Salisbury in the lords on Feb. 5, 1895, *Parl debs.*, 5th series, i, 32; Lady Gwendolen Cecil, *Salisbury*, ii, 5.

29. Selborne to Salisbury, Apr. 12, 1917. MS Selborne 6, fo. 212.

ago, with his simile of a naked precipice and a precipice with a rotten balustrade at the edge of it?"[30] That this line of thought continued to influence Selborne was apparent when four years later he used it in an article published during the crisis over the Parliament Bill. This time he had Salisbury referring to "a precipice with a sham and rotten parapet on its edge," the imagery the more striking because Salisbury, though not a timid man, was deathly afraid of heights.[31]

Little was said in diehard circles about the size of the proposed creation. Jem Salisbury, for one, assumed that it would be small,[32] but Curzon wrote as if the diehard aim were a large creation. This was Selborne's language at Lansdowne House, but the size of the creation does not figure in his later comments, and probably the question was immaterial to him so long as it was sufficient to dramatize the issue. Because the Parliament Bill was "a veiled revolution," it was "far more dangerous than a naked revolution."[33] Before the final vote of August 10 he summed up the diehard position: the peers must not die in the dark by their own hand, but in the light killed by their enemies. In taking this course they would follow their consciences. Not usually an eloquent speaker, he rose to new heights on an occasion so strongly engaging his emotions. To Leo Amery, a prominent diehard in the commons and Lord Milner's closest political ally, it was "one of the most moving speeches" that he had ever heard.[34]

When the final vote came in the lords, the diehards mustered 114 votes for the Lansdowne amendment in an amazing display of strength that trumpeted defiance of their leaders and the Liberal government. Yet, as earlier noted, the effort fell short

---

30. Selborne to Salisbury, Aug. 15, 1907, MS Selborne 5, fos. 175–6. See also MS Selborne 6, fos. 212–3; MS Selborne 1, fos. 127–8.

31. *The Unionist party and the referendum* (1911), 31. Salisbury's fear of heights is described by Lady Gwendolen Cecil in *Salisbury: the man and his policies*, ed. Blake and Cecil, 50.

32. Salisbury to Selborne, July 23, MS Selborne 6, fo. 102. *Parl. debs.*, lords, 5th series, ix, 927. Appendix to Sandars, "A diary of the events and transactions in connection with the passage of the Parliament Bill of 1911 through the house of lords."

33. Selborne to F.S. Oliver, Mar. 30, MS Selborne 74, fo. 73, Reprinted in *The crisis of British Unionism*, ed. Boyce, 56.

34. *Parl. debs.*, lords, 5th series, ix, 1072–4. See Dangerfield, *Strange death of Liberal England*, chap. 3. Amery, *My political life* (1953), i, 381.

when a third group of Unionist peers, this one led by another imperial proconsul, Lord Cromer, provided the winning margin in a vote of 131 to 114. Independently of the shadow cabinet, these peers saved the Bill.[35] The reaction from Selborne and Curzon was on lines to be expected. To Selborne, this "Judas group" consisted of "blacklegs," who had betrayed their party. To Curzon, its members were the "conscience peers."[36]

II

A major casualty of the diehard revolt was Balfour's party leadership, and once more Selborne and Curzon headed opposing sides. His going was due to three successive electoral defeats but was hastened when Selborne, working with Willoughby and Wyndham, founded the Halsbury Club. It reopened wounds created by the revolt; and though Balfour seemed to go voluntarily, he was in fact pushed. Discontent with his leadership flourished in the last days of the parliamentary crisis, and before it ended he was on his way to Bad Gastein to take the cure for what some saw as imagined health problems. Balfour was "a runaway commander,"[37] ran a caustic remark, and Robert Sanders, the Unionist whip, was as stinging when he noted that Balfour would have "to curtail his cure so as to be back in time for a golf handicap."[38] Curiously, Balfour, prior to departure, had made a serious effort to appease the diehards. On August 9 Selborne described the situation as "queer": Balcarres, with Balfour's approval, was doing everything possible "to defeat the blacklegs & to get abstainers to

35. Corinne Comstock Weston and Patricia Kelvin, "The 'Judas group'. and the Parliament Bill of 1911," *English Historical Review*, xcix (July 1984), 551–63. For a different view, see David Southern, "Lord Newton, the Conservative peers and the Parliament Act of 1911," ibid., xcvi (Oct. 1981), 834–40. Both articles are republished in *Peers, politics and power: the house of lords 1603–1911*, ed. Clyve Jones and David Lewis Jones, 519–39.

36. Weston and Kelvin, "The 'Judas group' and the Parliament Bill," 555, note 4. Selborne to Lady Selborne, Aug. 9, MS Selborne 102, fos. 24, 24v. See also MS Selborne 191, fo. 62.

37. Sir Edmund Cox to Willoughby, Aug. 22, WB/3/60.

38. *Real Old Tory politics: the political diaries of Robert Sanders, Lord Bayford, 1910–1935*, ed. John Ramsden (1984), 33.

leave Lansdowne to help" the diehards. But Lansdowne and Curzon would not "give him the least assistance."[39] Balcarres described the situation in the same terms. Following conversations with Curzon, Lansdowne, and Balfour, he wrote of Balfour's becoming a ditcher: "He pressed Lansdowne to support the duke of Norfolk [who finally voted with the diehards]. He pressed him to concentrate on home rule referendum. He advocated creation of peers up to 150." The outcome? "Lord Lansdowne would not budge. George Curzon won't let him: won't leave him."[40]

Had the change come earlier, it might have saved Balfour. Not by this time. Selborne later recapitulated the stages of his growing disillusionment. Balfour's flaw as a leader, manifested as early as 1903, was an inability to maintain party unity. During the tariff reform dispute he had alienated two men whom Selborne greatly admired, Devonshire and Chamberlain; and the Liberal landslide of 1906, which gave Liberals an overwhelming majority, had a sequel in the Parliament Act of 1911. This period, the most catastrophic of all, left the nation with single-chamber government while closing the door on an appeal to the people when there was a deadlock at Westminster. There was also the nagging doubt that Balfour was serious in constitutional matters. He was simply too philosophical, too aloof from human emotions to lead a great party successfully.[41] Selborne's patience was worn thin when he wrote to his wife during the diehard revolt: "If you want to see what a fool a philosopher can be, look at A.J.B." He added: "Besides he has behaved very badly to us."[42]

The reference was to the events of July 21 and their aftermath. At this juncture Balfour had failed to give the divided shadow cabinet a decisive lead; but worse than this, had sided with one faction against the other. Although Selborne's statements, written in 1937 without his papers at hand, are less direct,

---

39. Selborne to Lady Selborne, Aug. 9, MS Selborne 102, fos. 24–24v.

40. *Crawford papers*, 213.

41. MS Selborne 191, fo. 56. See also Fanning, "'Rats' versus 'Ditchers,'" 205. Selborne to Salisbury, Aug. 18, Hatfield House MSS 4M 70/144.

42. MS Selborne 102, fo. 21. The letter is dated July 26. In a sketch of Balfour written in 1916, Selborne wrote: "Philosophy is the worst possible training for politics." MS Selborne 80, fo. 288.

this was his reasoning when he wrote:

> ...when the struggle came over the line, which the house of lords was to take over the Parliament Act, Arthur Balfour's leadership failed again. To this day I do not know what his real opinion was. At the shadow cabinet, at which we finally ranged ourselves on different sides, he gave us no decided lead, but I certainly thought that he was against Halsbury and for Lansdowne. Nevertheless I believe the following story to be strictly accurate. The two sides set to work with all their might to raise & organize the Conservative Unionist peers, Curzon taking the lead for Lansdowne & I for Halsbury–one morning [22 July] Curzon quite by accident dropped into Balfour's house in Carlton Gardens about something or other, when just as he was leaving Balfour quite casually tossed him across a paper and said "now that you are here you may as well read this. I am going to circulate it to the shadow cabinet"–with growing horror Curzon read a memorandum in which Balfour stated that his position had been entirely misunderstood and by both parties to the dispute. Curzon saw at once that, if this paper was circulated, Lansdowne's position would be quite impossible. So he made Balfour promise to hold it up until he had seen Lansdowne. Lansdowne took the same view as Curzon & in deference to their remonstrances Balfour promised not to circulate the paper.[43]

Selborne understood that Balfour's reaction towards Curzon and Lansdowne was "one of mild & rather pained response." The account stands out in the memoirs because of its length. Very limited attention is accorded there to the diehard revolt and the days precedent to the Parliament Act; and it is the more significant because Selborne had never seen the memorandum.[44]

Balfour's biographer, Blanche Dugdale, who published Balfour's memorandum, attributes Curzon's and Lansdowne's consternation to the disclosure that Balfour was receptive to the idea of a limited creation of peers. Swamping the lords was out of the question; but the prohibition, according to Balfour, did not

---

43. MS Selborne 191, fos. 63–5. Balfour's memorandum is either given in full or discussed in a number of works, but it is uncommon to see a contemporary reaction of this dimension.

44. Ibid., fo. 65.

extend to making 50 or 100 peers. Had the memorandum been allowed to circulate, it would have undermined the hedgers, while giving the diehards what they most wanted, namely, the legitimation of their objective. Dugdale adds perceptively that its suppression was a sign and portent of a divergence between Balfour and the party, which before long convinced him to give up the party leadership.[45]

Selborne seems to have had no knowledge of an important sentence in the suppressed memorandum. According to Sandars, Balfour had written: "I need not say that I do not contemplate the possibility of any peer who believes in the wisdom of the Lansdowne amendment going into the lobby against it."[46] That is, Unionist peers ought not to vote with the Liberal government for the Parliament Bill. This statement would have been welcome to the diehards, but not to Curzon, always reluctant to foreclose any means of forestalling a peerage creation.

Balcarres also underlined the episode's high importance when he discussed Curzon's domination of Balfour and Lansdowne after the July 21 shadow cabinet. Had he not intervened, a formula might have been found to unite the party. The Parliament Bill would have passed, to be sure, but not at great cost to party unity. The desideratum was a fresh approach to the threat of a peerage creation–a *tertium quid*, as Balcarres put it. The preferred path lay somewhere between Selborne's stated willingness to force a large creation and Curzon's aversion from the most limited proposal.[47] That is, Balfour's suggestion of a limited creation of 50–100 peers or perhaps 100–200 was a viable option. Though it might be unacceptable on its merits to both sides, still it contained the seeds of a possible compromise.

Even as Balfour prepared his memorandum, Lansdowne, so Balcarres related, was burning his bridges at the Lansdowne House meeting.[48] He did this by limiting the choice before the

---

45. E. C. Dugdale, *Arthur James Balfour* (1936), ii, pp. 69–71. See also Jenkins, *Mr. Balfour's poodle*, 225–6; Akers-Douglas, *Chilston*, 355; Sandars, "A diary...of the Parliament Bill," fos. 206–7.

46. Ibid., fo. 207.

47. *Crawford papers*, 196, 197, 199–200.

48. Ibid., 199–200.

peers to a large creation or none at all, and then compounded the error by recommending the surrender policy. Why had he done this? Balcarres attributed the action to Curzon. He had learned from Lansdowne that he, too, favored a small creation and had no objection to the creation of 150–200 peers, only to one that would swamp the house of lords. Why, then, had he spoken so differently at the Lansdowne House meeting? According to Balcarres, relying on information from Jack Sandars, Lansdowne's position there was due to Curzon, and once taken could not be repudiated without an appearance of inconsistency. Combining this evidence of Curzon's influence over Lansdowne with their cooperation in suppressing Balfour's memorandum, Balcarres concluded that Curzon had prevented Lansdowne from expressing his whole mind to the peers at Lansdowne House and Balfour from sending written advice to his colleagues in the shadow cabinet.[49] No opinion more condemnatory of Balfour and Lansdowne was possible from the diehard standpoint; and given Balcarres' political sympathies, expressed on July 21, it may be supposed that he was repeating the consensus in that quarter of the party. The conclusion is reinforced by Selborne's vivid recollection of the aborted Balfour memorandum.

His detailed account of a memorandum that he had never seen, written long after the episode, certainly suggests that in his eyes the suppression was a grievous wrong. The lesson was that his personal policy had no future so long as Curzon's domination of Balfour and Lansdowne persisted. Either Curzon's influence over party policy was circumscribed or Selborne must abandon all hope of replacing the Parliament Act with the referendum and a reformed house of lords when the Unionists were returned to office. This was the alternative before him. After all, how could Balfour and Lansdowne be expected to carry out such a policy after their abject submission to Curzon in the summer of 1911?

And there was, of course, Curzon's inveterate hostility towards the referendum, which Selborne had experienced at first hand. That his own zeal for the referendum remained undiminished despite the August setback appears from his letter to Willoughby a few hours after the diehard defeat. The alacrity with

49. Ibid.

which he wrote and the conspicuous place allotted to the referendum in a very brief letter attest once more the adamantine purpose that had dominated his political conduct since South African days. Here is the letter:

20 Arlington St. S.W.
My dear Willoughby:

Before I go to bed let me express my great admiration of the way you & Lovat have done your work. May it always be my fortune to have you as a colleague to fight with. I ask for nothing better.

There is one important matter on which we do not see eye to eye at the present, and that is the referendum. I should not like you to misunderstand my position on it and therefore I ask you as a favour to read the article I sent you in the Oxford & Cambridge magazine.

as ever,
Selborne[50]

Selborne was author of this article, which was published on July 12, and Willoughby had already read it. Two days after receiving Selborne's letter, he wrote to him, declaring: "I will study your referendum pamphlet again, and try to get to you as near as I can." But clearly he had no zest for the referendum. "If we determine on an elected house of lords might not this h of l have the same powers as the h of l has always had?" he wondered. He would confine the referendum to deadlocks otherwise calling for a peerage creation; and he wrote: "I rather dread a free use of it, as leading to the initiative, etc."[51]

Selborne, however, had no qualms. He would forge ahead with the referendum whenever possible. Convinced that its adoption was indispensable to Unionist success, he continued to devote formidable energies to its promotion. His chosen vehicle was the Halsbury Club. Said to possess a "natural genius for organization based on sturdy common sense,"[52] he controlled the club's

50. Selborne to Willoughby, Aug. 10, WB/2/113. The article was published in July 1911.

51. MS Selborne 74, fos. 177–177v. See also Phillips, "Lord Willoughby and the politics of Radical Toryism," 209.

52. *Crawford papers*, 179. Balcarres wrote: "Selborne is the least attractive great man I ever met. I think he really is a great man, but his natural genius for organization based upon sturdy common sense, has obliterated any vestige of imagination, if such ever existed." According to Balcarres, Chamberlain stated that "W. [Willie] Selborne is the moving spirit" in the club. Ibid., 234.

agenda and set out to develop the machinery required to carry it out. The referendum was foremost in his mind when he wrote to Halsbury on October 2 about an organizational meeting that the latter could not attend. "The central work we have set ourselves," Selborne explained, "is to make up our minds how the constitution should be reconstructed when the radicals have done destroying it and to educate our party to make that its first work." But if the aim of the Halsbury Club in his view was to advance the referendum, there was an important corollary. Its members must stick together and do whatever they could "to infuse a more fighting spirit into the party."[53]

Choosing a name for the club was difficult; before settling on the Halsbury Club, the diehards canvassed other possibilities: the Phoenix, Defenders, Forwards, and the Unionist No-Surrender Club. The choice was, moreover, a misnomer if it led to the presumption that Halsbury was an active member. So minor was his role, in fact, that Selborne entertained seriously the idea of not inviting him to the organizational meeting. In his opinion Halsbury was much too conservative about the house of lords, for which Selborne was now prepared to prescribe radical surgery.[54] It was also well-known that the latter had great influence inside the Halsbury Club. Witness the line of enquiry pursued by Sir Arthur Steel-Maitland, head of the newly created office of chairman of the party organization. He had learned from Halsbury that the club was not meant to challenge the party leadership, but he also informed Balcarres that "from quite independent sources" he had corroborated that "Lord Selborne explicitly stated the same to his own friends."[55]

Other contemporaries had a different reading. Walter Long reported being told that the Club's founders "desired to destroy the existing leadership...and put their own people in."[56]

---

53. Selborne to Halsbury, Oct. 2, B.L. Halsbury papers, Add. MS 56374, fos. 196–7v.

54. Selborne to Willoughby, Aug. 18, WB/3/46, no pagination. Ibid., Aug. 26, WB/3/63, fo. 1. Selborne to Wyndham, Aug. 22, MS Selborne 74, fos. 192–3. Wyndham to Selborne, Aug. 23, MS Selborne 74, fo. 199. Wyndham urged that Halsbury be invited to participate. MS Selborne 74, fo. 209 (Oct. 7). See also Selborne to Salisbury, Oct. 18, Hatfield House MSS 4M/71/64.

55. Steel-Maitland to Balfour, Oct. 17, B.L. Add. MS 49861, fo. 351v. Fanning, "'Rats' versus 'Ditchers,' " 209, note 46.

56. Peter Fraser, "The Unionist debacle of 1911 and Balfour's retirement," *Journal of Modern History*, 35 (1936), 362–3.

He provided the names in a letter to G. E. Buckle, editor of *The Times*: they were Chamberlain and Selborne.[57] The modern historian Ronan Fanning was more impersonal when he wrote of the club's perpetuating "the spirit of the diehard revolt" and institutionalizing "the disaffection with the party leadership for long enough to serve as the catalyst which triggered Balfour's resignation."[58]

This is to stop short of alleging an outright attack on the Unionist leadership, but there were others whose views resembled Long's. Among them, surprisingly in light of his long friendship with Selborne, was Jem Salisbury, an insider who had participated in the organizational planning. Resigning suddenly on October 14, two days after the formal launching of the club, he attributed his action to the choice of name: it must "necessarily reawaken the friction of the summer, and be mortifying" to their friends who had differed from them. Addressing the leadership question, he continued: "Above all, to mortify the leaders whom we continue to acknowledge is for me indefensible." What was needed was "vigor without but...conciliation within." "To secure this vigor," the Halsbury Club "must be the leaven of the party but not its blister." Salisbury doubted, however, that other members felt as strongly this way. He referred also to sharing counsels and fighting battles at Lansdowne's side–to him unforgettable experiences.[59] Selborne's reply was reproachful. The club had responded to Salisbury's letter with "sorrow and surprise." Its members did not consider the name a "blister"; they thought it as little provocative as possible. And Selborne continued with what seems to be a reference to Salisbury's point about the leadership:

> You know my view and intention are the view and intention of those who will have the control of the Club...Your presence among us would go very far to help me to maintain that line, whereas your separation from us must inevitably, as Austen

---

57. Sir Charles Petrie, *Walter Long and his times* (1936), 169. The letter is dated Oct. 23.

58. "'Rats' versus 'Ditchers,' " 200. See also the *Crawford papers*, 231. Balcarres wrote on Oct. 15: "The formation of the Halsbury Club to record and consecrate the defiance of his leadership is one episode which cannot be ignored. Members of this Club differ on all constructive questions, e.g. tariff reform, second chamber, etc. They are united in disapproval of their leader's advice."

59. Salisbury to Selborne, Oct. 14, Hatfield House MSS 4M/71/54–55.

said, tend to give that very air to the Club which we wish most to avoid.[60]

But Salisbury was not needed to keep the club operative though Selborne was; and even if the latter had no intention of launching a frontal assault on Balfour and Lansdowne, still that impression would inevitably be conveyed if he undertook to keep party policy under his control and out of Curzon's reach.

Pertinent testimony on this point was forthcoming from Chamberlain, who recounted a conversation with Wyndham on the night of October 11, just before the Halsbury Club was formally launched. Wyndham, who had come to town at Selborne's request, reported that, after communicating with Milner, Carson, Smith, Amery, Willoughby, and others, he and Selborne had decided that the diehards should act in concert to maintain a proper influence in the party and "prevent the leaders being stampeded as they were last August by Curzon." Their aim was a diehard club, the name still to be determined, which would not be hostile to the party organization or Balfour and Lansdowne and would have a "forward policy." This consisted of abandoning Lansdowne's plan for reforming the lords and the Albert Hall pledge while sponsoring an elected second chamber. Diehards like Willoughby and Northumberland, Wyndham noted, also preferred to trust their fate at this time to the electors rather than rely "on a nomination scheme that Curzon could manipulate." After Wyndham and Selborne expressed interest in a series of reforms, Chamberlain had agreed to join them but only with an insistence that care be exercised to prevent their movement from appearing hostile to either Balfour or Lansdowne. It was Chamberlain who asked the key question: What would happen if Lansdowne retired? Could Selborne accept Curzon as the Unionist leader in the lords? Or Selborne, Curzon?[61]

Then there were Selborne's letters of late August to Willoughby and Wyndham. Without mentioning Curzon, these letters, combined with what Wyndham told Chamberlain on October 11, make it possible to insist that Selborne was dead set

---

60. Selborne to Salisbury, Oct. 18, Hatfield House MSS 4M/71/64. See also Selborne to Salisbury, Oct. 19. Ibid., 4M/71/68, recording Halsbury's distress at Salisbury's action. Halsbury also wrote to Salisbury, Oct. 18, ibid. 4M/71/64–6.

61. Chamberlain, *Politics from inside*, 358–9, 361.

on taking control of party policy away from Curzon. They must work together, Selborne exhorted, to heal the party's wounds and avoid the schism that a direct attack on the leadership might bring. Eschewing the idea of founding a new party after his earlier painful experience with Liberal Unionism, he preferred to capture "the party & Unionist machine lock, stock & barrel." He wanted to establish and promote a regular policy and plan of his own before the National Union assembled on November 15 in Leeds. Hence the need for a meeting for organizational purposes in late September, later changed to October 2. It was attended by such kindred spirits as Salisbury, Hugh and Robert Cecil, Chamberlain, Captain Ernest Pretyman, Sir Edward Carson, Lovat, Mayo, Smith, and Wyndham. He would exclude Halsbury, who seemed to him by this time too conservative. The group was divided on only one formidable point: the Cecils' devotion to free trade. On all else its members were agreed.[62]

A letter of August 22 enlarged on Selborne's strategy when he wrote: "Let us agree if we can on a common policy in respect to all important matters which now hold the field, and let us speak with one voice on the platform and in the councils of the party, and thus make our views prevail within the party." This was "the same thing as capturing the party and the party machine." He would have the front bench men of both sides of the party attend their first meeting. The theme of party unity echoed through another letter, this one to Willoughby on September 12. "My diagnosis of the position is that the party in an enormous majority agree with us," wrote Selborne, "and that, unless we play our cards very badly, *we can make our views predominate in the party, and guide the policy of the party.*" But they would spoil their game if they did anything to lead the average conservative to think that they were either spiteful towards the "abstainers" or careless about the party's unity.[63]

Hence his disapproval of a resolution that Leo Maxse, engaged in an all-out effort to oust Balfour as leader, had put down for debate at the forthcoming National Union meeting. Commending the diehard action of the summer, the resolution was

---

62. Selborne to Willoughby, Aug. 18, WB/3/46, no pagination.

63. MS Selborne 74, fos. 191–2. Selborne to Willoughby, Sept. 12, WB/3/69, fo. 2.

intended to heighten the already strong disaffection towards Balfour in the constituencies. Selborne condemned the tactic as both divisive and self-defeating. Concerned to keep the party as strong as possible so as to carry out his policy, he was suspicious of any move tending to weaken it and feared that Maxse's resolution would have "serious results in that direction."[64]

Selborne explained to Willoughby on August 26 how he would proceed with regard to Balfour. Their duty was clear, but "extremely delicate steering" was required because Balfour was loved by those in the party who had personal contact with him. Yet the vast majority of the party agreed with them. At the same time the party despised intrigue so it was necessary to proceed in a straightforward way. Selborne then turned to the forthcoming National Union Conference at Leeds. If he were there, he would attend the meeting and go on the platform. This was the guiding rule. A party member was obliged "to show all respect to the official leaders"; but this did not mean that they were free of criticism if they were leading in the wrong way or that one voted with them if their policies were wrong. Selborne expected Balfour to act "very right" at the National Union Conference so there was no logical reason for refusing to join him on the platform.[65] This, then, was Selborne's chosen course; and though it fell short of an overt attack on Balfour's leadership, the distance was minimal.

For Selborne, though hardly an imaginative man, was too politically experienced not to recognize how deeply the diehard revolt had humiliated Balfour; and he could hardly have expected Balfour's acquiescence as the Halsbury Club revived bitter memories of the summer and its very existence eroded his authority. Taking a high view of his position in the shadow cabinet and on one occasion terming it analogous to the prime minister's in the cabinet,[66] Balfour must have found the Halsbury Club intolerable; and if Selborne did not grasp this, others did.

---

64. Ibid.

65. WB/3/63, fos. 3–4.

66. Balfour to Sir William Anson, Sept. 18, B.L. Add. MS 49861, fos. 324–5. Jack Sandars, in "A note on the events leading to Mr. Balfour's resignation," B.L. Add. MS 49767, fo. 281 reported that Selborne asked Balfour to call a shadow cabinet on the question of the payment of members and Balfour replied that he did "not mean to have another shadow cabinet."

Lady Moyra Cavendish, writing on October 17 to Hugh Cecil from Devonshire House, a Curzon stronghold, termed Cecil a "wild revolutionary," who with his friends dwelt on their leaders' deficiencies rather than addressing the party's condition. "I think that your Halsbury Club," she wrote, "will have mortally wounded both Lord Lansdowne & Mr Balfour." They were all acting quite badly–the situation had changed since the division; and her letter closed with the germane query: "Why was not Lord Salisbury with you?"[67] Curzon's response was swift. A week later Balfour's and Lansdowne's supporters of July 21 assembled at Devonshire House with St. Aldwyn in the chair. Curzon took the lead in discussing "the situation as accentuated by the Halsbury Club" and the best means of keeping Balfour.[68]

In sum, Selborne and his friends founded the Halsbury Club without any concern for Balfour. Whatever his professions of affection, Selborne had no sympathy for Balfour the party leader. His paramount concern was to keep the referendum at the center of party policy; and whether Balfour stayed on was irrelevant when compared with the vastly more important goal of stabilizing the government at Westminster and in the empire. To achieve his goal, he must control party policy lest it go by default to Curzon. Hence Selborne's willingness to undertake "extremely delicate steering" that might or might not work. Steering was the more delicate because of the possibility that if Balfour resigned the party leadership, his successor could be Curzon. That this consideration was before Selborne appears from his letter of September 4 to Chamberlain, in which he mentioned without emotion that Balfour might go at any time and added that they had no guarantee as to who might endeavor to take his place. A postscript had this sentence: "I hear that George Curzon is still very busy."[69]

Balfour's resignation came less than a month after the Halsbury Club met for the first time. His thoughts had run intermittently in this direction ever since the shadow cabinet's vote of July 21 publicly revealed the schism in the Unionist front bench.

---

67. Lady Moyra Cavendish to Hugh Cecil, Oct. 17, Hatfield House MSS Qui 14/184.

68. Fraser, "The Unionist debacle of 1911," 363. *Crawford papers*, 235–6, 237.

69. MS Selborne 79, fo. 73. *The crisis of British Unionism*, ed. Boyce, 168.

Deeply affronted by the manner in which the dissentients flouted his authority, he was ill-prepared for the renewed challenge that the club represented. Before his resignation was announced, Chamberlain offered to secure a resolution of confidence in the leadership from the Halsbury Club. He went armed with the information that Balfour was going, and empowered to communicate this to Selborne, who was chairing the meeting. So great was the resistance that at one point he and Halsbury threatened resignation unless the resolution was approved. Balcarres left this account on November 6: "This resolution took two hours, which shows the troubled conditions of their minds. Doubtless they kept saying *cui bono*, and asked what impression such an announcement would make upon their supporters." And in the same note he wrote of Balfour: "He is more severe on the ditchers than before."[70]

After the resignation a leading member of the Halsbury Club came to see Balfour in a scene embarrassing to both. It was Selborne. Jack Sandars relates what occurred:

> After luncheon Selborne came to see Mr. Balfour, Mr. Balfour told me that the interview was brief, embarrassing and purposeless. Selborne, when he entered the room, seemed wholly at a loss what to say. He expressed his regret at the resignation, but he was unable to excuse himself for any part that he taken during recent months. Mr. Balfour said to me that he found he was quite unable to help Selborne out with any expressions appropriate to the occasion, and the interview ended with Selborne saying that the whole difficulty of the situation had been brought about by the iniquity of Lord Knollys.[71]

Despite the effort to divorce the resignation from the diehard revolt, these were clearly intertwined. There is a letter in the Curzon papers from Midleton to Curzon, dated October 15, describing Balfour as very angry with the diehards and, notably, with his diehard relatives; and a week later Balcarres informed Chamberlain that Balfour's fury was directed at Selborne in particular. Discussing his approaching resignation Balfour himself

---

70. *Crawford papers*, 240.

71. Jack Sandars, "Mr Balfour's resignation," B.L. Add. MS 49767, fo. 294. Cp. the account in Dugdale, *Arthur James Balfour*, ii, 89. See note 25 above for Selborne's attitude towards Knollys.

stated that he was leaving his post because of the "ditcher row, which was caused by his nearest relatives and oldest friends." The episode had affected him more keenly than anything else in his entire political career, and he resented it more.[72] Balfour's vulnerability can be sensed in a comment to Chamberlain in the first week of the diehard revolt. He said at this time that he allowed no one in his presence to speak of disloyalty in relationship to old and tried friends like Chamberlain, Selborne, Jem Salisbury, and George Wyndham.[73]

III

What then is known about the Halsbury Club? Of primary interest is its constitution, which was crafted to ensure Selborne's hegemony and enable him to continue promoting the referendum. Provision was made for a president (the nominal head), a chairman of the executive committee (Selborne's command post), and a secretary-treasurer (Willoughby). The executive committee, packed with Selborne's friends, was to establish sub-committees for the study of such topics as the constitution and defense; Selborne was to convene the first, Wyndham the second. The arrangements were to some less than satisfactory. An uneasy duke of Northumberland perceived in the form of the club a cloak for Selborne's domination; and noting that there was to be a constitution sub-committee, of which Selborne was a member, he remarked sarcastically, "of course, in all probability the chairman." This would tie the club to the referendum. "He is strongly in favour of the referendum," wrote Northumberland, "and I, for one, am by no means converted to it, though I am still open to conviction."[74]

---

72. Chamberlain, *Politics from inside*, 362. *Crawford papers*, 228, 229. St. Aldwyn to Curzon, Oct. 19. MSS Eur F 112/18.

73. Balfour to Chamberlain, July 27 [?], Chamberlain, *Politics from inside*, 350–1.

74. The executive committee membership is in MS Selborne 75, fo. 4 It includes Amery, Waldorf Astor, Carson, Hugh Cecil, Robert Cecil, Chamberlain, Dr. S. Lloyd, Lovat, Milner, Ormsby-Gore, Pretyman, Smith, Earl Winterton, and Wyndham. See also Northumberland to Willoughby, Oct. 9, WB/3/76; to Halsbury, Oct. 9, B.L. Add. MS 56374, viii, 201–201v. Willoughby to Robert Cecil, Nov. 30, B.L. Add. MS 51085, fos. 31–2.

Selborne did chair the sub-committee, which had a fluid membership, including at one time or another Robert Cecil, two MPs–J. F. Hope and M. Mackinder–Halsbury, Northumberland, Plymouth, and Willoughby. A report in 1912 reveals that numerous meetings, from which the sub-committee borrowed ideas, were held to discuss plans for a second chamber. Unable to agree on any of them, its members prepared three plans, based respectively on direct, indirect, and no election. In its revision the executive committee retained only the first and last plans; but Selborne wrote later of its favoring the elective principle. That a substantial amount of work went into the report appears from its contents and from Lansdowne's comment some years later that he had found it very valuable.[75]

Selborne's primary interest was in the second chamber's powers; and his sub-committee, as Northumberland had foreseen, carved out a role for the referendum. It was by no means, however, of the dimensions that Selborne wanted. The referendum would be applied to deadlocks between the houses, and either house, subject to certain conditions, could send a disputed measure to the people. Yet its members were cool to the idea of a compulsory referendum when the houses were agreed. This arrangement could be applied only to statutes embodying the sub-committee's scheme, and the provisions to this effect did not survive the executive committee's scrutiny.[76]

During the executive committee's work, a memorandum from Hugh Cecil to Selborne on July 31 revealed that even within this select group the referendum was unacceptable without substantial safeguards. Cecil had concluded that further restrictions were imperative. To satisfy Unionist opinion, the usage of the referendum should be infrequent and the questions asked must be neither complicated nor difficult. The referendum's critics would have a field day if anything but the simplest question were deemed subject to the referendum.[77] The sub-committee's report, as revised by the executive committee, reflected Cecil's critique,

---

75. Selborne to Salisbury, Apr. 12, 1917, MS Selborne 6, fo. 211. Lansdowne to Selborne, Aug. 21, 1917, MS Selborne 85, fos. 4–4v.

76. MS Selborne 75, fos. 55, 68–71.

77. Cecil to Selborne, July 31, 1912, MS Selborne 76, fos. 192–203. See especially fos. 197–200.

noticeably in a proposal for an elaborate system of free conferences that would make referendums rare.[78] On November 25 Selborne sent the sub-committee's revised report to Hugh Cecil, asking that it be kept completely confidential. Extraordinary precautions were to be taken to ensure secrecy. The report itself would be confined to the executive committee and the sub-committee. Only a general report would circulate to the membership, and Selborne would fill in the details orally (viva voce) when the club met on December 5.[79]

Although the Halsbury Club, in existence as late as June 29, 1914, was a prime means of keeping the referendum alive, its members' enthusiasm for Selborne's pet project was no more than lukewarm. Yet his interest never flagged. He urged its use in solving the Ulster problem and at one time even enlisted Curzon's support. In his memoirs he claimed that the whole Unionist party by 1914 was "keen and solid for greatly amending the Parliament Act & for reforming the house of lords" [80] and this statement was borne out when its leaders entered the wartime coalitions. They exacted pledges from Asquith and Lloyd George to fulfill the promise in the preamble of the Parliament Act to reform the house of lords, terminology encompassing both its powers and its composition. Though Selborne may have anticipated that in this environment, support for the referendum would grow, in fact, it did not.

Asquith characterized the pledge as a debt of honor but went no further than this, and it was the wartime coalition cabinet headed by Lloyd George that carried out the wartime pledges. He was responsible for the Bryce Conference on second-chamber reform (1917–8) and the appointment of a cabinet committee (1921–2) to study and report on the question. The cabinet committee, whose discussions reflected the Bryce Conference's influence, was known as the House of Lords Reform Committee: and its report, in the form of a series of resolutions, was referred to as C.P. 4039. Curzon, the Lloyd George Coalition president of the house of lords, was chairman of the cabinet committee; and

---

78. MS Selborne 75, fos. 142–5, 156.

79. Selborne to Cecil, Nov. 25, 1912. MS Selborne 74, fo. 220.

80. MS Selborne 191, fo. 65. Patricia Jalland, *The Liberals and Ireland: The Ulster question in British politics to 1914* (Brighton, Sussex, 1980), 204–5. Bonar Law Papers, 31/2/50.

when he became ill his place was taken by another Conservative, Lord Birkenhead (formerly F. E. Smith), Lloyd George's lord chancellor and ally, whose attitude towards reforming the house of lords is suggested by the candid statement that in his view the battle over the Parliament Act had already been fought and lost. Selborne and his friends seemed to him extremist on the question.[81]

Neither the Bryce Conference nor the cabinet committee led to reform of the house of lords, and both rejected categorically the referendum as a way to end deadlocks. A member of the Bryce Conference but not the cabinet committee, Selborne had no real influence on their conclusions, but members of both groups were well aware of his powerful interest in their proceedings. The Liberal chairman of the Conference, the distinguished constitutional scholar, Lord Bryce, collaborated with Lord Crewe, who as Liberal leader in the lords was one of the main authors of the Parliament Act; and together they framed paragraph 55 of the Bryce Report,[82] which supplied the majority's reasons for rejecting the referendum:

> The majority of the Conference...did not approve this plan on the ground (among others) that the use of the referendum once introduced could not be confined to the cases for which it was in this instance proposed, that it might tend to lower the authority and dignity of parliament, and that it was unsuited to the conditions of a large country, and especially of the United Kingdom, for different parts of which different legislation is sometimes required.[83]

The Report noted, however, that some members, presumably Lansdowne, Hugh Cecil, Selborne, and Balfour of Burleigh were inclined to adopt the referendum as the best way of solving deadlocks.[84] As for Bryce himself, he had no use for it. He would

---

81. MS Fisher 80, fo. 11.

82. Bryce to Crewe, Feb. 27, Apr. 7, Apr. 9, 1918. Crewe-Bryce correspondence, Crewe papers, Box C/13/1918. See also ibid., Box P/1/(8). I am grateful to Mary Duchess of Roxburge for permission to use the Crewe papers, which are in the Cambridge University Library. See also H.A.L. Fisher, *James Bryce, Viscount Bryce of Dechmont, O.M. 1838–1922*, 2 vols. (1927), ii, 86. Weston, "The Liberal leadership and the lords' veto, 1907-1910",514, note 13. For Selborne's view of Curzon about the time that the cabinet committee was appointed, see *The crisis of British Unionism*, ed. Boyce, 226–7.

83. *Conference on the reform of the second chamber* (1918), Cd.9038, 16.

84. Ibid.

mention it as little as possible in his Report lest even a brief reference arouse its supporters. To him it was a potential engine for democratic change, and he thought it strange that Conservatives like Hugh Cecil did not realize that this was the case.[85]

The cabinet committee followed the Bryce Conference's lead in rejecting the referendum and even based its action on paragraph 55 of the Bryce Report.[86] It also borrowed from the Report a proposal regarding the composition of the house of lords. But, according to P. A. Bromhead, an authority on this subject, the cabinet committee took an independent path in dealing with the lords' powers. Whereas the Bryce Conference considered the essential principle of the Parliament Act unsuitable as a permanent solution to the problem of differences between the houses, the cabinet committee would let stand the Act's suspensory veto.[87]

It can be seen in retrospect that the cabinet committee's decision in 1922 was epochal in the history of the house of lords. Should the Unionists or Conservatives, as they were now called, be returned to power, there would be no attempt to restore the lords' referendal function on which an independent legislative veto rested, contrary to Lansdowne's 1911 pledge at Lansdowne House. Since the cabinet committee was bipartisan, with a Conservative chairman, it is apparent that by 1922 both parties were committed to the idea that the Parliament Act was permanent.

This study of the referendal theory terminates, therefore, with a discussion of the proceedings in the cabinet committee that produced this result. Lloyd George was prime minister at the time, and the necessary first step is to consider his motivation in taking up once more the thorny subject of the lords' reform. Head of a wartime coalition rising out of a coup (December 1916) that toppled Asquith, he had emerged in the closing years of the war as architect of the allied victory over Germany. But as wartime gave way to peacetime, euphoria faded; and the strain of holding the coalition together grew. In particular, he had to deal with a growing restiveness among the Conservatives, who

85. Bryce to Crewe, Apr. 7, Apr. 9, 1918. Crewe papers, Box C/13/18 Fisher, *Life of Bryce*, ii, p. 186.

86. MS Fisher 80, fos. 5, 149.

87. Bromhead, *The house of lords and contemporary politics, 1911–1957* (1958), 241, 262.

yearned for their former independence. He needed their support the more because his anti-Asquith coup had divided his party into two parts: the coalition and Asquithian Liberals. Since the latter were a lost cause for Lloyd George, his problem became one of retaining the coalition Liberals while satisfying the Conservatives. His solution seems to have been to sponsor a limited reform of the house of lords while avoiding a plan hostile to the Parliament Act. The statement has been made tentatively for the simple reason that Lloyd George's intentions are not easily interpreted. On occasion he changed courses abruptly, and there are historians who consider him at bottom a compulsive, obsessive intriguer. With good reason, it would appear, when one notices his attitude towards the Parliament Act. Despite his conspicuous role in its passage and at times obvious devotion to its terms, he was quite capable of speaking at other times as if he were prepared to adopt in its place the system of free conferences that was acceptable to the Bryce Conference as a means of ending deadlocks between the houses.[88]

The decision to sponsor reform of the lords was sensible if he expected to keep the Conservatives in his coalition. Presumably, he had before him the considerations that Maurice Cowling advanced when he wrote:

> Defence of the house of lords had been a major Conservative platform at the 1910 election. Reform of the house of lords had been a major Conservative cause since the Parliament Act had been passed in 1911. It was prominent in the minds of the unemployed guardians of Conservatism through the years of coalition. As Labour became the major party of assault, it acquired added importance as an instrument of constitutional defence. The coalition platform at the 1918 election had given a firm commitment: it was a central issue whenever the National Union met in 1920, 1921, and 1922. Salisbury, Selborne and the Diehards [a deeply conservative group] made it one of their chief points of attack.[89]

---

88. MS Fisher 79, fo. 15. For Lloyd George and the Parliament Bill, see Weston, "The Liberal leadership and the lords' veto," *Historical Journal*, 508–37, passim. Also, *Crawford papers*, 415, 417. And finally, *Political diaries of C.P. Scott, 1911–1928*, ed. Trevor Wilson (1970), 415; *Historical Journal*, 24, 1(1981), 227.

89. *The impact of Labour 1920–1924* (Cambridge, 1971), 147.

Though Jem Salisury was obviously a beneficiary of his father's prestige, he was by this time a political leader who commanded respect in his own right; and he very early took the public position that the Conservatives should abandon the Lloyd George coalition.[90]

These were the circumstances when the prime minister appointed a cabinet committee reflecting the party makeup of the coalition. Curzon, who since 1916 had been lord president and leader of the lords, became chairman; and in addition the committee included Birkenhead; Austen Chamberlain, lord privy seal, a Conservative who wanted his party to remain in the coalition; and two Liberals, both of them Lloyd George's protégés. These were Winston Churchill, colonial secretary, and H.A.L. Fisher, president of the board of education. Two others were named but did not attend: Balfour and the Liberal Gordon Hewart, later lord chief justice. Birkenhead's attitude towards the Parliament Act has already received mention, Chamberlain was ill at a critical moment in the cabinet committee's deliberations, and Churchill and Fisher were determined to maintain the Parliament Act without modification. They worked closely with a fellow Liberal, Sir Alfred Mond, a prominent industrialist and minister of health. Though he was not a member of the cabinet committee, he submitted a paper to the coalition cabinet supporting Churchill and Fisher.[91]

The cabinet committee's deliberations were far advanced by the summer of 1922. On June 14 Curzon, without previously consulting his colleagues, prepared seven resolutions for the coalition cabinet. Of these resolutions, numbers ii, iii, and iv were devoted to his personal plan for solving deadlocks.[92] If Lloyd George in appointing Curzon chairman acted on the assumption that the Conservative leader would respect the integrity of the Parliament Act, he was now disabused. Curzon's plan, though it ignored the referendal theory, struck directly at the Parliament

---

90. Ibid., chap. iv. *Crawford papers*, 417.

91. See the committee report, printed for the cabinet, MS Fisher 80, fos. 142, 148. The membership changed in early July. Ibid., fos. 182–4. For Mond, see ibid., fos. 168–81.

92. MS Fisher 80, fos. 150v.–1. According to Winston Churchill, the cabinet committee had not agreed to the resolutions, nor had the cabinet discussed them. Ibid., fos. 154–5. In fact, the cabinet did discuss them, but at a later date.

Act's main principle. He would substitute for the Act's suspensory veto an idea gleaned from the Bryce Report, which had been discussed but not adopted. When there were disputes between the houses, Curzon would resort to a standing free conference committee. But if it were unsuccessful, he had his own suggestion for reaching a final settlement. It would rest with a joint session of the two houses.[93]

The resolutions comprising the Curzon plan were as follows:

> ii [Should disagreement rise between the houses] with regard to any public bill, other than a money bill, which cannot be settled by the ordinary practice of parliament, the bill, together with the amendments in dispute, shall be referred forthwith, or as soon as may be in the next following session of parliament, to a free conference of the two houses, which shall appoint their own chairman.
>
> iii That if the free conference fails to come to an agreement, or if either house of parliament disagree with the settlement arrived at by the free conference the bill, together with the amendments which may be in dispute, shall be referred in the next new session of parliament which occurs in the year following the free conference to a joint sitting of the two houses of parliament, the decision of which shall be final.
>
> iv That the two houses shall be represented in the joint sitting by a proportion of their members, the quota of the house of lords, which must depend upon the numerical strength and the composition of that house when reconstituted [It was to be limited to 350 members–some elected from outside the house, some from within, others nominated by the Crown], to stand in a definite relation to the quota of the house of commons, the quota in each case being determined by statute.

Number iv, which proved especially odious to the committee's Liberals, became at once the focus of their opposition to the Curzon plan.

They viewed it as potentially favorable to the Conservatives with their overwhelming majority in the lords. Given this advantage, that party, if joint sittings were adopted, might convert Liberal majorities in the house of commons into minorities

93. In developing his plan Curzon turned to the Ripon plan put forward by the Liberals during the Constitutional Conference of 1910. Chamberlain papers, Ac 10/2/57; Weston, "The Liberal leadership and the lords' veto," *Historical Journal* 508–37. Also MS Fisher 80, fos. 5, 11, 12 and Gollin, *The Observer and J.L. Garvin*, 231.

on disputed questions. Thoroughly alarmed at the prospect, which Curzon, too, thought possible,[94] the trinity of Churchill, Fisher, and Mond set out to destroy Curzon's plan. If this were its fate, with the referendum already out of contention, there would be no viable alternative to the Parliament Act to which critics could rally. It would be left by default in command of the field. This, in essence, was what happened.

The Conservative Lord Bayford (formerly Robert Sandars), whose career as party whip had given him familiarity with the currents of high politics, put on record the Liberal trinity's success when he wrote in his journal on July 15, 1922:

> The resolutions on the second chamber question that are to be submitted to the house of lords have been published, and are ridiculously inadequate. I have seen the cabinet papers on the subject. Curzon submitted a well thought out scheme by which the ultimate solution in cases of deadlock was to be a joint sitting [of the two houses]. This was attacked by Winston, Fisher, and Mond who want really to leave the Parliament Act alone; their views have prevailed.[95]

Bayford, however, made no mention of Lloyd George's part in the outcome, and perhaps knew nothing of it. Given his personal characteristics, the prime minister would have unhesitatingly left Curzon in the lurch or indeed anyone else if his own self-interest was at stake.[96] More than this can be said with confidence. Thanks to Lloyd George's intervention, the cabinet committee decided that the Parliament Act required no modification; hence the outcome to which Bromhead called attention.

That the wind was blowing this way appears from a letter that Maurice Hankey, secretary to the coalition cabinet, sent to Birkenhead on July 4. It was actually the minutes of the cabinet

---

94. See memoranda written by Fisher and Churchill. MS Fisher 80, fos. 90, 93–8, 99–103, 154–5, 156 ff. See fo. 90 for Curzon's concession.

95. *Real Old Tory politics*, 178.

96. Trevor Wilson, *The downfall of the Liberal party, 1914–1935*, (1966), 45–9, 414–8. Selborne, while recognizing Lloyd-George's services as war leader, was caustic about his personal characteristics. He would not want to go tiger hunting with Lloyd George because "he would leave anyone in the lurch anywhere if he thought it suited his purpose." He was "a born intriguer," and one could not believe a word that he said. Selborne considered that he had not "a real friend among his Liberal colleagues in the cabinet" and, in Selborne's view, "most of them evidently hated him." MS Selborne 80, fo. 287v.

meeting that morning. He was writing, Hankey stated, to remind Birkenhead of the decisions that had been taken regarding lords' reform. These were preliminary since neither Curzon nor Chamberlain was present because of illness. Hankey's description, which is full of interest, makes it manifest that Lloyd George's coalition cabinet was, despite its bipartisan makeup, in accord with Churchill, Fisher, and Mond. Its members are described in Hankey's minutes as in complete agreement after a full discussion of certain propositions. One of the most important of these was that any proposals involving substantial modification of the main features of the Parliament Act "would be highly contentious and in particular might alienate the government's Liberal supporters." Another, puzzling in light of the thrust of the meeting, was that the powers of delay given by the Parliament Act, compared with those in the joint sitting procedure sessions, indicated in iii and iv of C.P. 4039, would leave the lords with a stronger position under the Parliament Act. Why this was thought a desirable outcome is unclear, but perhaps it was intended to appeal to Conservative members of the coalition cabinet.

There is no difficulty in understanding the next proposition, however. The vital question regarding the joint sitting procedure was "the size of the house of lords' quota." Fixing it "would provoke the *most intense controversy and dissension.*" In conclusion, of the seven draft resolutions, those numbered ii, iii, and iv–that is, Curzon's deadlock plan–were "highly controversial." The coalition cabinet decided to refer the draft resolutions to the following committee, which was to report to the cabinet on July 7. The new cabinet committee included Birkenhead (chairman); Churchill; Fisher; the Conservative Sir Robert Horne, chancellor of the exchequer; the Liberal Edwin Montagu, secretary for India; and the Conservative Balcarres, now Earl of Crawford, first commissioner of works. Copies of Hankey's letter were to be sent to the new committee members and to Curzon and Chamberlain.[97]

There is in the Crawford papers Balcarres' own description of the coalition cabinet's discussions of July 4, the date of Hankey's cabinet minutes. It substantiates and supplements his

---

97. MS Fisher 80, fos. 182–4.

account. A member of the coalition cabinet, as well as the newly appointed Birkenhead cabinet committee, Balcarres wrote:

> We discussed house of lords reform at the cabinet. It is quite clear that Curzon's scheme which involves repeal of the Parliament Act would produce a crisis both inside the cabinet and in parliament as well. We should introduce a needless apple of discord, *for there is a pretty strong body of Unionist opinion which is quite prepared to muddle on upon the present lines.* Any announcement of repeal would cause endless trouble and possibly the gravest consequences. Why provoke dissensions unless victory is desired and certain as well? That is the view we all took.[98]

Balcarres added that they had decided to jettison Curzon's clauses about free conferences and joint sessions which were to replace the Parliament Act. There was however the problem of Curzon's response. As Balcarres put it, "What will Curzon say when he returns in two or three days? He does not like his schemes to be amended."[99]

Birkenhead could have been representative of that Unionist opinion, and likewise Balcarres. Nor should it be overlooked that, though a Conservative leader, Birkenhead was one of Lloyd George's closest allies. On July 6 Birkenhead's committee completed the work of emasculating Curzon's resolutions when it removed resolutions ii, iii, and iv and added a new resolution v, providing

> that the provisions of the Parliament Act, 1911, by which bills can be passed into law without the consent of the house of lords during the course of a single parliament, shall not apply to any bill which alters or amends the constitution of the house of lords as set out in these resolutions, or which in any way changes the powers of the house of lords as laid down in the Parliament Act and modified by these resolutions. 6th July 1922.

On that day, too, Balcarres reported that he, Birkenhead, Churchill, and Fisher had a conference on house of lords reform and agreed to recommend to the cabinet that it omit free conferences and joint sessions and "leave the Parliament Act untouched for the moment."[100]

---

98. *Crawford papers,* 425.

99. Ibid.

100. MS Fisher 80, fos. 185–8. *Crawford papers,* 425.

The response was swift. Under the dateline of July 7 Balcarres recorded that the "full cabinet" endorsed "this plan"–that is the emasculated Curzon resolutions plus the new resolution v–but that George Curzon was still to be considered. "He is enamoured of his own offspring," Balcarres wrote, "and I should not be in the least surprised if he objects to the truncation of his logical and well thought out scheme. He is to come to London today."[101] But Balcarres need not have troubled himself about Curzon. Disabled by phlebitis, the latter was more interested in finding a cure for his malady than in the coalition cabinet's activity. Nor is it likely that Curzon, had his health been better, would have sought a confrontation with Lloyd George on the issue. The prime minister, who was notoriously harsh towards Curzon, at times humiliated him in the presence of others; and the latter knew what to anticipate if on this occasion he were to cross him. The punishment may have been meted out in this case regardless of Curzon's course of action. He was ill in August 1922, and the illness could have arisen from Lloyd George's habitual mistreatment of him.[102]

These events reveal that the Conservative leadership was reconciled to the idea that the Parliament Act was inviolate, and the picture was completed when Balcarres wrote on July 20: "Salisbury, Selborne and one or two others are pushing the [lords'] reform, but I am sure nobody is really keen on the subject beyond a relatively small group."[103] The conclusion was justified. No matter what support was forthcoming from Salisbury and Selborne, the referendum was out of the running, its unpopularity evident from the Bryce Conference's and the cabinet committee's rejections. Curzon's was the only alternative plan, and it was diametrically opposed to the referendal theory. Nor,

---

101. Ibid.

102. Ibid., 426. Curzon to Lloyd George, Jan. 8, 1918, printed in Lord Beaverbrook, *Men and power 1917–1918* (1956), 396–7. Austen Chamberlain to Bonar Law, Jan. 6, 1921, ibid., 397–400. Taylor, *English history 1914–1945*, 190, note 1.

103. *Crawford papers*, 427. This is Balcarres' statement just before his reference to Salisbury's and Selborne's isolation. "In the afternoon I spoke in the house of lords about the reform resolutions. They are truncated and incomplete, but even so go a good deal further than most peers desire. There is a strong movement objecting to all change of our constitution though many would welcome a further curtailment of the Parliament Act. People are very unreasoning."

thanks to Lloyd George and his fellow Liberals, did it ever reach the public. As for the emasculated resolutions, these possessed little appeal for the lords. Sir Ivor Jennings, who printed them, goes to the heart of the matter when he writes: "Above all, and this was the fundamental Conservative objection, they did not substantially increase the powers of the house of lords." He adds that they were dropped after a cold reception.[104] No one was more vigorous in his attack upon them than Selborne, and Salisbury's critique awakened echoes of his father's version of the lords' legislative power. More than a decade later, in 1934, Balcarres wrote bitterly that they had fought the coalition government "all they knew" and that they had made "the great gaffe of defeating the proposals put forward by W. Peel [secretary of state for India] and myself on lords reform and the Parliament Act."[105]

Not until 1949 was the Act changed, and then it was to reduce the ability of the house of lords to delay legislation from two years to one. The Conservative response came from the fifth marquis of Salisbury (Jem Salisbury's son), who had great influence with Conservative peers during the Attlee government (1945–51). He persuaded them not to oppose "measures which had specifically been included in the program on which the Socialist party had been returned to power, leaving themselves free to amend or reject anything else."[106] Earlier (October 31, 1945) he had expounded more fully the political ideology on which this advice rested. If the lords refused powers that the Labor party's leaders deemed essential in carrying out their nationalization program, he urged their leaders to seek "the ordinary constitutional remedy." It was for them to go back to the country to renew their mandate; and it would be forthcoming if the country supported them. This was "the proper constitutional course" since the British people's authority was superior to that of the government and

---

104. Jennings, *Parliament*, 437. See also Cannadine, *The decline and fall of the British aristocracy*, 468.

105. *Crawford papers*, 552. *Parl. debs.* (lords), li, 5th series, cols. 537–8, 546–9 (Selborne); 969–70 (Salisbury).

106. Bromhead, *The house of lords and contemporary politics*, 262. See also the anonymous reviewer of this book in the *Times Literary Supplement*, Apr. 4, 1958. He considered the fifth marquis' doctrine without constitutional precedent. Yet, clearly Salisbury was familiar with his grandfather's activitis and ideology. See Bromhead, *The house of lords*, 113.

parliament. "If the government are hampered in their work," he pointed out, "they can always go back to the sovereign people of this country from which parliament gets its authority."[107] So much for the commons' superiority as enshrined in the Parliament Act and the concept of parliamentary sovereignty on which it depended. Two years later, in a move suggesting that these ideas were still deemed relevant in political discourse, the Conservative Political Centre circulated a tract entitled *The house of lords: a survey of its history and powers.* It contained a lengthy quotation from Lord Salisbury's celebrated speech of June 26, 1869, which had so influential a role in creating the referendal theory.[108]

In another speech, this one on March 9, 1955, after the second Parliament Bill's passage, Salisbury once more expounded the Conservative attitude towards the Parliament Acts. At the time of his speech, Churchill was Conservative prime minister but was expected soon to retire in favor of Sir Anthony Eden; and in this transitional period Salisbury, speaking for the government's policy regarding the lords, conveyed that his party was more interested in that house's composition than its powers. But with this reservation. The government was unwilling to tie itself to the proposition that in no circumstances should that house, however constituted, have no greater power than it now possessed. This was a decision for both parliament and the British people to make.[109] A modern historian, interpreting this speech, thought it unlikely that the Conservatives would in the future seek to increase the lords' power beyond the residue left by the 1949 Act.[110] If this conclusion on the face of it seems puzzling, since Salisbury had actually left his party room for maneuver, the fact remains that no further action has been taken.

A few tentative conclusions will bring to an end this long discussion of the referendal theory and its offspring, the referendum. To begin with, it can be urged that Lord Salisbury's definition of the referendal theory in late Victorian England, and the

---

107. *Parl. debs.* lords, 5th series, cxxxvii, 613.

108. MS Selborne 181/15, 17.

109. *Parl. debs.* lords, 5th series, cxci, 855. See also the reference to the idea that the house of commons represented the electorate at all times.

110. Bromhead, *The house of lords*, 242.

techniques which he adopted to defend it, brought that house a generation of legislative independence though this should be qualified to state that it was exercized only when the Liberals were in power. Moreover, the theory enjoyed an Indian summer of popularity in Conservative ranks in the late 1940s and early 1950s when the lords were confronted with Attlee's nationalization program. Selborne's advocacy of the referendum, on the other hand, enjoyed no such popularity. Although it reached the top of the Unionist agenda before the Parliament Act, it was there for only a limited period of time before the First World War changed the political scene beyond recall. In the immediate years before the great war the referendum was associated with the die-hard revolt and the founding of the Halsbury Club that led to Balfour's resignation. As a result of these experiences Selborne became convinced that the house of lords had to be replaced by an efficient second chamber, which would be elected, and that the referendum was more necessary than ever as a popular check on what he saw as an autocratic executive. He wrote in 1911, after the Parliament Bill became law: "There is no more a house of commons than a house of lords. There is nothing but the cabinet, subject to the continuous but slight check of the crown and the violent but occasional check of the electors."[111]

Any real hope of securing an efficient second chamber disappeared with the war. As he put it, a great number of young men entered the party after 1918 who "knew nothing about this great constitutional question; and the attempt to arouse them to the danger of leaving the Parliament Act unamended and the lords unreformed fell to the ground because neither Balfour nor Stanley Baldwin gave the needed help."[112] Had he known about the fate of Curzon's resolutions, he might have added Lloyd George to his list of those who failed to recognize the need to solve the constitutional problem posed by the unreformed house of lords.

Given post–1867 developments, which culminated in the full-blown parliamentary sovereignty embodied in the Parliament

---

111. Selborne to his son, Dec. 6. Cited in Spring, "Land and politics in Edwardian England," 34.

112. MS Selborne 191, fos. 65–6.

Act of 1911, the appearance of an autocratic executive in the second half of the twentieth century comes as no surprise. Although the process is far advanced today, when compared with Lord Salisbury's and Selborne's time, they waged their vigorous campaigns for the lords' referendal function in terms that would be familiar to the present generation. It is one measure of Salisbury's political genius that in opposition to the executive–in this case Gladstone–he secured the Second Home Rule Bill's defeat without injuring the lords and consolidated his gains in the spectacular victory of 1895. Just as clearly, Selborne failed to achieve his goal of staving off single-chamber government at Westminster. But not for lack of effort. His sponsorship of the referendum from 1907 to his retirement in 1922 constituted a last desperate attempt to preserve a measure of equilibrium at Westminster and hence in the government of the empire. That he made the attempt at all and stayed with it so long makes him a memorable figure in the modern history of the house of lords and also of the times in which he lived. For a political leader whose domestic career is ignored in histories of late Victorian and Edwardian England, this is no small achievement though it obviously would not have satisfied Selborne.

But if Selborne–and Curzon, too–was a loser in the political sense, so was the nation. In this respect. Whatever the drawbacks of the pre–1911 house of lords, the extended controversy over its referendal function, to which Curzon subscribed as much as Selborne, and over the referendum, on which they differed, had kept steadily before the nation for more than four decades the concept of a popular check on an autocratic executive. But the electorate in what was in many ways a quasi-democratic state was apathetic in the crucial general elections of 1910, and the passage of the Parliament Bill went far to make the house of lords the sham that Lord Salisbury and Selborne had decried. Thereafter the house of commons was independent of the electorate between general elections, though not of the executive. That house's traditional powers had long since passed to the prime minister, as Salisbury and Selborne well knew; and the power of No. 10 Downing Street reached a new height in the eleven years (1979–90) of Mrs. Margaret Thatcher's prime ministership–in part because of her personal attributes.

As the *Economist* of July 6–12, 1991 put it:

A parliamentary system that worked well would not have produced the poll tax [a major cause for Mrs Thatcher's fall from power]; a huge majority of MP's privately opposed it from the outset. Nor would an effective parliament have spent so much time in recent years avoiding any detailed debate about Britain's European future. And these two cases illustrate more general worries: about the power and patronage of the prime minister; about the secrecy that still cocoons Whitehall; about the degraded level of adversarial debate in the house of commons; about the relative failure of the commons to keep a proper check on the executive.[113]

In these circumstances serious discussion began for the first time since the Parliament Act of 1911 about the need for constitutional change.

The publication of a document entitled Charter 88 in November 1988 was of cardinal importance in starting a movement for constitutional reform. Among the far-reaching proposals now advanced, many of them reflecting the American experience, were a written constitution and a written Bill of Rights, electoral reform, an effective second chamber, a revitalization of local government, even a freedom of information act. In these years, too, the doctrine of parliamentary sovereignty, which constituted an obstacle to constitutional change, was irretrievably weakened as Britain became part of the European community. Whether anything will come of this ferment remains to be seen, but present signs suggest that as the movement intensifies at the least effective constraints will be placed upon the executive authority.[114]

---

113. *The Economist*, November 5–11, 1977, "Blowing up a tyranny," 11–16. At another point the *Economist* reports: "Because it has this almost automatic majority, the government has gained virtually total control of the house [of commons]. There is not in Britain's parliament any method for defending the citizen against the power of the executive sitting in its midst (and outside it the Ombudsman is not a strong reed)." The *Economist*, which would like to see an efficient second chamber, points out that the present situation did not always prevail, but it is quite clear that its editorial staff knows nothing about the activities of Lord Salisbury and Selborne and their warning against a sham house of lords.

114. Charter 88 is described in the *Economist*, Nov. 19, 1989, p. 60; and for comment on the American system see ibid., Oct. 13, 1990, 13–4. Also helpful is Martin Pugh's review of vol. 21, part 4 of the *British Journal of Political Science* in the *Times Literary Supplement*, Nov. 15, 1991, p. 23. There are also pertinent materials in the *TLS*, Nov. 22, 1991, 11–2; ibid., Nov. 29, p. 14; and the *London Review of Books*, Dec. 5, 1991, p. 7; ibid., Oct. 22, 1992, pp. 16–8.

Index

The House of Lords and Ideological Politics

Albert Hall declaration and the referendum, 182

Amery, Leo, 210, 213

Anson, Sir William, 121

Anti-Corn Law League, 14, 16, 19, 21

Argyll, duke of, 54

Army Regulation Bill, 68-71

Arrears Bill
- tests Salisbury's leadership, 102
- Lady Gwendolen's view, 102

Asquith, H.H., 87, 149, 167, 197-199, 217
- to Balfour on George V's promise to create peers in 1911, 87
- on single chamber government, 149
- on Curzon's search for an hereditary peerage, 197-199
- his wartime promise to reform the house of lords, 217
- and the Parliament Act, 217

Attlee government, 189

Austin, Alfred, 122, note 10

Baker, Robert of Writle, 19, 20

Balcarres, Lord, 26th earl of Crawford, 158, 180, 190, 195, 202, 203, 205-206, 208, 224-226, 227
- on Selborne, 158, 180
- on voting pattern in shadow cabinet, 1911, 190
- compares Curzon and Selborne, 195
- describes Curzon as vindictive, 195
- as does Jack Sandars, 195
- Balfour's changes, 202-203
- Lansdowne and the diehards, 203
- Selborne's view of Balfour as a failed leader, 203
- Balfour had sided with one faction, 203
- Selborne's statement in his memoirs, 204
- *on the tertium quid*, 205
- sees Lansdowne as burning his bridges, 205-206
- attributes this to Curzon's influence, 206
- this could have been the view in diehard circles, 206
- Balcarre's sympathies, 206
- mentioned, 208
- member of the Birkenhead Committee, 225, 226

Balfour, Arthur, 9, 86, 88, 100, 156, 161, 163, 167, 168-169, 172, 174, 182, 187, 202, 213-215, 221, 224
- lacks credibility with Jem Salisbury and Selborne, 168-169
- a flawed leader, 168
- on the Parliament Act, 169
- on Ireland and India, 169
- Jem Salisbury a free trader, 169
- his statement on the breakup of the shadow cabinet, July 21, 1911, 174
- Balfour at Hackwood, 182
- and his issuance of the Albert Hall pledge, 182

and the king's promise to create peers, 187
his electoral record, 202
alienates Selborne, 203-206
the diehard revolt and the Halsbury Club, 207-215, passim
his resignation, 209, 213-215

Balfour of Burleigh, 104, 170, 178
introduces a referendum bill, 170
St.Loe Strachey its author, 170

Ballot Bill, 67

Bankes, George, 21, 27, 28, 35, 38

Bath, Lord, 193

Beaumont, Lord, 24

Beaverbrook, Lord, 197

Bentinck, Lord George, 22, 23-24, 28, 31, 67, note 25

Bigge, Arthur (Lord Stamfordham), 198-199

Birkenhead, Lord (formerly F.E. Smith),
replaces Curzon as chair of cabinet committee, 217-218
believes Parliament Act to be permanent, 218, 221, 225

Birmingham caucus, 90

Blake, Lord, 1, 2

Bright, John, 44, 45, 107

Bromhead, P.A., 219, 228

Brooks, David, 122, note 12, 134

Brougham, Lord, 34, 35, 38, 44-45, 48, 72, note 62

Bryce, James, Lord Bryce, 89-127, passim

Bryce Conference, 218-227

Buckle, G.E., 209

cabinet committee, 223

cabinet government after 1867, 81-83

Cairns, earl of, 57-58, 61, 62, 64, 65, 69, 99, 100, 102, 104, 114, 126

Campbell-Bannerman, Sir Henry,
his veto plan would limit lords' veto to six months, 166
too radical for his cabinet, 166
Lord Crewe's warning that it would encourage the Conservative adoption of the referendum, 166

Carnarvon, Lord, 61, 64, 65, 69, 70-72, 78, 98, 101, 102, 104, 147, 161, 165

Carson, Edward, 210

Catholic Emancipation, 13, 14

caucus, 82, 83, 86, 87, 88, 89, 98-99, 101
used by Salisbury to discredit Liberal MPs, 82, 98-99
terms them "wirepullers," 83, 86
not present in the lords, 85-86
reasons for disliking the caucus, 86-87
on mechanisms that expedited the flow of legislation, 87
limitations that ought to be placed on its operation, 87
his willingness for Conservatives to remain permanently in opposition, 87
the difficulty of satisfying both the classes and the masses, 87

Cavendish, Lady Moyra, 213

Cecil, Hugh, 197, 213, 216, 217, 218, 219

Cecil, Lady Gwendolen, 77, 83, 98, 114, 122, 123, 147-148, 162, 175-176
"stump oratory," 77
on Gladstone's temporary majority, 123
her reading of the general election of 1895, 135
on Salisbury's political skills, 147
on Curzon and Jem Salisbury, 175-176
on the shadow cabinet of 1911, 189
and principle, 194

Cecil, Lady Maud, 158, 164, 203

Cecil, Robert, 172

Chamberlain, Austen, 10, 159-160, 171-172, 182, 185, 210, 221
hostile to referendum, 171-172
Hackwood and Albert Hall declaration, 182
working with Curzon, 185

Chamberlain, Joseph, 82, 86, 88, 126, 157, 159-160, 171-172, 221
Chaplin, Henry, 154
Charter 88, 231
Churchill, Randolph, 2, 48-49, 89, 154-155, 221
Churchill, Winston, 89, 221, 223, 228
Clarendon, Lady, 31
Clarendon, Lord, 26, 31, 57
closure, 85-86, 87-89, 97, 124, 126
not used in the lords, 85-86
Salisbury would limit its use, 87
unpopular, 89
employed as a Conservative weapon in 1893, 124, 126
Cobden, Richard, 16, 29, 37, 164
Collings, Jesse, 124
Conservatism,
and Salisbury, 87-88, 133-134, 155
and Rosebery, 134-135, 155
Conservative hostility to legislating, 87
Conservatives more realistic than Liberals on post-1867 era, 194
Constitutional Conference of 1910, 167, 181, 182
Cranborne, Lord, 64
Crewe, Lord, 166, 182, 218
Cromer, Lord, 200, 202
Curzon,
personal qualities, 143-145, 174, 175, 176, 180, 195, 196, 197
rivalry with Selborne, 143-146, 151, 184-188, 189, 202, 221
no interest in home rule, 144-145, 146, 174, 175
rejects referendum, 145-146, 174
alliance with Austen Chamberlain, 171-172, 185
opposes sending the referendum to a select committee of the shadow cabinet, 173
and shadow cabinet breakup in 1911, 175
distinguished imperial proconsul, 175
not liked by either Selborne or Jem Salisbury, 175
expected to become prime minister, 175
Jem Salisbury breaks with him in 1911, 175-176
his unpopularity, 175-176
and Lord Kitchener, 176
Jem Salisbury's wife sympathetic to Kitchener, 176
favors reform of the house of lords' composition, 176, 185
interest in house of lords' reform, 176
accepted referendal theory, 176
his own view of the lords, 176
upset by LaBouchere, 176
articles about the lords in *National Review* for 1888, 176
and Lord Rosebery, 177
chairs a committee on the lords, 177
report of 1908, 177
hereditary peerage and a seat in the lords, 177
Curzon's support for Rosebery, 177
relationship between the Rosebery plan and Lansdowne resolutions, 177
accepts the referendal theory, 177, 179
distrusts the electorate, 178
would circumscribe the use of the referendum, 179
opposes women's suffrage, 179
leads the Hedgers, 190
and the Judas group, 196
his role in the failure to amend the Parliament Act in 1922, 217-227
chairman of Lloyd George's cabinet committee, 221
its membership, 221
his personal plan, 221-222
destroyed by Liberals on his committee, 222-223
opposition of Winston Churchill, H.A.L. Fisher, and Sir Alfred Mond, 223
and the curious role of Lloyd George, 223
Maurice Hankey's letter, 223-224
Curzon's emasculated resolutions, 225, 226, 227
Balcarre's account, 226

the Conservative objection to the resolutions, 227

Derby, 15th earl, 71

Devonshire, duke of, 66, 84, 115, 130, 131, 132, 140, 156, 213
see Lord Hartington

Dicey, A.V., 84-85, 156-157, 170

diehard manifesto, 191-192, 200

diehard revolt, 98, 177, 196

diehard revolt and Curzon, 197

diehard whips, 190

diehards, 190-193
described as Selborne's friends, 193

diehards or ditchers, 190

Disraeli, Benjamin, 18, 24-26, 28, 54, 55, 58, 60-62, 65, 71, 81

Dugdale, Blanche, 204-205

Egremont, Max, 199

Fanning, Ronan, 209

Finlay, Sir Robert, 183

First Home Rule Bill
broke up the Liberal party, 100
Lord Devonshire's speech, 115
and George Curzon, 115

Fisher, H.A.L., 221, 223

Fitzroy, Almeric, 193

Garvin, James, L., 126

Gell, P. Lyttelton, 155

Gladstone, William, vi, 39, 42, 43, 44, 45, 46, 51, 53, 54, 67, 70, 76, 77, 78, 81, 82, 84, 86, 99, 100, 105-106, 115, 116, 118, 119, 120
praises Wellington, 42, 47
Paper Duties Bill, 70
finds referendal theory too radical, 76
his Midlothian speeches, 77-78
Gladstone and the Old Liberals, 84-85
and Irish land war, 100
on Conservatives as the greatest innovators of the day, 105-106
Ecclesiastical Titles Bill, 111
his adoption of home rule breaks up his party, 118
breakup of the Liberal party in 1886, 119

Granville, Lord, 42, 61

Greville, Charles, 26

Halsbury Club
and Balfour's resignation, 202, 215
an exchange of letters on the referendum between Selborne and Willoughby de Broke, 207
founded by Selborne, working with Willoughby de Broke and Wyndham, 210

Hamilton, Edward, 133

Hartington, Lord, 140

Hatfield House, 121, 156

hedgers, 190

Hewart, Gordon, 221

Irish Church Bill, 51-80
referendal theory, 53-54, 59, 65-68, 70-80
and Suspensory Bill, 55-59, 60, 71
Salisbury's speeches, 56-57, 62, 63, 66, 71-72
Stanley amendment, 56-58
disestablishment of the Irish Church, 58, 59, 60, 72
his break with Cairns in the final vote, 65
his speeches recalled in the early 1890s and in 1911, 66-67
abolition of army purchase, 68
his letter to Lord Carnarvon, 70-72
and Ballot Bill, 70-72, 73
learns from the Midlothian campaigns, 73-77, 79
and "stump oratory," 77-80
the lords' function revised, 78
the lords win a great propaganda victory, 121
his article on constitutional revision, 121

Jenkins, Roy, 153

Judas group, 202

Kelso, 98, 200, 200, note 21, 201
Kemp, Betty, 36-37
King George V, 187, 189, 197, 198, note 25
promise to create peers, 187
and the Parliament Bill, 198
and Selborne, 198
and Curzon, 198, 199
Kitchener, Herbert, 176
Knollys, Lord, 198

Labouchere, Henry, 90, 176
Lansdowne, Lord
on the Parliament Act, 153
and the referendum, 172, 173
his Reform Bill of 1911 and the Rosebery plan, 173
the Lansdowne resolutions and Curzon, 177

Lansdowne House meeting, 191
Lansdowne House Meeting
Lord St. Aldwyn a key figure, 190
but Curzon rallies Lansdowne's followers, 190
the Lansdowne memorandum on Selborne's speech, 191
Lansdowne on economic policy, 170, 172, 173
Lansdowne resolutions in the lords on November 1, 1910, 174
Law, Andrew Bonar, 173
Lecky, W.E.H., 132-133
"legislating by picnic," 81
Liberal party and first home rule bill, 118
Liberal Unionists, 84-85, 115, 116, 117, 118, 156
Life Peerages Bill of 1869, 54
Lloyd George, David, 84, 162, 217-227
his Finance Bill and the Parliament Act of 1911, 84, 162
ensures the permanence of the Parliament Act in 1922, 219-227
his personal characteristics, 220
the Curzon resolutions and their fate, 221-227
Lord Birkenhead's role, 224-226
Lloyd George's attitude towards Curzon, 226-227
see also Lord Curzon
logrolling, 122, 166
Long, Walter
on Halsbury Club, 208
Lords, house of, weaknesses in late Victorian England, 99
Lovat, Lord, 190, 192
Low, Sidney, 83
Lowther, Speaker, 193
Lucy, Sir Henry, 117, 121, 135, 146
Lyndhurst, Lord, 31

"machine men," 85-86
Maine, Sir Henry, 84-85
Malmesbury, earl of, 21, 26, 27, 30, 32-34, 38
Marsh, Peter, 2, 118-119
Maxse, Leo, 156-157, 175, 211-212
holds a symposium on the referendum in the *National Review*, 156-157
hostile to Curzon, 175
sponsors a resolution to oust Balfour as party leader, 211-212
Selborne opposed, 211-212
Mayo, Lord, 190
Middleton, Captain, 159
Middleton, R.W.E., 89
Midleton, Lord
and Curzon, 196
Milner, Lord, 155, 160, 210
Mond, Sir Alfred, 221, 223, 224
Monkswell, Lady, 131
Morley, John, 126

National Liberal Federation, 82-83, 123
National Review Symposium, 177
National Union of Conservative and Constitutional Associations, 82-83
Newcastle Program, 122, 123, 126
Northcote, Sir Stafford, 1, 13, 81, 93, 101, 154
Northumberland, earl of, 215, 216

Norwich program, 134

Old Liberals, 84-90, 94
    see also Liberal Unionists

Ormsby-Gore, Lord William, 197

Ostrogorski, Mosei, 71, 84, 88, 89-90, 94, 95

Palmer, Lady Sophia, 100-101

Palmerston, Lord, 32, 44, 150

Parliament Act and referendal theory, 153

Parliament Act of 1911, 9, 153, 198, 201, 223, 229-230

parliamentary government
    expounded by the 3rd Earl Grey and Walter Bagehot, 4-20, 83
    based on concept of ministerial responsibility, 4
    treats house of commons as dominant since 1832, 4, 7
    no role in it for public opinion, 6
    final decision-making in the cabinet, 6-7
    Wellington's contribution, 7-8
    the Liberal Parliament Act of 1911 based on its principles, 8
    and party organization, 82
    and the Old Liberals, 84-85

Parliamentary Reform Bills,
    of 1832, 15, 37
    of 1867, 48, 55, 82, 87
    of 1884, 101

Parnell, Charles Stewart
    paralysis of the house of commons, 86

Peel, Sir Robert, 13, 14, 15, 23, 24, 25, 26, 27, 28, 29, 35, 36, 37, 38, 39, 194

Primrose League, 89

Queen Victoria, 60, 68-71, 107, 114

Radical Liberals, 86, 88
    referendal theory, 1-4, 6-9, 13, 14, 15, 16, 19, 53-55, 66-68, 70, 71, 76, 81, 83, 84, 85, 89, 105, 116, 154, 189, 219, 227, 228, 229, 230
    protects the lords' legislative veto, 1
    reasons for its adoption, 3-4, 8-9
    effect on Conservatives, 9
    contrary to parliamentary government, 9
    opposed to the ascendancy of the commons, 9
    Franchise Bill rejected by lords in 1884 in language of the referendal theory, 105
    any possibility of the referendal theory's revival ended in 1922, 219

Reform Act of 1832, 14, 15, 37

Reform Act of 1867, 52, 54, 55, 82, 87, 94, 103, 136-137, 230

Richmond, 5th duke of, 13, 14, 15, 17, 18, 19, 20, 24, 25, 26, 27, 28, 30, 31, 34, 38, 64
    and the referendal theory, 13, 14
    imparts an ideological tone to parliamentary debates on repeal of the Corn Laws, 26
    Peel's response evokes parliamentary sovereignty, 29, 36-37
    Lord Stanley's famous speech, 32, 38
    opposition from Wellington and Lord Brougham, 33, 34, 35, 38

Richmond, sixth duke of, 64, 100, 104

Ronaldshay, earl of, 175

Rosebery, 133, 134, 177

Russell, Lord John, 15, 16, 27, 31, 44

Sadler, Michael, 14

St. Aldwyn, Lord, 182, 190, 213

Salisbury, 3rd marquis of,
    personal qualities, vi, 1-3, 42-43, 47, 48, 51, 53-54, 68, 79-80, 84, 85, 89, 101, 116-119, 121, 123, 124, 138-139, 147, 180-181, 230
    referendal theory, 1-4, 13, 42-43, 57, 70, 81, 85, 87, 116, 154, 230
    goals, 2-3, 8-9, 49, 51, 116
    journalist, 3
    Paper Duties Bill, 3, 45, 49, 70
    and class warfare, 3, 52, 100, 147
    dislike of direct taxation, 3, 52, 146-149

distrusts Gladstone, 3-4
on "parliamentary government," 4-10, 47, 52
the referendum and home rule, 9, 140
relations with Wellington, 39-42
on public opinion as the arbiter between the two houses, 42-43, 116
and the Radical Liberals, 43-45
more radical than Gladstone, 43, 230
dislikes sham, 47, and 47, note 83, 122, note 10
and the Reform Act of 1867, 48, 49, 54, 64, 65, 82, 87
on Disraeli as party leader, 65
Salisbury's letter to *The Times* in 1895 recalls the lords' stand in 1869, 66
Lord Lansdowne in 1911 quoted Salisbury's language on the second reading of the Irish Church Bill, 66
and the duke of Devonshire did so on the second reading of the Irish Church Bill, 66
Salisbury finds power leaving Westminster for the platform, 77
Lady Gwendolen Cecil discerns a new stump oratory, 77
at Hackney and Liverpool he describes the lords as representing the nation's permanent opinion, 77-78
describes lords as more trustworthy than the commons, 81-82
associates the National Liberal Federation with the caucus and American machine politics, 82, 85-86
and post-1867 party organization, 82-84
denounces "wirepullers," 85-88, 99
has negative view of law-making, 87
on the caucus and the guillotine, 88, 97, 126, 134-135, 136, 139, 188, 189
and the Primrose League, 93-97
Salisbury at Liverpool, 97
denounces a house of commons enslaved by the caucus and muzzled by the caucus and cloture, 97
at Sheffield, 97
and duration of parliament, 97
at Kelso advises the lords against compromise with the commons, 98
on a powerful prime minister, 99
on Gladstone and the general election of 1880, 100
general election of 1895, 117, 118
preceded by his defeat of the Second Home Rule Bill in 1893, 117-118
lords treated as main arena by historians, 118
but the Bill in the commons for six months and in the lords for only a few weeks, 118
the incongruity points to the lords' action as only ratification, 118
the commons' proceedings more important, 118
Gladstone's position, 118-121, 122
sees home rule as destructive of the empire, 119
Salisbury's difficulties, 121
sets out to unshackle the lords' veto in his "constitutional revision," 121-122
his article on constitutional revision, 121-122, 124, 128, 130
Lady Gwendolen Cecil, 122, 123
on a sham house of lords, 122, note 10
concept of a "motley majority," 122-123
also of "predominant partner," 123
wide-spread obstruction in the commons, 123
the Newcastle program, 123
stages "great scenario" at Westminster, 124
role of Jesse Collings, 124
Joseph Chamberlain's role, 125
obstruction in the commons, 125-126
and lavish use of closure and the guillotine, 125-126
intended to discredit Gladstone, 125-126

Joseph Chamberlain and Lord Wolmer lead campaign, 125-126
Lord Wolmer's role, 126
Salisbury's speech at the Junior Constitutional Club, 127
Salisbury and the general election of 1895, 133
his emphasis on principle in politics, 136-137
on the home rule issue and the referendum, 137-146
on Ulster, 138-139
favors the referendum, 140-141, 146
the intellectual link between Salisbury's ideology and the diehard mentality in 1911, 200

Salisbury, 4th marquis of, 10, 160, 161, 168, 169, 172, 182, 195, 200, 221
referred to as "Jem Salisbury," 10
allied with Selborne, 10, 168
their reputations for probity, 168
distaste for Balfour, 168-169
in 1911 they spearheaded the diehard revolt, 169
and Balfour's resignation as party leader, 169
imperialists, 169
on retaining Ireland, 169
and the referendum, 169
breaks with Curzon, 175-176
and Lady Gwendolen Cecil, 175-176
praises sincerity, 195
with Selborne author of the diehard manifesto, 200
a founder of the Halsbury Club, 209
his view of its purpose, 209
devotion to Lansdowne, 209
resigns from the Halsbury Club, 209
Selborne's reproach, 209-210

Salisbury, 5th marquis of, 189, 227, 228, 229
revives the referendal theory, 189
would resist the Attlee government's nationalizing policies, 227, 228, 229
unclear whether the Conservatives will seek change in the Parliament Acts, 228

Saltoun, Lord, 174, note 55

Sandars, Jack, 157, 172, 195-196, 206

Sandars, Robert, Lord Bayford, 202, 223

Second Home Rule Bill, 67, 81, 82, 100, 116, 118, 119-127
defeated in 1893, 118
Peter Marsh's interpretation, 118
Gladstone's political strength, 119
Salisbury's unwillingness to endanger the lords, 119
meeting of Feb. 28, 1893, 121, note 9

Selborne, 1st Lord, 76, 100-101, 157

Selborne, 2nd lord
Salisbury's son-in-law and ideological heir, 10, 143, 156
the 4th marquis of Salisbury, known as Jem, his closest friend and ally, 10, 68, 160
a zealous advocate of the referendum, 10, 141-144, 156
discord between him and Curzon, 143-146
admirer of Joseph Chamberlain, 143, 149, 159, 160
as Lord Wolmer and Chief Unionist Whip active in defeating the Second Home Rule Bill, 143-144, 156, 159
his personal qualities, 157, 158, 159, 160, 164-165, 168
becomes high commissioner for South Africa, 157
a successful imperial proconsul and nation builder, 157
married Lady Maud Cecil, 158
entered the Colonial Office as under-secretary, 159-160
his associates and his relatives, 159-161
establishes a lasting bond with George Wyndham, 160
unlike the Cecils, Selborne embraced tariff reform, 161
while in South Africa adopts the referendum, 162
sees it as a source of stability at Westminster and in the empire, 163
his distrust of the Liberals when he was in South Africa, 163-164

would allow the use of the referendum even when the two houses were in agreement, 167
flaws in his scheme, 167
Selborne would also reform the house of lords and keep the crown out of the political arena, 168
considered Balfour a flawed leader, 168
worked closely with Jem Salisbury, 168
their characteristics, 168
distrusted Lloyd George, 168-169
his "Notes on the Referendum," 172
his communications with Balfour before leaving South Africa, 172
on Lansdowne's Reform Bill, 177
his speech at the Lansdowne House meeting, 191
discerns no glory in "dying in the ditch," 191
but would resist to the end, 191
the diehards echo his views, 191
their nominal leader, Lord Halsbury, 191
but Selborne, Halsbury's chief of staff, probably the real leader, 191
He and Jem Salisbury wrote the diehard manifesto, 191, 200
Willoughby de Broke prominent in the diehard movement but not its leader, 192
the condition of the Unionist party when Selborne returned from South Africa, 194
emphasizes principle, 194
and the Judas group, 196
Selborne's course of action in 1911 reflected Salisbury's ideology, 199
would force a peerage creation to avoid a silent revolution, 199
sees Sir Henry Campbell-Bannerman's veto plan in this light, 199-200
above all, there should be no "sham" house of lords, 200, 230
recalls Salisbury's speech at Kelso, 200
and invokes Salisbury's "precipice" imagery, 200
his memorandum on Balfour's leadership, 203-206
Curzon's continued hostility towards the referendum, 206
Selborne on an aborted Balfour memorandum, 206
his letter to Lord Willoughby de Broke, 207
and the response, 207
Selborne's administrative ability, 207
founds the Halsbury Club, 207-208
sees it as a vehicle by which to unite his following, 208
his influence on the Club, 208
and the First World War, 229
a memorable figure in the modern history of the house of lords, 230
a final appraisal of his attempt to achieve his goals, 230
see also Arthur Balfour, the Selborne-Curzon rivalry, shadow cabinet

Selborne-Curzon rivalry, 143-146, 151, 184-185, 189, 195

shadow cabinet, 172-174
struggle over the referendum, 174
its breakup, July 21, 1911, 174, 203, 204
Balfour's description, 174
two strong willed imperial proconsuls at loggerheads, 179
Selborne and Curzon compared, 180
and Balfour's leadership, 181
on the referendum, 183
discussion of the need to agree on the machinery for a referendum, 184
a question of credibility, 184
Austen Chamberlain aligned with Curzon, 185

shadow cabinet committee, 183, 184

Stanley, Lord, 14th earl of Derby, 7, 15-18, 30-33, 38, 39, 121
memorable speech of May 25, 1645, 32-33
and Salisbury, 39, 40
Stanley amendment, 56, 93, 94

Stead, William T., 121, note 9
Steel Maitland, Sir Arthur, 208
Stoddart, Jane, 165, 166, 174, note 55, and 178, note 67
on the referendum, 165
and logrolling, 166
her influence, 178, note 67
Strachey, John St.Loe, 84-85, 156-157, 170
Suspensory Bill, 39, 54-55, 56-60, 67
see Irish Church Bill

Tate, archbishop, 59-60
Third Home Rule Bill,
Tory Rebellion, 153
Townshend, Charles, 153

Unionist arguments in favor of the referendum, 155
their view of the political system after the Parliament Act of 1911, 155
feared the introduction of an omnipotent cabinet, 155
considered the constituencies the remaining battlefield, 155
Unionist electoral victory of 1895, 81-82, 117, 133
Unionist party, 9, 117, 133
Unionists in 1922 considered Parliament Act permanent, 189
Unionists more realistic than Liberals in interpreting the post-1867 constitution, 194

Wellington, duke of, 30
letter to Lord Stanley (later 14th earl of Derby), 7
described by Bagehot, 7-8, 19-20, 30
and Reform Bill of 1832, 13, 15, 26, 30
Catholic Emancipation, 13, 30, 33
on referendal theory, 33-34, 37, 38
and Salisbury, 39-42
Gladstone on his leadership, 41-42, 70
Willoughby de Broke, Lord, 192-193, 206-207, 210, 211, 212, 215
Wyndham, George, 184, 197, 199, 210
on Curzon's motives in 1911, 199
his conversation with Austen Chamberlain, 210
on the Halsbury Club, 210
not aimed at the party leadership, 210
its forward policy, 210
on Willoughby and the duke of Northumberland, 210
Austen Chamberlain to join the Halsbury Club, 210
Curzon an issue, 210
and Selborne's intentions, 210